KL...
SOWSNEK-KERNEWEK

CORNISH-ENGLISH /
ENGLISH-CORNISH
POCKET DICTIONARY

Kesva an Taves Kernewek
Cornish Language Board

Yoran
2015

Trugarez da Divi Kervella ha Jean-Eric Balnoas

Special thanks to Mikael Kilfenn, the best Breton driver who is able to keep his left on the Cornish roads

ISBN 978-2-36747-003-0
EAN 9782367470030

© Cornish Language Board & Yoran 2015

Yoran, 71 hent Mespiolet
29170 Fouenant – Breizh
yoran.embanner@gmail.com
http://yoran-embanner.com/

INTRODUCTION

The Cornish language

Cornish is the traditional language of Cornwall. It was spoken as a community language until about 1800, and then fell into disuse until it was revived in the early twentieth century. It is one of the six Celtic languages, belonging with Breton and Welsh to the Brythonic branch; the other branch, called Goidelic, comprises Scots Gaelic, Irish and Manx.

The history of the language may be divided into phases. Very little is known about the Primitive Cornish phase (600 to 800 AD). From the Old Cornish phase (800 to 1200) we have lists of names and a Cornish-Latin word-list. The heyday of the traditional language was the second part of the Middle Cornish phase (1200 to 1575). From this phase we have five plays and a long poem, all in verse, and the translations of thirteen homilies, in prose. Cornish retreated from east to west, so that by the time of the Late Cornish phase (1575 to 1800), it was spoken only in the west. From this phase we have poems, articles, stories, letters, translations, and one play. By 1800 Cornish had ceased to be used as an everyday means of communication. The last native speaker is reputed to be Dolly Pentreath (d. 1777).

During the nineteenth century, a few people in the far west had a traditional knowledge of pieces of Cornish, but so far as we know, they could not converse in the language. From the mid-century onwards, others began to compose new material in Cornish. The Revived Cornish phase is considered to date from 1904, when Henry Jenner published his *Handbook of the Cornish Language*. During the inter-war years, the revival was led by Robert Morton Nance and A.S.D. Smith. In the 1970s, the emphasis changed from writing Cornish to speaking it; a few parents raised their children to speak Cornish. In 2003, Cornish was recognized under Part II of the European Charter for Minority Languages.

The pocket dictionary

This pocket dictionary is one of a series published in Brittany by Yoran Embanner. It has been compiled by Dr Ken George under the auspices of the Cornish Language Board (Kesva an Taves Kernewek). Although it contains a surprising number of words for its size, they have necessarily been selected from a larger corpus. The choice of words reflects to a large extent that in the sister dictionary containing Breton and English. Given its format, the dictionary cannot be considered as more than an instrument to discover the Cornish language, since it contains only the basic vocabulary of everyday life.

The use of Cornish in naming houses, children, boats, etc. is to be welcomed, but the proposers of a name must be aware that one cannot just take words from a Cornish dictionary and put them together in the same way as one would in English. The rules of syntax for Cornish are different from those in English. The Cornish Language Board will be pleased to advise in this matter.

Presentation

Head-words are printed in **Large Helvetica Bold** type; their pronunciations are given within square brackets, using the International Phonetic Alphabet. There follows grammatical information *in italics*. Many Cornish nouns have their plural form shown using **+** where suffixes are added (e.g. **dydh +yow** for **dydhyow**) or **-** where letters are replaced (e.g. **kiger -oryon** for **kigoryon**). Collective nouns in Cornish have their singulative form shown (nearly always as the suffix **+enn**); e.g. **gwydh** 'trees' **+enn** (i.e. **gwydhenn**) 'tree'.

Homographs are distinguished by left superscripts.

Initial mutations

In common with the other Celtic languages, Cornish is subject to initial mutations, whereby a consonantal sound at the beginning of some words may change to another consonantal sound under certain circumstances. These changes are represented in writing, but only the non-mutated (radical) forms of words are usually given in dictionaries. This means that if you hear or read a word which is mutated, then the word will not appear in the dictionary in this form, but with a different initial letter. For example, if you hear the expression **an gador vras** then you may need to look up **an**, **kador** and **bras** in order to interpret it as 'the large chair'. You may have to look for:

b	instead of	**v**, **p** or **f**
d		**dh** or **t**
g		**k**, **h**, **w** or **hw**
p		**b** or **f**
t		**d** or **th**
k		**g** or **h**
m		**v** or **f**
ch		**j**

Since this aspect of using the dictionary can cause difficulties for learners, a summary of the initial mutations in Cornish is now given. There are five possible states of mutation, and they are conventionally numbered in text-books as follows:

1	radical (dictionary form)
2	soft mutation
3	spirant mutation
4	hard mutation
5	mixed mutation

These numbers are used as right superscripts in this dictionary.

Soft mutation

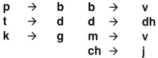

p	→	b		b	→	v
t	→	d		d	→	dh
k	→	g		m	→	v
				ch	→	j

When followed by **o**, **u**, **ro** or **ru**, **g** usually changes to **w**; otherwise **g** is lost altogether, e.g. **garr** 'leg', **an arr** 'the leg'.

Soft mutation occurs principally:
- after a large number of individual words, of which the commonest are the verbal particles *a*, *na, ny*; the possessives *dha, y*; the prepositions *a*, *dhe*, *re*, *war*; the numbers *dew*, *diw*:
- after the article in all feminine singular nouns

8

and in masculine plural nouns denoting persons:

- in adjectives following a feminine singular noun, or a masculine plural noun denoting persons.

Spirant mutation

p	→	**f**
t	→	**th**
k	→	**h** (but **kr** and **kl** are unaffected)

Spirant mutation occurs principally:
- after the possessives *ow, hy, aga*.
- after the numbers *tri, teyr*.

Hard mutation

b	→	**p**
d	→	**t**
g	→	**k**

Hard mutation occurs principally:
- after the present participial particle *ow*;

- after the conjunctions *mar, a* 'if'.

Mixed mutation

b	→	**f**	after *'th*	**v**
d	→	**t**	after *'th*	**t**
m	→	**f**	after *'th*	**v**

When followed by **o**, **u**, **ro** or **ru**, **g** usually changes to **hw**; otherwise **g** changes to **h**.

This form of mixed mutation occurs principally:
- after the adverbials *kyn, maga, may, ple, p'eur, py, yn*:
- after the verbal particle *y*.

A modified form of mixed mutation occurs after *'th*.

Pronunciation and spelling of Cornish

Since sound-recording apparatus had not been invented at the time when Cornish was spoken traditionally, we have no direct evidence of how it was pronounced. The nearest that we can get to its pronunciation is the description made by Edward Lhuyd during his visit to Cornwall in 1701. This applies to the Late Cornish phase, and because the sounds of Cornish (like those of any other language) changed with time, it is not applicable to the Middle Cornish phase on which the revived language is based. Otherwise we have to rely on the interpretation of the written texts.

This is complicated because four different spelling systems were used for writing traditional Cornish; those of Old, Middle and Late Cornish, and that of Edward Lhuyd. Only the last of these was reasonably fixed, and only the last attempted seriously to indicate the pronunciation. (It could be argued that a fifth system was the modification of the Late Cornish spelling in the light of Lhuyd's work). In the twentieth century, Jenner's orthography and Nance's Unified Cornish were fixed, but their links to the pronunciation were tenuous.

During the 1980s, the compiler of this dictionary carried out an extensive study of the historical phonology of Cornish, and his recommended pronunciation was intended to approximate that of the traditional language *c.*1500. Nance's orthography, known as Unified Cornish, was improved so as to fit the pronunciation more closely, and to be more phonemic. A phonemic orthography is one in which each phoneme (contrastive sound-unit) is represented by a unique grapheme (letter or group of letters). Using such an orthography, one can work out what the phonemes are from the written word. To determine the pronunciation then depends on knowing the way in which each phoneme is pronounced (its realization), which may vary according to its position in an utterance. The near one-to-one relationship between writing and sound enables learners of Cornish to acquire a fairly accurate pronunciation with ease and speed. The orthography is most phonemic when applied to stressed syllables; in unstressed syllables it is sometimes partly etymological.

The improved spelling (as used in this dictionary) and recommended pronunciation, known as ***Kernewek Kemmyn***, were adopted by the Cornish Language Board in July 1987. They have been criticized by N.Williams in his book *Cornish Today*, but his criticisms are largely unfounded, as shown by Paul Dunbar and the present editor in their reply *Kernewek Kemmyn – Cornish for the 21st Century*. Although the pronunciation of Cornish is readily deducible from its spelling, the pronunciation has been included in this dictionary, to conform with others in the same series.

Vowels

Cornish vowels have three possible lengths, depending on the stress and on the nature of the following consonants. [ː] indicates that the vowel is long, and [·] that it is of mid-length. The vocalic system is most fully developed in stressed vowels. It has the nine phonemes /i, ɪ, e, a, ɔ, o, u, œ, y/, which are represented respectively in **Kernewek Kemmyn** by the nine graphemes *i, y, e, a, o, oe, ou, eu, u*. The recommended pronunciations are as follows:

SPELLING	STRESSED			UNSTRESSED
i	[iː]	[iˑ]	[i]	[ɪ]
y	[ɪː]	[ɪˑ]	[ɪ]	[ɪ]
e	[ẹː]	[ẹˑ]	[ẹ]	[ɛ]
a	[aː]	[aˑ]	[a]	[a]
o	[ɔː]	[ɔˑ]	[ɔ]	[ɔ]
oe	[oː]	[oˑ]	[ɤ]	[ɤ]
ou	[uː]	[uˑ]	[u]	[u]
eu	[œ]	[œ]		
u	[yː]	[yˑ]	[y]	[ɪ] in final syllables

Note that [ẹ] and [ɛ] are replaced in the pronunciations in the dictionary by [e].

Diphthongs

The Cornish diphthongs are as follows:

SPELLING	SOUNDS
ey	[eɪ]
ay	[aɪ]
oy	[ɔɪ]
iw	[iʊ]
yw	[ɪʊ]
ew	[ẹʊ]

14

aw	[aʊ]
ow	[ɔʊ]
uw	[yʊ]

Semi-vowels

These are [j] and [w], spelled respectively *y* and *w*.

Consonants

The following stressed Cornish consonants have the same values as the English ones:

SPELLING	SOUNDS
p-, t-, k-	[p, t, k]
b, d, g	[b, d, g]
ch, f, th	[tʃ, f, θ]
j, v, dh	[dʒ, v, ð]
sh, h, ng	[ʃ, h, ŋ]
m, n, l, r	[m, n, l, r]

s at present stands for both [s] and [z].

The grapheme *gh* in Cornish is pronounced [x] (as *ch* in *loch*) when at the end of a word and following a vowel; otherwise it is pronounced [ɦ] (the sound of *h* in *aha*). The following consonants may be doubled: [pp, tt, kk], [ff, θθ, xx, ss], [mm, nn, ll, rr]; and the corresponding graphemes are also doubled (except that [θθ] and [xx] are represented respectively by *tth* and *ggh*). Unstressed consonants are pronounced the same as the stressed consonants, except that ***mm, nn, ll*** and ***rr*** are reduced to [m, n, l, r] respectively.

Bibliography

Brown, W. (2001) *A grammar of modern Cornish*. Cornish Language Board, Saltash; 3rd edn. This is the most comprehensive description of the revived language.

Dunbar, P.A. and George, K.J. (1997) **Kernewek Kemmyn - Cornish for the 21st century**. Cornish Language Board, Saltash.

George, K.J. (ed.) (2009) *Gerlyver Kernewek Kemmyn - An Gerlyver Meur*. Cornish Language Board, Saltash. This large Cornish-English / English-Cornish dictionary includes etymologies, morphologies and extensive notes.

Sandercock, G.M. (2004) *Holyewgh an Lergh*. This is a course-book for beginners, tried and tested through many editions over the last 20 years.

Abbreviations used in both sections

abst.	abstract
Anat.	anatomy
Astron.	astronomy
Biol.	biology
e.g.	for example
f	feminine
fig.	figuratively
geog.	geography
intrans.	intransitive
m	masculine
Mus.	music
neg.	negative
obj.	object
occasl.	occasional
pl	plural
poss.	possessive
sg.	singular
trans.	transitive
T.V.	television
v	verb

The compiler wishes to thank Graham Sandercock for proof-reading the text of this pocket dictionary.

KERNEWEK-SOWSNEK
CORNISH-ENGLISH

Grammatical abbreviations used in this section

av	*asverb*	adverb
b	*benow*	feminine noun
es	*erthyglenn stroeth*	definite article
esk	*eskarm*	exclamation
g	*gorow*	masculine noun
hd	*hanow dewel*	dual noun
hg	*hanow-gwann*	adjective
hk	*hanow kuntellek*	collective noun
hp	*hanow person*	person
le	*le*	place
lp	*liesplek*	plural
m	*mellenn*	conjunction
niv	*niverenn*	numeral
pv	*perthyglenn verbel*	verbal particle
rg	*rag-ger*	preposition
rv	*rann verb*	part of a verb
v	*verb*	verb

A

¹a [ˈaː] *esk* ah
²a² [a] *pv* (verbal particle)
³a² [a] *rg* of, from
⁴a⁴ [a] *m* if
a-ban² [aˈban] *m* since
a-barth [aˈbarθ] *rg* for the sake of, beside, in the name of, along with; **a-barth Duw** for God's sake
abas [ˈaːbas] *g* **+ow** abbot
abatti [aˈbatːi] *g* **+ow** abbey
abel [ˈaːbel] *hg* able, capable, competent, fit
Aberfala [aberˈfaːla] *le* Falmouth
Aberplymm [aberˈplimː] *le* Plymouth
a-bervedh [aˈberveð] *av* inside, indoors, aboard; **a-bervedh yn** inside
a-borpos [aˈbɔrpɔs] *av* purposely, on purpose
a-brys [aˈbriːz] *av* early, timely, on time, in good time
acheson [aˈtʃeˈzɔn] *g* **+yow** cause, reason
a-dal [aˈdaːl] *rg* opposite, facing
adamant [ˈaˈdamant] *g* **+ow** diamond
a-der [aˈdeːr] *rg* without, outside, except
a-dermyn [aˈdermin] *av* in time, on time, punctually
a-dhelergh [aðeˈlerx] *av* behind
a-dherag [aðeˈraːg] *rg* before, beforehand, in front of
a-dhesempis [aðeˈzempis] *av* immediately, forthwith, suddenly
a-dhia² [aˈðiˈa] *rg* since; **a-dhia Nadelik** since Christmas

a-dhistowgh [a'ðiˑ'stɔwx] *av* immediately

adhves ['aðves] *hg* ripe, mellow

adhvesi [að'veziˑ] *v* ripen

a-dhyghow [a'ðiˑfiɔw] *av* on the right hand

adhyskans [a'ðiˑskans] *g* **+ow** education

a-dreus [a'drœːz] *av* across, indirectly, transversely: *rg* across; **kewsel a-dreus** talk at cross-purposes

a-dro [a'drɔː] *av* around: *rg* about, concerning, approximately

a-dryv [a'drɪːv] *av* behind: *rg* behind

afina [a'fiˑna] *v* decorate, garnish, adorn

afinans [a'fiˑnans] *g* **+ow** decor, decoration, garnish

Afrika ['afrɪka] *le* Africa

Afrikan ['afrɪkan] *g* **+s** African

afrikanek [afriˑkaˑnek] *hg* African

aga³ [ˌaga] *rh* their

agan [agan] *rh* our

agas [agas] *rh* your

ages [ag'eːz] *m* than

agh ['aːx] *esk* fie, ugh

agh ['aːx] *b* **+ow** offspring

a-gledh [a'gleːð] *av* on the left hand

a-gynsow [a'gɪnzɔw] *av* recently, lately, just now

ahanan [a'haˑnan] *av* hence, from us, of us

ahwer [a'hweːr] *g* **+yow** trouble, sorrow, distress

a-hys [a'hɪːz] *av* full length, outstretched, from end to end

a-ji [a'dʒiː] *av* inside: *rg* inside

akont [a'kɔnt] *g* **+ow** financial account, reckoning

akontya *v* count, reckon, esteem

akord [a'kɔrd] *g* agreement, harmony (abst.), reconciliation

akordya [a'kɔrdja] *v* agree, harmonize (abst.),

reconcile

akwityans [aˈkwiˑtjans] *g* **+ow** receipt

alamand [ˈaˑlamand] *g* **+ow**; **+ys** almond

alargh [aˈlarx] *g* **elergh** swan

Alban [ˈalban] *le* Scotland: *g* **+yon** Scotsman

Albanes [alˈbaˑnes] *b* **+ow** Scotswoman

Albani [alˈbaˑni] *le* Albania

albom [ˈalbɔm] *g* **+ow** album

alemma [aˈlemːa] *av* hence

a-lemmyn [aˈlemːɪn] *hg* present

alena [aˈleˑna] *av* thence

alhwedh [ˈalhweð] *g* **+ow** key

alhwedha [alˈhweˑða] *v* lock

alhwedh-korkynn [ˌalhweðˈkɔrkɪn] *g* **alhwedhow-korkynn** corkscrew

alhwedhor [alˈhweˑðɔr] *g* **+yon** treasurer (male)

alhwedhores [alhweˈðɔˑres] *b* **+ow** treasurer (female)

alkan [ˈalkan] *g* **alkenyow** metal

Almann [ˈalman] *g* **+ow** German man

Almannes [alˈmanːes] *b* **+ow** German woman

Almayn [ˈalmaɪn] *le* Germany

almaynek [alˈmaɪnek] *hg* German

Almaynek [alˈmaɪnek] *g* German language

¹**als** [ˈals] *b* **+yow** cliff

²**als** [ˈals] *g* **+yow** joint

altenn [ˈalten] *b* **+ow** razor

alusen [aˈlyˑzen] *b* **+ow** alms, charity (gift of money)

amal [ˈaˑmal] *b* **emlow** edge, border, side, rim

amanynn [aˈmaˑnɪn] *g* **+ow** butter

amanynna [ˌamaˈnɪnːa] *v* butter

amari [aˈmaˑri] *g* **+ow**; **+s** cupboard, locker

ambos ['ambɔs] *g* **+ow** promise, contract, vow, covenant; **ambos demmedhyans** engagement to marry

ambosa [am'bɔ·zaː] *v* promise

Amerika [a'merɪka] *le* America; **Amerika Dyghow** South America; **Amerika Kledh** North America; **Amerika Latin** Latin America

Amerikan [a'merɪkan] *g* **+yon** American

amerikanek [amerɪ'ka·nek] *hg* American

amiral ['amɪral] *g* **-elyon** admiral

amkan ['amkan] *g* **+ow** aim, objective, goal

amm ['amː] *g* **+ow** kiss

amma ['amːa] *v* kiss

ammeth ['amːeθ] *b* agriculture

amontieth [,amɔn'tiˑeθ] *b* computing, computer science

amontydh [a'mɔntɪð] *g* **+yon** computer scientist

amovya [a'mɔ·vja] *v* agitate

amovyans [a'mɔ·vjans] *g* **+ow** agitation

amseryow [am'zˑerjɔw] *lp* menstrual period

amyttya [a'mɪtːja] *v* admit, acknowledge, concede

an [an] *es* the

anall ['aˑnal] *hk* **+enn** *b* breath

analladow [ana'la·dɔw] *hg* impossible

andhemmedhys [,anðe'meˑðɪs] *hg* unmarried, single

andhewanadow [anðeʊa'na·dɔw] *hg* impermeable

androw [an'drɔw] *g* **+yow** afternoon

androweyth [an'drɔweɪθ] *g* **+yow** afternoon-time

anella [a'nelːa] *v* breathe

anes [an'eːz] *hg* uneasy, troubled, wearied

aneth ['aˑneθ] *g* **+ow** wonder, adventure, marvel; **gul aneth a** wonder at

anewn [an'ɛʊn] *hg* unfair

anfeus ['anfœs] *b* ill luck, misfortune, misery

anfeusik [an'fœˑzɪk] *hg* unfortunate, unlucky

angoes ['angɤs] *g* anguish

anken ['anken] *g* **+yow** misery, grief, trouble

ankevi [an'keˑvi] *v* forget

ankewar [an'gewar] *hg* incorrect

ankombra [an'kɔmbra] *v* bother, hamper, embarrass

ankor ['ankɔr] *g* **+yow** anchor

ankorya [an'kɔˑrja] *v* anchor

ankoth [an'kɔˑθ] *hg* unknown, strange, outlandish

ankow ['ankɔw] *g* Death (personified)

ankres ['ankrɛs] *g* disquiet, distress

ankresus [an'kreˑzys] *v* disturbing

ankresya [an'kreˑzja] *v* disturb

annia [a'niˑa] *v* annoy, tire, weary, vex, aggrieve

anpryvyon [an'prɪˑvjɔn] *lp* insects

anragwelys [anrag'weˑlɪs] *hg* unforeseen

anrewlys [an'rɛʊlɪs] *hg* irregular

anserghek [an'sɛrxɛk] *hg* independent

ansertan [an'sɛrtan] *hg* uncertain

Antarktika [ant'arktika] *le* Antarctica

anvlasus [an'vlaˑzys] *hg* tasteless, insipid, bland

anvodhek [an'vɔˑðek] *hg* involuntary

anvovadow [anvɔ'vaˑdɔw] *hg* spritually immovable

anwayadow [anwa'jaˑdɔw] *hg* physically immovable

anwoes ['anwɤs] *g* **+ow** chill, cold in the head

anwortosys [anwɔr'tɔˑzɪs] *hg* unexpected

apert [a'pert] *hg* obvious, evident, open

apposya [a'pɔˑzja] *v* examine (of knowledge), test by questions

apposyans [a'pɔˑzjans] *g* **+ow** examination, test

apron ['aprɔn] *g* **+yow** apron

Arab ['aˑrab] *g* **Arabyon** Arab

Arabek [aˑraˑbek] *hg* Arabic: *g* Arabic language

Arabi [aˑraˑbi] *le* Arabia

arader ['aˑrader] *g* **ereder** plough

a-rag [aˑraːg] *rg* before, in front of, in the presence of: *av* forward

arall ['aˑral] *hg* other, another; **yn fordh arall** on the other hand

aras ['aˑras] *v* plough

aray ['aˑraɪ] *g* **+ow** order, array, arrangement, layout

araya [aˑraɪa] *v* put in order

arbenniger [ˌarbeˑniˑger] *g* **-oryon** specialist, expert

arbennik [arˈbenːik] *hg* special; **yn arbennik** specially

arbrovji [arˈbrɔvji] *g* **+ow** laboratory

ardak ['ardak] *g* **ardagow** delay

arenebedh [areˑneˑbeð] *g* **+ow** area

arenep [aˈreˑnep] *g* **-enebow** surface

areth ['aˑreθ] *b* **+yow** speech, address, oration, declamation, lecture

arge ['arge] *g* **+ow** dam

argelli [arˈgelːi] *v* risk

argemmynnans [ˌargeˈmɪnːans] *g* advertising

argerdh [ˈargerð] *g* **+ow** process

argh ['arx] *b* **+ow** chest, coffer, bin, ark

arghans ['arxans] *g* silver, money, finance; **arghans byw** mercury; **arghans tiogeth** housekeeping money

arghanser [arˈfianzer] *g* **-oryon** banker

Arghantina [arfianˈtiːna] *le* Argentina

arghantti [arˈfianti] *g* **+ow** bank (for money)

arghena [arˈfieˑna] *v* put shoes on

arghpedrevan [ˌarfipeˈdreˑvan] *g* **+es** dinosaur

26

argoll ['argɔl] *g* risk
argyans ['argjans] *g* **+ow** argument
Arktik ['arktɪk] *le* Arctic
arliw ['arliw] *g* **+yow** tint
arliwa [ar'liwa] *v* tint
arloedh ['arlʏð] *g* **arlydhi** lord, master
arloedhes [ar'loˑðes] *b* **+ow** lady, mistress of a
  house
arnowydh [ar'nɔwɪð] *hg* modern
art ['art] *g* **+ow** art; **artow fin** fine arts
arta ['arta] *av* again, once more, on a future occasion
artydh ['artɪð] *g* **+yon** artist
arv ['arv] *b* **+ow** weapon, arm
arva ['arva] *v* arm
arvedhenn [ar've·ðen] *b* **+ow** insult
arvethesik [ˌarve'θe·zɪk] *g* **-igyon** employee,
  hireling
arvethor [ar've·θɔr] *g* **+yon** employer, boss
arvor ['arvɔr] *g* **+yow** coast, coastland
arvregh *b* **+ow** forearm
arvreusi [ar'vrœ·zi] *v* criticize
arwask ['arwask] *g* **+ow** oppression
arwaska [ar'wa·ska] *v* oppress
arwoedh ['arwʏð] *b* **+yow** sign, symbol, emblem,
  armorial device, symptom
a's [as] *rh* her, it (obj.)
a's [as] *rh* them
asen ['a·zen] *g* **-es** donkey, ass
asenn ['a·zen] *b* **+ow** rib, spoke of wheel, stave of
  barrel
Asi ['a·si] *le* Asia
Asiek [a'si·ek] *hg* Asiatic
askell ['a·skel] *b* **eskelli** wing, fin, naker shell

askell-dro [askel'drɔ:] *b* **eskelli-tro** helicopter

askeller [as'keller]; **-oryon** winger

askell-groghen [ˌa·skel'grɔ·xen] *g* **eskelli-kroghen** bat (creature)

askloes [as'klʏs] *hk* **+enn** chips

askorn ['a·skɔrn] *g* **eskern** bone

askorr ['a·skɔr] *g* produce

askorra [as'kɔr:a] *v* produce

askorras [as'kɔr:as] *g* **+ow** product

askus ['askʏs] *g* **+yow** excuse

asow ['a·zɔw] *hk* **+enn** ribs

asper ['a·sper] *hg* harsh

aspians [a'spi·ans] *g* **+ow** reconnaissance

assay ['as:aɪ] *g* **+s** rehearsal, trial, try, attempt, essay

assaya [as'aɪa] *v* attempt, try

assentyans [a'sentjans] *g* **+ow** assent

astel ['a·stel] *v* discontinue, suspend, cease, break off

astell ['a·stel] *b* **estyll** board, plank, splint; **astell an oeles** mantelpiece

astiveri [ˌastɪ've·ri] *v* compensate

astiveryans [ˌastɪ've·rjans] *g* **+ow** compensation

asverb ['azverb] *g* **+ow** adverb

aswiwa [az'wiʊa] *v* adapt

aswonn ['azwɔn] *v* know (persons or places), recognize, acknowledge, realize, be familiar with

aswonnvos [az'wɔnvɔs] *g* knowledge, acquaintance

atal ['a·tal] *hk* **+enn** rubbish, mine-waste

atalgist [a'talgɪst] *b* **+yow** dustbin

athletieth [aθleˈti·eθ] *b* athletics

Atlantek [at'lantek] *hg* Atlantic

attendya [a'tendja] *v* notice, pay attention, take note of

attes [at:'e·ɪz] *hg* comfortable, at ease

attyli [at'tɪ·li] *v* repay

a-ugh [a'yːx] *rg* above, over, aloft

aval ['aˑval] *g* **+ow** apple

avalennek [ˌavaˑlenːek] *b* **-egi** apple orchard

aval-gwlanek [ˌavalˈgwlaˑnek] *g* **avalow-gwlanek** peach

aval-kerensa [ˌavalkeˈrenza] *g* **avalow-kerensa** tomato

avan ['aˑvan] *b* **+enn** raspberries

a-vann [a'vanː] *av* above

a-varr [a'varː] *av* early

avel [a'veːl] *rg* like, as

a-ves [a've:z] *hg* outside, away

avi ['aˑvi] *g* **+ow** liver

avi ['aˑvi] *g* **+ow** envy, jealousy, ill-will

avis ['aˑvɪs] *g* **+yow** advice, opinion, consideration

avisya [a'viˑsja] *v* advise, observe, make known

avlavar [av'laˑvar] *hg* dumb, mute, speechless

avleythys [av'leɪθɪs] *hg* hardened, obdurate, tough

avodya [a'voˑdja], leave, go away, get out, escape, withdraw

avon ['aˑvɔn] *b* **+yow** river

avonsya [a'vɔnsja] *v* advance, progress, promote, exalt

avonsyans [a'vɔnsjans] *g* **+ow** advance, promotion

a-vorow [a'voˑrɔw] *av* tomorrow; **a-vorow gorthugher** tomorrow evening

avowa [a'vɔwa] *v* avow, confess, acknowledge

a-wartha [a'warθa] *av* above, aloft, on top

awel ['awel] *b* **+yow** wind, gale, weather

awen ['awen] *b* inspiration, muse, genius, poetic imagination

awen ['awen] *b* **+ow** jaw

aweyl [a'weɪl] *b* **+ys**; **+yow** gospel

29

awgrym [ˈaʊgrɪm] *g* mathematics

awos [aˈwɔːz] *m* because, though, for the sake of, in spite of; **war neb 'wos** on any account

a-wosa [aˈwɔːza] *av* afterwards, later on

awtour [ˈaʊtur] *g* **+s** author

ayr [ˈaɪr] *g* air

ayra [ˈaɪra] *v* air

ayrborth [ˈaɪrbɔrθ] *g* **+ow** airport

ayrgylgh [ˈaɪrgɪlx] *g* **+yow** atmosphere

aysel [ˈaɪzel] *g* **+yow** vinegar

B

baban [ˈbaˑban] *g* **+es** baby

badhya [ˈbaˑðja] *v* bathe

bagas [ˈbaˑgas] *g* **+ow** group, troop, bunch; **bagas ilewydhyon** orchestra

bal [ˈbaːl] *g* **+yow** mine, area of tin-working

balegi [baˈleˑgi] *v* project

balegva [baˈlegva] *b* **+ow** balcony

balyer [ˈbaˑljer] *g* **+yow** barrel

banadhel [ˈbaˑnaðel] *k* **banadhlenn** broom-plant, besom

banana [baˈnaˑna] *g* **+s** banana

band [ˈband] *g* **+ys** musical band

baner [ˈbaˑner] *g* **+yow** flag, banner

bankenn [ˈbanken] *b* **+ow** topographical bank

banna [ˈbanːa] *g* **bannaghow** drop, bit, jot

banow [ˈbaˑnɔw] *b* **bynewi** sow (female pig)

bara [ˈbaˑra] *g* bread

baramanynn [ˌbaraˈmaˑnɪn] *g* **+ow** sandwich

bardh [ˈbarð] *g* **berdh** bard (male), poet (male)

bardhes [ˈbarðes] *b* **+ow** bard (female), poet (female)

bardhonek [barˈðɔˑnek] *hg* poetic: *g* **-ogow** poem

bardhonieth [ˌbarðɔˈniˑeθ] *b* poetry

bargen-tir [ˌbargenˈtiːr] *g* **bargenyow-tir** farm, holding of land

barr [ˈbarː] *g* **+ys** bar (in pub), tribunal

barr [ˈbarː] *g* **+ow** summit, top, climax, branching bough

barras [ˈbarːas] *g* **+ow** crisis

barrenn [ˈbarːen] *b* **+ow** twig

barrlenn [ˈbarlen] *b* **+ow** lap

barthusek [barˈθyˑzek] *hg* miraculous

barv [ˈbarv] *b* **+ow** beard

barvek [ˈbarvek] *hg* bearded

bas [ˈbaːz] *hg* shallow

basa [ˈbaˑza] *v* stun

basnett [ˈbasnet] *g* **+ow** helmet

bason [ˈbaˑsɔn] *g* **+yow** large basin

batalyas [baˈtaˑljas] *v* fight

batel [ˈbaˑtel] *b* **+yow** battle

bath [ˈbaθ] *g* **+ow** coin

batri [ˈbatri] *g* **+ow** battery

baya [ˈbaɪa] *g* **+ys** bay (coastal indentation)

bedh [ˈbeːð] *g* **+ow** grave, sepulchre, tomb

bedha [ˈbeˑða] *v* dare, venture, presume

bedhek [ˈbeˑðek] *hg* daring, venturesome, presumptious

bedhygla [beˈðɪgla] *v* moo

begh [ˈbeːx] *g* **+yow** burden, load

beghya [ˈbeˑxja] *v* burden, oppress, load, impose upon

beghyek [ˈbexjek] *hg* pregnant

31

bejeth [ˈbeˈdʒeθ] *b* **+ow** face

ben [ˈbeːn] *b* **hy ben** the other (f.)

benel [ˈbeˈnel] *hg* feminine

bennath [ˈbenːaθ] *b* **+ow** blessing, benediction

benniga [beˈniˈga] *v* bless

benow [ˈbeˈnɔw] *hg* female

benyn [ˈbeˈnɪn] *b* **+es** woman

bera [ˈbeˈra] *v* flow

¹bern [ˈbern] *g* **+yow** care (solicitude), interest (concern); **ny vern** it does not matter, never mind

²bern [ˈbern] *g* **+yow** heap, rick, stack

bernya [ˈbernja] *v* pile up, stack

¹berr [ˈberː] *hg* short

²berr [ˈberː] *b* **+ow** shank, calf of leg

berrhe [berˈheː] *v* shorten

berrwelyek [berˈweˈljek] *hg* myopic

besow [ˈbeˈzɔw] *hk* **+enn** birch-trees

best [ˈbeːst] *g* **+es** beast, animal

besydh [ˈbeˈzɪð] *g* **+yow** baptism

besydhya [beˈzɪˈðja] *v* baptise

beudhi [ˈbœˈði] *v* drown

bewin [ˈbewɪn] *g* beef

bibyn-bubyn [ˌbiˈbɪnˈbyˈbɪn] *g* **bibynes-bubyn** shrimp

bil [ˈbiːl]; **bil an garr** calf of leg

bili [biˈli] *hk* **+enn** pebbles

bilvil [ˈbilvɪl] *g* **+yow** billion

bismer [bisˈmeːr] *g* contempt, infamy, scandal

blam [ˈblaːm] *g* **+ys** blame, fault

blamya [ˈblaˈmja] *v* blame, censure, find fault with

blas [ˈblaːz] *g* **+ow** taste, smell, relish

blasa [ˈblaˈza] *v* taste, smell, relish

bleudh [ˈblœːð] *hg* soft, tender, delicate

bleujenn [ˈblœˈdʒen] *b* **+ow, bleujyow** *hk* flower, bloom, blossom; **bleujenn an gog** bluebell

bleujennydh [blœˈdʒenːɪð] *g* **+yon** florist

bleus [ˈblœːz] *g* **+yow** flour

blew [ˈblew] *hk* **+enn** hair

blewenn [ˈblewen] *b* **+ow, blew** *hk* individual hair; **blewenn an lagas** eyelash

bleydh [ˈbleɪð] *g* **+i** wolf

bleyn [ˈbleɪn] *g* **+yow** tip, point, peak, forefront

bloedh [ˈbloɪð] *g* year of age, age in years

blogh [ˈblɔːx] *hg* bald, hairless, close-shaven

blonek [ˈblɔˈnek] *g* **-egow** fat, grease, lard

blydhen [ˈblɪˈðen] *b* **blydhynyow** year; **Blydhen Nowydh Da!** Happy New Year!; **nessa blydhen** next year

blydhenyek [blɪˈðeˈnjek] *hg* annual

boba [ˈbɔˈba] *g* **bobys** simpleton

bodh [ˈbɔːð] *g* **+ow** will, inclination, consent; **bodh da** goodwill

bodhar [ˈbɔˈðar] *hg* deaf

bodharel [bɔˈðaˈrel] *hg* deafening

bodharhe [ˌbɔðarˈheː] *v* deafen

bodhesik [bɔˈðeˈzɪk] *g* **-igyon** amateur

boekka [ˈbɤkːa] *g* **+s** hobgoblin, imp, scarecrow

boel [ˈbɔːl] *b* **+yow** axe

boemmenn [ˈbɤmːen] *b* **+ow** blow, buffet, stroke

boes [ˈbɔːz] *g* **+ow** food, meal, fodder; **boes soper** supper; **boes war'n voes** meal-time

boesti [ˈbɔˈsti] *g* **+ow** restaurant, eating-house

bogh [ˈbɔːx] *g* **+es** buck, billy-goat, he-goat

bogh [ˈbɔːx] *hg* **+ow, diwvogh** *hd* cheek (Anat.)

boghes [ˈbɔˈxes] *hg* few, little; **boghes venowgh** seldom

boghosek [bɔˈfiɔˑzek] *hg* poor, indigent, destitute: *g*-**ogyon** pauper

boghosogneth [ˌbɔfiɔˈzɔgneθ] *b* poverty, destitution, want

boks *g* **byksyn** box-tree

bold [ˈbɔld] *hg* bold, daring

bolgh [ˈbɔlx] *g* **+ow** pass (topographical), col

bolla [ˈbɔlːa] *g* **bollow** bowl, small basin

bollenn [ˈbɔlːen] *b* **+ow** lamp-bulb

bolonjedh [bɔˈlɔndʒeð] *g* will

bombard [ˈbɔmbard] *g* **+ow** bombard (Mus.)

bones [ˈbɔˑnes] *v* be

bonk [ˈbɔnk] *g* **+ys** bump, knock, bang

bora [ˈbɔˑra] *g* **+ow** dawn

¹bos [ˈbɔːz] *v* be; **na yll bos** impossible

²bos [ˈbɔːz]; **+ow** abode, dwelling-place

³bos [ˈbɔːz] *g* **+ow** bush

Bosni [ˈbɔzni] *le* Bosnia-Herzegovina

Bosvenegh [bɔzˈveˑnex] *le* Bodmin

botas [ˈbɔˑtas] *hk* **+enn** boots; **botas palvek** flippers

botell [ˈbɔˑtel] *g* **+ow** bottle

both [ˈbɔːθ] *b* **+ow** hump, boss, stud, hub

bothell [ˈbɔˑθel] *b* **+ow** blister

boton [ˈbɔˑtɔn] *g* **+yow** button

botona [bɔˈtɔˑna] *v* button

bour [ˈbuːr] *g* **+yow** embankment

bowji [ˈbɔudʒi] *g* **+ow** cowshed

bownder [ˈbɔunder] *b* **+yow** lane

braggya [ˈbragːja] *v* threaten, menace

braggyans [ˈbragːjans] *g* bragging

braggyer [ˈbragːjer] *g* **+s** braggart

bramm [ˈbramː] *g* **bremmyn** fart

bramma ['bramːa] *v* fart

bran ['braːn] *b* **brini** crow

¹bras ['braːz] *hg* big, large, great, generally, overall, mostly, chiefly, for the most part

²bras ['braːz] *g* **+ow** plot, conspiracy

brashe [bras'heː] *v* enlarge, magnify

braster ['braːster] *g* **+yow** greatness, size

brastir ['braːstir] *g* **+yow** continent

brath ['braːθ] *g* **+ow** bite

brav ['braːv] *hg* grand, fine

Brazil [bra'zɪl] *le* Brazil

bre ['breː] *b* **+ow** hill

bregh ['breːx] *b* **+ow, diwvregh** *hd* arm (limb)

breghel ['breˑxel] *g* **bregholow** sleeve

breghellik [bre'fielˑɪk] *g* **-igow** bracelet

brennik ['brenːɪk] *hk* **-igenn** limpet

brennya ['brenːja] *v* direct

bresel ['breˑzel] *b* **+yow** war, dispute, strife

Breten ['breˑten] *le* Britain; **Breten Veur** Great Britain; **Breten Vyghan** Brittany

Breton ['breˑtɔn] *g* **+yon** Breton man

Bretoneger [ˌbretɔ'neˑger] *g* **-oryon** Breton speaker

bretonek [bre'tɔˑnek] *hg* Breton

Bretonek [bre'tɔˑnek] *g* Breton language

Bretones [bre'tɔˑnes] *b* **+ow** Breton woman

breusi ['brœˑzi] *v* judge

breuslys ['brœzlɪs] *b* **+yow** assize-court, court of law

breusydh ['brœˑzɪð] *g* **+yon** judge, referee

breyn ['breɪn] *hg* rotten, decayed

breyna ['breɪna] *v* decay, rot

breynder ['breɪnder] *g* rot

bri ['briː] *b* esteem, value, worth, importance,

reputation; **gul vri a** take account of; **ny wra vri (orth)** he takes no notice (of)

brialli [bri'al:i] *hk* **briallenn** primroses

brigadenn *b* **+ow** brigade

brith ['bri:θ] *hg* streaked, striped, variegated: *hk* **+enn** tartan, freckle

brithel ['bri·θel] *g* **brithyli** mackerel

bro ['bro:] *b* **+yow** country, land

brocha ['bro·tʃa] *g* **brochys** brooch

broder ['bro·der] *g* **breder** brother; **broder dre lagha** brother-in-law

broenn ['brʊn:] *hk* **+enn** rushes

brogh ['bro:x] *g* **+es** badger

bronn ['brɔn:] *b* **+ow, diwvronn** *hd* breast; **ri bronn** suckle

bronnlenn ['brɔnlen] *b* **+ow** bib

bronnvil ['brɔnvil] *g* **+es** mammal

¹bros ['bro:z] *g* **+ow** sting, prick, stimulus, sharp point

²bros ['bro:z] *hg* extremely hot; **+ow** stew

brosa ['bro·za] *v* sting

brosweyth ['brɔzweɪθ] *g* embroidery

brosya ['brɔ·zja] *v* stitch, embroider

browagh ['brɔʊax] *g* **+ow** terror

browaghweyth [ˌbrɔʊax'weɪθ] *g* **+ow** terrorism

broweghyades [ˌbrɔʊefi'ja·des] *b* **+ow** female terrorist

broweghyas [brɔ'we·xjas] *g* **-ysi** male terrorist

bryansenn [bri'anzen] *b* **+ow** throat, windpipe, gullet

bryjyon ['bri·dʒɔn] *g* boiling, convection: *v* boil

brykedh ['bri·keð] *hk* **+enn** apricots

brykk ['brik] *g* **+ow** brick

bryntin [ˈbrɪntin] *hg* noble, splendid

¹brys [ˈbriːz] *g* **+yow** mind, intention, way of thinking **orth ow brys**; **dhe'm brys vy** in my opinion

²brys [ˈbriːz] *g* **+yow** womb

Brython [ˈbrɪˈθɒn] *g* **+yon** Briton, Brythonic Celt

bryw [ˈbrɪw] *hg* broken, injured, bruised: *g* **+yon** bruise

brywi [ˈbrɪwi] *v* bruise, crush, crumble

brywvannek [brɪʊˈvanːek] *hg* sore

brywyon [ˈbrɪʊjɒn] *hk* **+enn** crumbs

budhynn [ˈbyˈðɪn] *g* **+ow** meadow

bugel [ˈbyˈgeles] *b* **+edh** shepherd

bugeles [byˈgeˈles] *b* **+ow** shepherdess

bugh [ˈbyːx] *b* **+es** cow

bughik-Duw [ˌbyˈxɪkˈdyw] *b* **bughesigow-Duw** ladybird

Bulgarek [bylˈgaˈrek] *g* Bulgarian language

Bulgari [bylˈgaˈri] *le* Bulgaria

burjes [ˈbyrdʒes] *g* **burjysi** townsman, burgess

burjestra [byrˈdʒeˈstra] *b* **-trevow** borough

bush [ˈbyːʃ] *g* **+ys** crowd, mass

buthuk [ˈbyˈθyk] *hk* **+enn** earthworms

byghan [ˈbɪˈfian] *hg* small, little

byghanhe [bɪfianˈheː] *v* reduce, make smaller

bykken [ˈbɪkˈen] *av* ever, always; **Kernow bys vykken!** Cornwall for ever!

bynk [ˈbɪŋk] *b* **+yow** platform, bench

¹bys [ˈbiːz] *g* **+ow** world

²bys [bɪs] *rg* until, till, as far as, up to; **bys y'n eur ma** till now; **bys a-vorow!** until tomorrow!

³ bys [ˈbiːz] *g* **bysies** finger, digit; **bys bysow** ring finger

bysi ['bɪˈzi] *hg* busy, occupied, diligent; **bysi yw dhyn** we must

bysow ['bɪˈzɔw] *g* **bysowyer** ring (for finger)

bysowek [bɪˈzɔʊek] *b* **-egi** keyboard

bys-troes [ˌbɪsˈtroːz] *g* **bysies-troes** toe

byth ['bɪːθ] *av* ever

bythkweth ['bɪθkweθ] *av* ever, never

byttegyns [bɪtːeˈgɪns] *av* nevertheless, yet, however

byw ['bɪw] *hg* alive, quick, active

bywa ['bɪwa] *v* live

bywder ['bɪʊder] *g* **+yow** activity

bywdern ['bɪʊdern] *g* **+ow** canteen

bywek ['bɪwek] *hg* lively, active, sprightly

bywhe [bɪʊˈheː] *v* activate

bywnans ['bɪʊnans] *g* **+ow** life

bywoniethel [ˌbɪwɔniˈeˈθel] *hg* biological

CH

chambour ['tʃambur] *g* **+yow** bedroom, chamber

chanel; **An Chanel** The English [sic] Channel

chanj ['tʃandʒ] *g* change

chanjya ['tʃandʒja] *v* change, alter

chapel ['tʃaˈpel] *g* **+yow** chapel

chaptra ['tʃaptra] *g* **chapters** chapter

charj ['tʃardʒ] *g* **+ys** charge, care, responsibility

chatel ['tʃaˈtel] *hk* **+enn** cattle, chattels, capital

chek ['tʃeːk] *g* **+ys** cauldron

chekk ['tʃek] *hg* Czech; **Repoblek Chekk** Czech Republic

Chekk ['tʃek] *hg* Czech language

chekkenn [ˈtʃekːen] *b* **+ow** cheque

chekkya [ˈtʃekːja] *v* check

cher [ˈtʃeːr] *g* **+yow** mien, demeanour, state of mind

chershya [ˈtʃerʃja] *v* caress, treat kindly

chevisya [tʃeˈviːzja] *v* borrow

chevisyans [tʃeˈviːzjans] *g* borrowing

chi [ˈtʃiː] *g* **chiow** house, building

China [ˈtʃiːna] *le* China

chinek [ˈtʃiːnek] *hg* Chinese

Chinek [ˈtʃiːnek] *g* Chinese language

choklet [ˈtʃɔklet] *hk* **+enn** chocolate

chons [ˈtʃɔːns] *g* **+yow** chance, luck, lot, opportunity

chymbla [ˈtʃɪmbla] *g* **chymblys** chimney

D

¹da [ˈdaː] *hg* good, wholesome, of full measure, in-law; **da yw genev** I like, I enjoy; **da lowr** mediocre

²da [ˈdaː] *b* **+es** doe (female deer)

dadhel [ˈdaðel] *b* **dadhlow** argument, dispute, discussion

dadhelva [ˈdaðelva] *b* **+ow** debate

dadhla [ˈdaðla] *v* discuss, debate

daffar [ˈdafːar] *g* equipment

dager [ˈdager] *g* **dagrow** tear (weeping), drop (of fluid)

dagrewi [daˈgreʊi] *v* weep, shed tears

dalghenn [ˈdalxen] *b* **+ow** grip, hold, grasp; **kavoes dalghenn yn** take hold of, get a grip on

dalghenna [dalˈfienːa] *v* hold, seize, grasp, retain

39

dall ['dalː] *hg* blind: *g* **dellyon** blind person

dalla ['dalːa] *v* blind

dalleth ['dalːeθ] *g* **+ow** start, commencement, origin, beginning: *v* begin, start, commence

dallether [da'leˑθer] *g* **-oryon** beginner

dallhe [dalˈheː] *v* blind

damaj ['daˑmadʒ] *g* **+ys** damage

dampnya ['dampnja] *v* condemn, damn

dampnys ['dampnɪs] *hg* damned

damsel ['damsel] *b* **+s**, young lady, unmarried woman miss

danek ['daˑnek] *hg* Danish

Danek ['daˑnek] *g* Danish language

Danmark ['danmark] *le* Denmark

dannvon ['danvɔn] *v* send, dispatch

dans ['dans] *g* **dyns** tooth

daras ['daˑras] *g* **+ow** door

darbar ['darbar] *g* **+ow** gadget

darbari [dar'baˑri] *v* prepare, make ready, equip

dargan ['dargan] *b* **+ow** prediction, forecast, prophecy

dargana [dar'gaˑna] *v* forecast

darn ['darn] *g* **+ow** bit, fragment, piece, part

darnas ['darnas] *g* **+ow** portion, fraction (in general)

daromres [dar'ɔmres] *g* **+ow** traffic, oscillation: *v* frequent

darvos ['darvɔs] *g* **+ow** event, happening

dasentra [daz'entra] *v* re-enter

daskavoes [das'kaˑvʏs] *v* recover (trans.), find again

dasknias [das'kniˑas] *v* ruminate

daskorr [das'kɔr] *v* restore, give back

daslenwel [das'lenwel] *v* refill

dasleverel [ˌdasle'veˑrel] *v* repeat

40

dasseni [das'se·ni] *v* echo

dassevel [das'se·vel] *v* rebuild

dasskrif ['das:krif] *g* **+ow** copy

dasskrifa [das'skri·fa] *v* copy

dasskrifys [das'skri·fɪs] *hg* rewritten

dasson ['das:ɔn] *g* **+yow** echo

dastewynnya [daste'wɪn:ja] *v* reflect (of light), shine back

dastoemma [das'tʏmma] *v* reheat

dasvywa ['dasfɪwa] *v* revive, live again

dasweles [daz'we·les] *v* revise

daswrias [daz'wri·as] *v* resew

daswul ['daswyl] *v* remake

dates ['da·tes] *hk* **+enn** date

datum ['da·tym] *g* **data** datum

davas ['da·vas] *b* **deves** sheep

de ['de:] *av* yesterday

deantell [de'antel] *hg* dangerous

debreni [de'bre·ni] *v* itch, tickle

debron ['debrɔn] *g* **+ow** itch, tickling, urge

dedhwi ['de·ðwi] *v* lay eggs

defendya [de'fendja] *v* defend, erase, delete

defola [de'fɔ·la] *v* pollute, defile, violate

defolans [de'fɔ·lans] *g* **+ow** pollution

defoler [de'fɔ·ler] *g* **-oryon** polluter

defowt [de'foʊt] *g* **+ow** defect, failure

deg ['de:g] *niv* **+ow** ten

degadow [de'ga·dɔw] *hg* portable

degea [de'ge·a] *v* close, shut

degemmerer [ˌdege'me·rer] *g* **-oryon** recipient

degemmeres [ˌdege'me·res] *v* receive, take possession of, accept

degemmerva [ˌdege'merva] *b* **+ow** reception room

41

deger ['de·ger] *g* **-oryon**; **deger gravath** stretcher bearer

deges [de'gɪːz] *hg* closed, shut

deghesi [de'fie·zi] *v* fling, cast, hurl

degi ['de·gi] *v* carry

degrena [de'gre·na] *v* shiver, shudder, tremble

dehweles [de'hwe·les] *v* return, come back, atone

dehwelyans [de'hwe·ljans] *g* **+ow** return, forgiveness, atonement

del ['de:l] *hk* **+enn** leaves, foliage

delatya [de'la·tja] *v* delay

delatys [de'la·tɪs] *hg* delayed

deleva [de'le·va] *v* yawn

delinja [de'li·nja] *v* draw (as in art), delineate

delinyans [de'li·njans] *g* **+ow** drawing, delineation

delit [de'li:t] *g* **+ys** delight, pleasure, fun

delivra [de'livra] *v* deliver, release

delk ['delk] *g* **+ow** necklace

dell² [del] *m* as, so, since, how, in as much as; **dell hevel** as it seems; **dell grysav** as I believe

delledhek [de'le·ðek] *hg* suitable, worthy

delow ['delɔw] *g* **+yow** statue

demmedhi [de'me·ði] *v* marry, get married

demmedhyans [de'me·ðjans] *g* **+ow** wedding, marriage

demmedhys [de'me·ðɪs] *hg* married

den ['de:n] *g* **tus** man

dena ['de·na] *v* suck

dendil ['dendɪl] *v* earn, gain, deserve

denewes [de'newes] *b* **+ow** heifer

denladra [den'ladra] *v* kidnap

denses ['denzes] *g* humanity, mankind

denvyth [den'vɪ:θ] *g* nobody

42

der [der] *rg* through

deray [deˈraɪ] *g* **+s** disorder, disarray, confusion

dergh *hg* bright

derivador [ˌderiˈvaˑdɔr] *g* **+yon** reporter, announcer

derivas [deˈriˑvas] *g* report: *v* report, tell

¹derow [ˈdeˑrɔw] *g* **+yow** beginning, start

²derow [ˈderɔw] *hk* **derwenn** oak-trees

derowel [deˈrɔˑwel] *hg* original

desedha [deˈzeˑða] *v* fit

desedhek [deˈzeˑðek] *g* **desedhogow** commission (group of persons)

desempis [deˈzempɪs] *av* immediately, at once

desirya [deˈziˑrja] *v* desire

desk [ˈdeːsk] *g* **+ow** desk

desyghys [deˈsɪˑxɪs] *hg* desiccated

deu [ˈdœː] *hg* over, ended

deur [ˈdœːr]; **ny'm deur** it does not matter to me

deuv [ˈdœːv] *g* **+yon** son-in-law

devedhek [deˈveˑðek] *hg* future: *g* **-ogow**

devedhyans [deˈveˑðjans] *g* **+ow** origin, arrival, genealogical descent

devedhys *hg* come

dever [ˈdeˑver] *g* **+ow** duty

devera [deˈveˑra] *v* drip, dribble, trickle

deves [ˈdeˑves] *g* **devosow** rite, custom, ceremony

devnydh [ˈdevnɪð] *g* **+yow** material, stuff, ingredient; **gul devnydh a** use

devnydhyer [devˈnɪˑðjer] *g* **-yoryon** consumer, user

devos [ˈdeˑvɔs] *v* arrive

devri [deˈvriː] *av* certainly, indeed, definitely, seriously, truly

dew² [ˈdew] *niv* two (m.); **an dhew** both (m.)

dewana [deˈwaˑna] *v* penetrate

dewblek ['deʊblek] *hg* double

dewdhek ['deʊðek] twelve: *g* **-egow** dozen

dewdhen ['deʊðen] *g* couple, pair, man and woman

dewelin [deʊ'e·lɪn] *d* elbows

dewgroch ['deʊgrɔtʃ] *d* pair of crutches

dewi ['dewi] *v* burn, blaze, flare, kindle

dewis ['dewis] *g* **+yow** choice, option, selection: *v* choose, select, pick

dewlagas [deʊ'la·gas] *d* eyes

dewlin ['deʊlɪn] *d* knees

Dewnens ['deʊnens] *le* Devon

dew-ugens [,deʊ'y·gens] *niv* forty, two-score

dewweder [deʊ'we·der] *hd* **-wedrow** pair of spectacles

dewwynkya [deʊ'wɪnkja] *v* blink

dewynn ['dewɪn] *g* **+ow** ray (e.g. of light), beam (radiation)

dewynnell [de'wɪ:nel] *b* **+ow** radiator

dha² [ða] *rh* your (sg.), thy; **dha weles!** see you (to one person)

dh'agan [ðagan] to our

dhe² [ðə] *rg* to, at; **dhe wir** really

dhe-ves [ðə've:z] *av* away

dhiworth [ðɪ'wɔrθ] *rg* from

di ['di:] *av* thither, to that place

dialloes [di'al:ʏs] *hg* unable, powerless, impotent, incapable

diank [di'ank] *g* **+ow** escape: *v* escape

diarghen [di'arxen] *hg* barefoot

dibarow [dɪ'ba·rɔw] *hg* odd (of numbers), unmatched, unique, unequalled, unlike others

dibarth [dɪ'barθ] *b* **+ow** separation, departure, segregation, parting

diberth [dɪˈberθ] *v* separate, part

dibita [dɪˈbiˑta] *hg* pitiless

diblans [dɪˈblans] *hg* distinct, separate

didhan [dɪˈðaːn] *hg* amusing, funny: *g* **-enyow** amusement

didhana [dɪˈðaˑna] *v* amuse, entertain, charm

didhemmedh [dɪˈðemːeð] *hg* divorced

didroessa [dɪˈdrɤsːa] *v* unpack

didros [dɪˈdrɔːs] *hg* silent, noiseless

diedhomm [dɪˈeˑðɔm] *hg* unnecessary

diek [ˈdiˑek] *hg* lazy, idle, slothful

dien [ˈdiˑen] *hg* whole, complete, entire; **yn tien** completely, entirely

dieskis [diˈeskɪs] *hg* barefoot

difenn [ˈdiˑfen] *g* **+ow** prohibition, ban: *v* forbid, ban, prohibit

difennyas [dɪˈfenːjas] *g* **-ysi** defender

difeudhell [dɪˈfœˑðel] *b* **+ow** extinguisher

difeyth [dɪˈfeɪθ] *g* **+yow** desert

difres [dɪˈfreːz] *v* protect, relieve: *g* **+ow** relief

difun [dɪˈfyˑn] *hg* awake

difuna [dɪˈfyˑna] *v* awaken, wake up

difunell [dɪˈfyˑnel] *b* **+ow** alarm clock

difurvya [dɪˈfyrvja] *v* deform

digamma [dɪˈgamːa] *v* straighten out

digelmi [dɪˈgelmi] *v* untie, detach, solve, dissociate, disentangle

digemmyska [ˌdigeˈmɪˑska] *v* sort

digeredh [dɪˈgeˑreð] *g* **+ow** excuse

digeredhi [ˌdigeˈreˑði] *v* excuse

digeudh [dɪˈgœːð] *hg* carefree, merry

digila [dɪˈgiˑla] *hg* lonely

digodennell [ˌdigɔˈdenːel] *b* **+ow** decoder

45

digolm [dɪˈgɔlm] *g* solution to a problem

digolonnek [dɪgɔˈlɔnːek] *hg* downhearted

digorkynna [dɪgɔrˈkɪnːa] *v* uncork

dihaval [dɪˈhaˑval] *hg* different

dihevelepter [dɪˈheveˈlepter] *g* **+yow** difference, dissimilarity

dihigenna [dɪhɪˈgenːa] *v* unhook

dilea [dɪˈleˑa] *v* remove, cancel, delete

dilestra [dɪˈleˑstra] *v* disembark

dillas [ˈdɪlːaz] *hk* **+enn** clothes, clothing, dress

dillasva [dɪˈlazva] *b* **+ow** wardrobe

Dinedin [dɪnˈeˑdɪn] *le* Edinburgh

diner [ˈdiˑner] *g* **+ow** penny

dinerenn [dɪˈneˑren] *b* **+ow** penny-piece

dinewi [dɪˈneʊi] *v* shed

dineythi [dɪˈneɪθi] *v* give birth, beget, generate

dineythyans [dɪˈneɪθjans] *g* **+ow** birth

diogeledh [ˌdiɔˈgeˑleð] *g* security

direwl [dɪˈreʊl] *hg* irregular, unruly, disorderly: *g* anarchy

dirolya [dɪˈrɔˑlja] *v* unroll

diruska [dɪˈryˑska] *v* peel, flay, scrape off skin

dis [ˈdiːs] *g* **+yow** dice

disebilya [dɪseˈbiˑlja] *v* unplug

disedha [dɪˈseˑða] *v* unseat

dises [dɪsˈeːz] *g* **+ys** disease, disquiet, inconvenience

disjunya [dɪsˈjyˑnja] *v* disconnect

diskarga [dɪsˈkarga] *v* unload, discharge

diskians [dɪˈskiˑans] *hg* ignorant

disklerya [dɪsˈkleˑrja] *v* declare

disklusa [dɪsˈklyˑza] *v* unstick

diskudha [dɪsˈkyˑða] *v* discover, uncover, reveal, disclose

diskwedhes [dɪsˈkweˑðes] *v* show, exhibit

diskwedhyans [dɪsˈkweˑðjans] *g* **+ow** show, exhibition, demonstration

diskwitha [dɪˈskwiˑθa] *v* relax

disliw [dɪsˈliw] *hg* discoloured

dismygi [dɪsˈmɪˑgi] *v* guess, invent, find out

dismyk [ˈdɪsmɪk] *g* **-ygow** guess

disobaya [ˌdɪsˈɔbaɪa] *v* disobey

disordyr [dɪsˈɔrdɪr] *g* disorder

displegya [dɪsˈpleˑgja] *v* unfold, develop, explain

displesya [dɪsˈpleˑzja] *v* displease

displetya [dɪsˈpleˑtja] *v* display, unfurl

displetyans [dɪsˈpleˑtjans] *g* **+ow** display

dissernya [dɪsˈsernja] *v* discern, distinguish

distag [dɪˈstaːg] *hg* detached, untethered

distaga [dɪˈstaˑga] *v* detach, untether, sever, secede

distennys [dɪsˈtenːɪs] *hg* distracted

distowgh [ˈdiˑstɔux] *av* immediately, suddenly, instantly

distrui [dɪsˈtryˑi] *v* destroy, undo, ruinate

distruyans [dɪsˈtryˑjans] *g* destruction

distyr [dɪˈstiːr] *hg* insignificant, meaningless, of no account

diswaytys [dɪsˈwaɪtɪs] *hg* disappointed

diswrians [dɪsˈwriˑans] *g* **+ow** ruin, undoing

diswruthyl [dɪsˈwryˑθɪl] *v* undo

diswul [dɪsˈwyːl] *v* undo, ruin, spoil

divarva [dɪˈvarva] *v* shave (trans.)

diveghya [dɪˈveˑxja] *v* unburden, unload

diveri [dɪˈveˑri] *v* pour

divers [ˈdiˑvers] *hg* various, diverse

divlas [dɪˈvlaːz] *g* **+ow** disgust: *hg* disgusting, tiresome

divlasa [dɪˈvlaˑsa] *v* be disgusted with, offend, be ashamed of

diw² [ˈdiw] *niv* two (f.); **an dhiw** both (f.)

diwarr [ˈdiwar] *d* legs

diwedh [ˈdiʊeð] *g* **+ow** end, finish, outcome; **an diwettha** last, latest

diwedhes [diˈweˑðes] *hg* late

diwedhyn [dɪˈweˑðɪn] *hg* rigid, stiff, unbending

diwes [ˈdiwes] *g* **diwosow** drink

diwettha [diˈweθːa] *hg* later; **an diwettha** last

diweyth [diˈweɪθ] *hg* unemployed

diwiska [diˈwiˑska] *v* undress, unclothe

diwiver [dɪˈwiˑver] *g* **+yow** radio, wireless

diwlagatell [diʊlaˈgatːel] *d*; **+ow** binoculars

diworth [dɪˈwɔrθ] *rg* from

diwotti [diˈwɔtːi] *g* **+ow** public house, alehouse

diwros [ˈdiʊrɔs] *b* **+ow** bicycle

diwros-tan [ˌdiʊrɔzˈtaːn] *b* **diwrosow-tan** motorbike

diwrosyer [diʊˈrɔˑzjer] *g* **-yoryon** cyclist

diwskoedh [ˈdiʊskɤð] *d* shoulders

diwskovarn [diʊˈskɔˑvarn] *d* ears

diwvregh [ˈdiʊvrex] *d* arms

diwvronner [diʊˈvrɔnːer] *g* **+yow** brassiere, bra

diwyethek [diʊˈjeˑθek] *hg* bilingual

diwysyans [dɪˈwɪˑzjans] *g* **+ow** industry (manufacture)

diyskynn [diˈɪˑskɪn] *g* **+ow** descent

diyskynna [ˌdiɪsˈkɪnːa] *v* descend, go down, dismount

doen [ˈdoːn] *v* carry, transport, bear, support

does [ˈdoːz] *hg* dense (physically)

doeth [ˈdoːθ] *hg* prudent

48

dohajydh [dɔha'dʒɪːð] *g* **+yow** afternoon, noon to sunset

doktour ['dɔktur] *g* **+s** doctor (title)

dolli ['dɔliː] *b* **+ow** doll

domhwel ['dɔmhwel] *v* overthrow, subvert, overturn

domhwelyans [dɔm'hwe'ljans] *g* **+ow** political revolution

domino [dɔ'miːnɔ] *g* **+yow** domino

dones ['dɔ'nes] *v* come

dons ['dɔns] *g* **+yow** dance; **dons meyn** stone circle

donsya ['dɔnsja] *v* dance

dopi ['dɔːpi] *v* dope

dopyans ['dɔːpjans] *g* doping

dor ['dɔːr] *g* **+yow** ground, soil, earth; **an nor** the world

dordoll ['dɔrdɔl] *g* **+ow** burrow

dorfols ['dɔrfɔls] *g* **+ow** geological fault

dorgell ['dɔrgel] *b* **+ow** cellar, vault, bunker

dorgi ['dɔrgi] *g* **dorgeun** terrier

dorhys ['dɔrhɪs] *g* **+ow** geographic longitude

dorles ['dɔrles]; **+ow** geographic latitude

dorn ['dɔrn] *b* **+ow, diwdhorn** *hd* hand (when used as an instrument), fist

dornas ['dɔrnas] *g* **+ow** handful

dornel ['dɔrnel] *hg* manual

dornla ['dɔrnla] *g* **dornleow** handle, handhold

dornlyver [dɔrn'lɪˈver] *g* **-lyvrow** handbook

doronieth [ˌdɔrɔ'niˈeθ] *b* geography

dos ['dɔːz] *v* come; **dos ha bos** become; **deus a-ji!** come in!

doust ['duːst] *g* dust, chaff

dout ['duːt] *g* **+ys** doubt, dread, fear

49

doutya ['duːtja] *v* doubt

dov ['dɔːv] *hg* tame, domestic

dovhe [dɔv'heː] *v* tame, domesticate

dovydhyn [dɔv'ɪˈðɪn] *k* poultry

down ['dɔun] *hg* deep, profound

dowr ['dɔur] *g* **+ow** water, river

dowra ['dɔura] *v* sprinkle

dowrell ['dɔurel] *b* **+ow** watering-can

dowrer ['dɔurel] *g* **An Dowrer** Aquarius

dowrvargh ['dɔurvarx] *g* **-vergh** hippopotamus

draylell ['draɪlel] *b* **+ow** sledge

draylya ['draɪlja] *v* drag

dre² [dre] *rg* through, by means of; **dre vras** generally, overall

drefenn ['dreˑfen] *m* because, on account of

dregynn ['dreˑgɪn] *g* wrong

drehedhes [dreˈheˑðes] *v* reach, attain

drehevel [dreˈheˑvel] *v* build, raise, erect, construct, lift up

drehevyans [dreˈheˑvjans] *g* **+ow** building, edifice

dren ['dreːn] *g* **dreyn** thorn, prickle, bone of fish

dres [dres] *rg* beyond, over, besides, during **dres oll** above all

drewydh ['drewɪð] *g* **+yon** druid

dri ['driː] *v* bring, take with one

drog ['drɔːg] *hg* bad, wicked, naughty: *g* **+ow** evil, ill, vice; **drog yw genev** I am sorry

droglamm ['drɔglam] *g* **+ow** accident, misadventure, adversity

drogober [drɔg'ɔˑber] *g* **+ow** misdeed, crime

drogoberer [ˌdrɔgɔ'beˑrer] *g* **-oryon** evil-doer, miscreant, criminal

drok-penn ['drɔkpen] *g* **drogow-penn** headache

drolla ['drɔlːa] *g* **drollow** novella
droppya ['drɔp:ja] *v* drop
drudh ['dry:ð] *hg* precious, cherished
du ['dy:] *hg* black, sombre, dark
duk ['dy:k] *g* **+ys** duke
dur ['dy:r] *g* **+yow** steel
dustuni [dys'ty'ni] *g* **dustuniow** evidence,
  testimony, reference for character
dustunier [ˌdysty'ni·er] *g* **-oryon** witness (person),
  referee for character
Duw ['dyw] *hp* God; **Duw genes** goodbye; **Duw
  genowgh hwi** goodbye
duw ['dyw] *g* **+ow** god
duwon ['dywɔn] *g* **kemmeres duwon** be sorry
dybrer *g* **-oryon** eater
dybri ['dɪbri] *v* eat
dydh ['dɪ:ð] *g* **+yow** day; **y'n jydh ma** today; **dydh
  da** good day
dydhweyth ['dɪ·ðweiθ] *av* by day, in the daytime: *b*
  +yow
dydhyas ['dɪ·ðjas] *g* **+ow** date (specific day)
dyenn ['dɪ·en] *g* **+ow** cream; **dyenn dyns** tooth-
  paste
dyerbynna [ˌdɪer'bɪnːa] *v* meet, encounter
dyffrans ['dɪfrans] *g* **+ow** difference: *hg* different
dyffransegi ['dɪfran'ze·gi] *v* differentiate (maths.)
dyghow ['dɪ·ɦɔw] *hg* right (opposite to left)
dyghtya ['dɪxtja] *v* manage, treat, prepare, serve,
  appoint, deal with
dyghtyans ['dɪxtjans] *g* **+ow** management
dyghtyer ['dɪxtjer] *g* **-yoryon** manager
dy'goel [dɪ'goːl] *g* **+yow** feast-day, holiday
dyllo ['dɪlːɔ] *v* publish, release, emit

dyllo ['dɪlːɔ] *hg* lively
dynamekter [dɪnamˈekter] *g* dynamism
dynnargh ['dɪnːarx] *g* **+ow** welcome, greeting
dynnerghi [dɪˈnerxi] *v* greet, salute, welcome
dynsel ['dɪnzel] *v* bite
dyowl ['djɔul] *g* **dywolow** devil
dyskador [dɪsˈkaˌdɔr] *g* **+yon** teacher (male)
dyskadores [ˌdɪskaˈdɔˌres] *b* **+ow** teacher (female)
dyskans ['dɪˈskans] *g* **+ow** lesson, instruction, knowledge
dyskas ['dɪˈskas] *g* **+ow** teaching, doctrine, moral
dyski ['dɪˈski] *v* learn, teach, train, instruct
dyskybel [dɪsˈkɪˌbel] *g* **dyskyblon** pupil
dythya ['dɪˈθja] *v* recite

E

e' [e] *rh* him, it
ebel ['eˈbel] *g* **ebeli** colt
ebil ['eˈbɪl] *g* **+yer** peg, stopper
ebilya [eˈbɪlja] *v* plug
e-bost ['eˈbɔst] *g* **+yow** e-mail
ebron ['ebrɔn] *b* sky
ebrow ['ebrɔw] *hg* Hebrew
Ebrow ['ebrɔw] *g* **+yon** Hebrew
Ebrowek [eˈbrɔwek] *g* Hebrew language
edhel ['eˈðel] *hk* **edhlenn** poplar-trees, aspen-trees
edhen ['eˈðen] *b* **ydhyn** bird
edhomm ['eˈðɔm] *g* **+ow** need, want
edrega [eˈdreˈga] *b* regret
edrek ['edrek] *g* **-egow** regret, remorse, repentance;

edrek a'm beus I regret

efan ['eˑfan] *hg* broad, extensive, spacious

efander [e'fander] *g* space (in general)

efanvos ['eˑfanvɔs] *g* space (Astron.)

effeyth ['efˑeɪθ] *g* **+yow** effect; **effeyth chi gweder** greenhouse effect

effeythus [e'feɪθys] *hg* effective

eghek ['eˑxek] *g* **eghogyon** salmon

eghenn ['eˑxen] *b* **+ow** kind, species, sort, variety; **dres eghenn** exceedingly

egin ['eˑgin] *g* **+yow** bud

eglos ['eglɔs] *b* **+yow** church

ekologieth [ekɔlɔ'giˑeθ] *b* ecology

ekologydh [ekɔ'lɔgɪð] *g* **+yon** ecologist

el ['eːl] *g* **eledh** angel

elester [e'leˑster] *hk* **elestrenn** irises (yellow plants)

elgeth ['elgeθ] *b* **+yow** chin

elin ['eˑlɪn] *g* **+yow, dewelin** *hd* elbow; **+yow** angle

elow ['eˑlɔw] *hk* **+enn** elm-trees

Elzas [el'zas] *le* Alsace

emperour ['emperur] *g* **+s** emperor

empereureth [ˌempeˈruˑreθ] *b* **+ow** empire

ena ['eˑna] *av* there, then, at that place or time

enebi [en'eˑbi] *v* oppose

enebieth [ene'biˑeθ] *b* opposition

enep ['eˑnep] *g* **enebow** surface, face, page of book

enev ['eˑnev] *g* **+ow** soul

eno ['eˑnɔ] *av* yonder, there

enor ['eˑnɔr] *g* **+s** honour

enowi [e'nɔʊi] *v* light up, kindle

ensampel [en'sampel] *g* **-plow** example; **rag ensampel** for example

53

¹envi ['envi] *g* enemy (enemies), foe(s)

²envi ['envi] *g* **+ow** ill-will, grudge, envy

enyval [e'nɪˈval] *g* **+es** animal, beast

epskop ['epskɔp] *g* **epskobow** bishop

¹er ['er] *rg* for, by, on account

²er ['eːr] *g* **+yon** eagle

erberjour [er'berdʒur] *g* **+s** quartermaster

erbynn [er'bɪnː] *rg* against, in readiness for, by the time that

erbynner [er'bɪnːer] *g* **-oryon** opponent

erbys ['erbɪs] *g* **+yow** thrift (saving money), economy

erbysi [er'bɪˈzi] *v* save (amass money), economize, retrench

erbysiedh [ˌerbɪˈziˈeð] *g* **+ow** economy (system)

erbysieth [ˌerbɪˈziˈeθ] *b* economics

erbysyon [er'bɪˈzjɔn] *lp* savings

ergh ['erx] *hk* **+ow** snow

erthylya [er'θɪˈlja] *v* abort

ervin ['ervɪn] *hk* **+enn** turnips

ervira [er'viˈra] *v* decide, resolve

ervirans [er'viˈrans] *g* **+ow** decision, verdict

¹es [es] *m* than (short form of **ages**)

²es ['eːz] *g* comfort, ease, convenience: *hg* easy

esedh ['eˈzeð] *b* **+ow** seat, throne

esedha [e'zeˈða] *v* sit down

esedhek [e'zeˈðek] *g* **-ogow** session

esedhva [e'zeðva] *b* **+ow** siege

esedhvos [e'zeðvɔs] *g* **+ow** eisteddfod, session

esel ['eˈzel] *g* **eseli** member, limb

eskar ['eskar] *g* **eskerens** enemy, foe

eskarogeth [ˌeska'rɔˈgeθ] *b* hostility

eskeansek *hg* eliminatory

54

eskeas [es'keˑas] *v* exclude, eliminate

eskerdh ['eskerð] *g* **+ow** expedition

eskis ['eskɪs] *b* **+yow** shoe; **eskis prenn** clog

eskresek [es'kreˑzek] *hg* eccentric (off-centre)

esow ['eˑzɔw] *g* **+yow** privation

esperthi [es'perθi] *v* export

esporth ['espɔrθ] *g* **+ow** export

Essa ['esːa] *le* Saltash

ester ['eˑster] *hk* **esterenn** oysters

estewlel [es'teʊlel] *v* expel

estonek [es'tɔˑnek] *hg* Estonian

Estonek [es'tɔˑnek] *g* Estonian language

Estoni [es'tɔˑni] *le* Estonia

estren ['eˑstren] *hg* strange, alien; *g* **+yon** stranger (male), alien, foreigner

estrenes [es'treˑnes] *b* **+ow** stranger (female), alien, foreigner

estrenyek [es'treˑnjek] *hg* foreign

estrigys [es'triˑgɪs] *hg* absent

estyllenn [es'tɪlːen] *b* **+ow, estyll** *hk* shelf

esya ['eˑzja] *v* make easy, facilitate

etek ['eˑtek] *niv* eighteen

eth ['eːθ] *niv* eight

ethenn ['eˑθen] *b* **+ow** odour, scent, vapour, steam

etholans [e'θɔˑlans] *g* **+ow** election

eun ['œːn] *hg* straight

eur ['œːr] *b* **+yow** hour, time, o'clock; **y'n eur ma** presently

Eurasi [œ'raˑsi] *le* Eurasia

euro ['œˑrɔ] *g* **+yow** euro

Europa [œ'rɔˑpa] *le* Europe

europek *hg* European

euryer ['œˑrjer] *b* **+yow** watch (timepiece)

euskadek [œs'ka·dek] *hg* Basque

Euskadek [œs'ka·dek] *g* Basque language

Euskadi [œs'ka·di] *le* Basque country

euthega [œ'θe·ga] *v* terrify

euthyk [' œ·θɪk] *hg* dreadful, horrible, terrible: *av* terribly

ev ['e:v] *rh* he, him, it

eva ['e·va] *v* drink

evredhek [ev're·ðek] *hg* handicapped

evy [e'vi:] *rh* me

evyas ['evjas] *g* **-ysi** drinker

ewik ['e·wɪk] *b* **-igow** doe (female deer)

ewin ['e·wɪn] *g* **+es** finger-nail, claw, talon

ewn ['eʊn] *hg* correct, just, proper, valid

ewnder ['eʊnder] *g* **+yow** equity, justice, legal right

ewnhe [eʊn'he:] *v* repair, rectify, mend

ewnheans [eʊn'he·ans] *g* **+ow** repair

ewnhynsek [eʊn'hɪnzek] *hg* just, upright

ewnter ['eʊnter] *g* **ewntres** uncle

ewyn ['eʊɪn] *hk* **+enn** froth, foam, effervescence, head on a glass of beer

eyl ['eɪl] *hg* second; **an eyl y gila** each other; **pub eyl dydh** every other day

eylenn ['eɪlen] *b* **+ow** second of time

Eynda ['eɪnda] *le* India

eyndek *hg* Indian

Eyndek *g* **Eyndogyon** Indian

eythin ['eɪθɪn] *hk* **+enn** gorse, prickles

F

fagel-wiow *b* tendonitis
faglenn ['faglen] *b* **+ow** torch
faktor ['faktɔr] *g* **+yow** factor (maths.)
falgh ['falx] *b* **fylghyer** scythe
falghun ['falxyn] *g* **+es** falcon
fall ['fal:] *g* failure
fals ['fals] *hg* false, treacherous
fals ['fals] *b* **+yow** scythe
fantasi ['fantazi] *g* **+s** fantasy
fara ['fa·ra] *g* behaviour, conduct, demeanour: *v*
    behave
fardell ['fardel] *g* **+ow** parcel, package, bundle
fardellik [far'del:ɪk] *g* **-igow** packet
fardellow [far'del:ɔw] *lp* luggage
fars ['fars] *g* **+ys** farce (theatre)
farwell [far'wel:] *esk* farewell
fas ['fa:s] *g* **fasow** face
fast ['fa:st] *hg* firm, fast, fixed
fastya ['fa·stja] *v* fasten
fatell² ['fa·tel] *av* how
fatla ['fatla] *av* **fatla genes?** how are you?
fav ['fa:v] *hk* **+enn** beans
faveradow [fave·ra·dɔw] *hg* favourable
fekyl ['fe·kɪl] *hg* false, perfidious
felghya ['felxja] *v* scythe
fell ['fel:] *hg* cruel, fierce, grim
felsys ['felzɪs] *hg* split, cracked
fenester ['fe·nester] *b* **-tri** window
fenten ['fenten] *b* **fentynyow** spring, fountain,
    surface well
fer ['fe:r] *g* **+yow** fair; **Fer Krowswynn** Royal

fer ['feːr] *b* **+yow, diwfer** *hk* shin

feryl ['feˑrɪl] *g* **+yow** pharmacist

ferylva [feˑrɪlva] *b* **+ow** pharmacy (establishment)

fest ['feːst] *av* very, extremely; **fest yn ta** very well

fesya ['feˑzja] *v* drive away, put to flight, chase off

feth ['feːθ] *g* **+ow** fact

fetha ['feˑθa] *v* defeat, beat, conquer, vanquish, overcome

fethans ['feˑθans] *g* **+ow** defeat

fethus ['feˑθys] *hg* luxuriant, beautiful, well-formed

fethys ['feˑθɪs] *hg* defeated

fi ['fiː] *g* disdain

¹fia ['fiˑa] *v* disdain

²fia ['fiˑa] *v* flee; **fia dhe'n fo** take flight

fienas [fiˑeˑnas] *g* **+ow** anxiety

figur ['fiɡyr] *g* **+ys** figure (shape)

figurenn [fɪˈɡyˑren] *b* **+ow** figurine

¹fin ['fiːn] *b* **+yow** end

²fin ['fiːn] *hg* delicate, refined

finel ['fiˑnel] *hg* final

finweth ['finweθ] *b* **+ow** limit

finwetha [fɪnˈweˑθa] *v* limit

fisegieth [ˌfɪseˈɡiˑeθ] *b* physics

fisment ['fisment] *g* **fismens** countenance, face, complexion

fisten ['fiˑsten] *g* hurry

fistena [fɪsˈteˑna] *v* hasten, make haste, hurry

flamanek [flaˈmaˑnek] *hg* Flemish

Flamanek [flaˈmaˑnek] *g* Flemish language

flamm ['flamː] *g* **+ow** flame

flattra ['flatra] *v* flatter

fleghik ['fleˑxɪk] *g* **fleghesigow** infant, little child

58

Flemen ['fleˑmen] *g* **+yon** Fleming

fler ['fleˑɪr] *g* **+yow** stink, stench, bad smell

flerys ['fleˑrɪs] *hg* stinking

flogh ['flɔːx] *g* **fleghes** child

flogholeth [flɔˑfiɔˑleθ] *b* childhood, infancy

flogh-wynn [flɔxˈwɪnː] *g* **fleghes-wynn** grandchild

florenn ['flɔˑren] *b* **+ow** lock of door

¹flour ['fluːr] *hg* perfect

²flour ['fluːr]; *g* **+yow** deck of ship

flows ['flɔʊs] *g* nonsense, idle talk, humbug

fo ['fɔː] *g* **fohow** flight, escape, retreat

fog ['fɔːg] *b* **+ow** focus

fogella [fɔˈgelːa] *v* focus

folenn ['fɔˑlen] *b* **+ow** page of book, sheet of paper

foll ['fɔll] *hg* foolish, mad; *g* **fellyon** fool, madman

fols ['fɔls] *g* **+yow** split, cleft, rift, schism, fissure

folsa ['fɔlza] *v* split

fondya ['fɔndja] *v* found, establish, institute, lay foundations

fondyer ['fɔndjer] *g* **-oryon** founder

fordh ['fɔrð] *b* **+ow** road, way, manner

forgh ['fɔrx] *b* **fergh** fork, tool, prong

forn ['fɔrn] *b* **+ow** oven, stove, kiln

forn-doemma [fɔrnˈdʏmːa] *b* **fornow-toemma** boiler for domestic heating

fors ['fɔrs] *g* **+ow** force; **na fors** no matter; **ny wrav fors** I don't care

forsakyans [fɔrsaˈkjans] *g* abandonment

fos ['fɔːz] *b* **+ow** wall, rampart

¹fow ['fɔw] *hk* **+enn** beech-trees

²fow ['fɔw] *b* **+ys** cave, den

fowesik [fɔˈeˑzɪk] *g* **-igyon** refugee

fowt ['fɔʊt] *g* **+ys**; **+ow** lack, fault

59

Fowydh ['fɔwɪð] *le* Fowey
fram ['fra:m] *g* **+yow** frame
framya ['fra·mja] *v* framya
frankedh ['frankeð] *g* freedom, liberty
frega ['fre·ga] *v* tear up, shred, rip
fresk ['fre:sk] *hg* fresh
freth ['fre:θ] *hg* eager, fluent, eloquent
freudh ['frœ:ð] *g* **+ow** violence, disturbance, commotion, brawl
freudhek ['frœ·ðek] *hg* violent
froeth ['fro:θ] *hk* **+enn** fruit; **froeth kiwi** kiwi fruit
fronn ['frɔn:] *b* **+ow** brake, curb, restraint
fronna ['frɔn:a] *v* brake, restrain, curb
fros ['frɔ:z] *g* **+ow** current, flow, stream
Frynk ['frɪŋk] *g* **+yon** Frenchman
Frynkeger [frɪŋ'ke·ger] *g* **-oryon** French-speaker
frynkek ['frɪŋkek] *hg* French
Frynkek ['frɪŋkek] *g* French language
Frynkes ['frɪŋkes] *b* **+ow** Frenchwoman
fugieth [fy'gi·eθ] *b* fiction
fur ['fy:r] *hg* wise, cautious, discreet
furv ['fyrv] *b* **+ow** form, shape, mould for casting
furvas ['fyrvas] *g* **+ow** format
furvell ['fyrvel] *b* **+ow** mould
furvya ['fyrvja] *v* form, mould (shape)
furvyans ['fyrvjans] *g* **+ow** formation
fusenn ['fy·zen] *b* **+ow** rocket
fust ['fy:st] *g* **+ow** club (weapon)
fydh ['fi:ð] *b* **+yow** faith, trust, reliance
fydhya ['fi·ðja] *v* trust, confide, hope
fydhyans ['fi·ðjans] *g* confidence, trust, faith
fyll ['fɪl:] *g* **+ow** fiddle, violin
fyllel ['fɪl:el] *v* fail; **fyllel a** lack

60

fylm ['fɪlm] *g* **+ow** film (cinema, T.V., video)
fylmya ['fɪlmja] *v* film, shoot a film
Fynn ['fɪn:] *g* **+yon** Finn
Fynndir ['fɪndir] *le* Finland
fynnek ['fɪn:ek] *hg* Finnish
Fynnek ['fɪn:ek] *g* Finnish language
fyslek ['fɪslek] *hg* fussy, fidgetty: *g* **fyslogyon** nuisance
fytt ['fɪt] *g* **+ys**; **+ow** match, bout

G

gal ['gaːl] *g* **+yon** criminal
galar ['gaˑlar] *g* **+ow** grief
galari [gaˑlaˑri] *v* lament
galargan [gaˑlargan] *b* **+ow** lament
Galia [gaˑliˑa] *le* Gaul
galianek [ˌgaliˑaˑnek] *hg* Gaulish
Galianek [ˌgaliˑaˑnek] *g* Gaulish language
galithek [gaˑliˑθek] *hg* Galician
Galitha [gaˑliˑθa] *le* Galicia
galladow [gaˑlaˑdow] *hg* possible
galloes ['galːɤs] *g* **+ow** power: *v* be able
galloesek [gaˑloˑzek] *hg* powerful
galow ['gaˑlɔw] *g* **+yow** invitation, call
galwesigeth [ˌgalweˑziˑgeθ] *b* **+ow** profession
galwesik [galˈweˑzɪk] *hg* professional: *g* **-igyon** professional
galweyth ['galweɪθ] *g* **+yow** crime
galweythel [galˈweɪθel] *hg* criminal
gam ['gaːm] *g* game (object of hunt)

'gan [gan] *rh* us

ganow ['gaˑnɔw] *g* **+ow** mouth; **orth ganow** face to face

gans ['gans] *rg* with, by

garan ['gaˑran] *b* **+es** crane (bird and machine)

garlont ['garlɔnt] *b* **+ow** garland

garm ['garm] *b* **+ow** shout

garma ['garma] *v* shout

garow ['gaˑrɔw] *hg* rough

garr ['garː] *b* **+ow, diwarr** *hd* leg

garrenn ['garːen] *b* **+ow** stem

garth ['garθ] *g* **+ow** yard, enclosure

gasa ['gaˑza] *v* leave, abandon; let, permit, allow

gass ['gas] *g* **+ow** gas

gava ['gaˑva] *v* forgive; **gav dhymm!** excuse me!

gaver ['gaver] *b* **gever** goat; **An Aver** Capricorn

geler ['geˑler] *b* **+yow** coffin

gell ['gelː] *hg* light brown

gelvin ['gelvin] *g* **+es** beak

gelwel ['gelwel] *v* call, invite

genesigeth [ˌgeneˈziˑgeθ] *b* **+ow** birth

genesik [genˈeˑzɪk] *g* **-igyon** native

genynn ['geˑnɪn] *g* **+ow** gene

genys ['geˑnɪs] *hg* born

ger ['geːr] *g* **+yow** word

ger-da [gerˈdaː] *g* **geryow-da** fame

gerlyver [gerˈlɪˑver] *g* **-lyvrow** dictionary

gerva ['gerva] *b* **+ow** vocabulary, lexicon

geryow ['geˑrjɔw] *lp* lyrics

gerys-da [ˌgerɪzˈdaː] *hg* famous

ges ['geːz] *g* **+yow** mockery, joke, fun; **gul ges a** make fun of

gesya ['geˑzja] *v* mock, joke

geveligow [ˌgeve'liˑgɔw] *lp* pliers

gevelik [ge've·liˑk] *b* tweezers

gevell ['ge·vel] *g* **+yon** twin (male); **An Evellyon**
The Twins (Gemini)

gevelles [gev'el:es] *b* **+ow** twin (female)

gevyans ['ge·vjans] *g* **+ow** forgiveness

giow ['giˑɔw] *hk* **+enn** tendons, ligaments

gis ['giːz] *g* **+yow** fashion, custom, manner

gis-leveryans [ˌgiˑslev'e·rjans] *g* **gisyow-l.**
pronunciation

gitar [gɪ'taːr] *g* **-eryow** guitar

glan ['glaːn] *hg* clean: *av* completely, quite

glanhe [glan'heː] *v* clean

glann ['glanː] *b* **+ow** bank (of river)

glas ['glaːz] *hg* blue, green (of plants)

glasrudh ['glasryð] *hg* purple, violet

glaveri [glav'e·ri] *v* slobber

glaw ['glaw] *g* **+yow** rain; **glaw a wra** it is raining
gul glaw rain

glawlenn ['glawlen] *b* **+ow** umbrella

glena ['gle·na] *v* cling, stick; **glena orth** stick to

glesin ['gle·sɪn] *g* **+yow** lawn

glin ['gliːn] *g* **+yow, dewlin** *hd* knee

glori ['glɔ·ri] *g* glory

glow ['glɔw] *hk* **+enn** coal

glus ['glyːz] *g* **+ow** glue

glusa ['gly·za] *v* glue

gluth ['gly·θ] *g* **+ow** dew

glyb ['glɪːb] *hg* wet

glybya ['glɪ·bja] *v* wet

glyttra ['glɪtra] *v* glitter

gnas ['gnaːz] *b* **+ow** quality, character

gnasenn ['gna·zen] *b* **+ow** trait

gober ['gɔ·ber] *g* **gobrow** pay, income, salary; **gober omdennans** pension

gobrena [gɔ'bre·na] *v* hire, rent

gobrenans [gɔ'bre·nans] *g* **+ow** lease

godewel [gɔ'de·wel] *v* hush

godeyl ['gɔ·deɪl] *g* fertilizer

godh ['gɔ·ð] *b* **+ow** mole

godhen ['gɔ·ðen] *g* **godhnow** sole of foot

godhevek [gɔð'e·vek] *hg* patient

godhevel [gɔð'e·vel] *v* suffer

godhevyans [gɔð'e·vjans] *g* **+ow** suffering

godhonieth [ˌgɔðɔ'ni·eθ] *b* **+ow** science

godhoniethek [gɔðˌɔni'e·θek] *hg* scientific

godhonydh [gɔ'ðɔ·nɪð] *g* **+yon** scientist

godhvos ['gɔðvɔs] *v* know

godhynsel [gɔ'dɪnzel] *v* nibble

godoemm ['gɔ·dɤm] *hg* lukewarm

godra ['gɔdra] *v* milk

godramm [gɔ'dram:] *g* **+ow** cramp

godriga [gɔ'dri·ga] *v* stay for a short time, visit

godriger [gɔ'dri·ger] *g* **-oryon** visitor

godrik ['gɔdrɪk] *g* **-igow** short stay, visit

godroghya [gɔ'drɔ·xja] *v* rinse

godros ['gɔdrɔs] *v* threaten: *g* **+ow** threat

goedh ['goː·ð] *b* **+ow** goose

goedhan ['gɔ·ðan] *g* **+es** moth

goedhboell ['gɤðbɤl] *g* chess

Goedhel ['go·ðel] *g* **Goedheli** Irishman

¹**goel** ['goː·l] *g* **+yow** sail

²**goel** ['goː·l] *g* **+yow** festival

³**goel** ['goː·l] *g* **+yow** wake (after a funeral)

goelann ['go·lan] *b* **+es** seagull

goeles ['go·les] *g* **+ow** bottom

goelya ['goˑlja] *v* sail
goelyas ['goˑljas] *v* keep watch
goemmon ['gɤmːɔn] *hk* **+enn** seaweed
¹goen ['goːn] *b* **+yow** downland
²goen ['goːn] *g* **+yow** gown
goera ['goˑra] *g* hay
goes ['goːz] *g* **+ow** blood
goesa ['goˑza] *v* bleed
goeth ['goːθ] *g* pride
goethus ['goˑθys] *hg* proud
goghi ['goˑxi] *hk* **+enn** wasps
gogledh ['gɔgleð] *g* north
gogosk ['gɔˑgɔsk] *g* **+ow** nap
gohelus [gɔˈheˑlys] *hg* shy
gohydh ['gɔˑhɪð] *b* **+ow** daughter-in-law
gokki ['gɔkːiː] *hg* silly, stupid
gokkineth [gɔˈkiˑneθ] *b* stupidity
gol ['gɔːl] *g* **+yow** goal (in sport)
golewder [gɔˈleʊder] *g* **+yow** brightness
golghi ['gɔlxi] *v* wash
golghva ['gɔlxva] *b* **+ow** bathroom
goli ['gɔˑli] *g* **+ow** wound
golia [gɔˈliˑa] *v* wound
golok ['gɔˑlɔk] *b* **-ogow** look
golow ['gɔˑlɔw] *g* **+ys** light
golowi [gɔˈlɔwi] *v* illuminate
golowji [gɔˈlɔʊdʒi] *g* **+ow** light-house
golowys [gɔˈlɔwɪs] *lp* traffic lights
gols ['gɔls] *g* head of hair
golslin ['gɔlslin] *g* **+yow** shampoo
golusek [gɔˈlyˑzek] *hg* rich
golvan ['gɔlvan] *g* **+es** sparrow
gonis ['gɔˑnɪs] *g* **+yow** service (in general, not in

church): *v* cultivate crops

gonisogeth [ˌgɒniˈzɔˈgeθ] *b* **+ow** culture

gonisogethel [gɒnizɒgˈeˈθel] *hg* cultural

goniwl [ˈgɒˈnɪʊl] *g* haze

gordhiwedh [gɒrˈðiʊeð] *g* **+ow** conclusion

gordhyllans [gɒrˈðɪlːans] *g* **+ow** sacking

gordoemma [gɒrˈdʌmːa] *v* overheat

gordoemmheans [gɒrdʌmˈheˈans] *g* overheating

goredhomm [gɒreˈðɒm] *g* **+ow** emergency

gorenn [ˈgɒˈren] *b* **+ow** abscess

gorfenna [gɒrˈfenːa] *v* finish

gorfennys [gɒrˈfenːɪs] *hg* finished

gorfordh [ˈgɒrfɒrð] *b* **+ow** motorway

gorhel [ˈgɒrhel] *g* **-holyon** ship

gorhemmynn [gɒrˈhemːɪn] *g* **+ow** command, order

gorhemmynna [ˌgɒrheˈmɪnːa] *v* command

gorhemmynnadow [gɒrˌhemɪˈnaˈdɒw] *g* greetings

gorher [ˈgɒrher] *g* **+yow** cover, lid

gorheri [gɒrˈheˈri] *v* cover

gorhota [gɒrˈhɔˈta] *g* **-hotow** overcoat

gorladha [gɒrˈlaˈða] *v* massacre

gorladhva [gɒrˈlaˈðva] *b* **+ow** massacre

gorm [ˈgɒrm] *hg* dark brown

gormel [ˈgɒrmel] *v* praise

gormola [gɒrˈmɔˈla] *b* **gormoledhow** praise

gormrudh [ˈgɒrmryð] *hg* maroon

gorow [ˈgɒˈrɒw] *hg* masculine (grammatical gender)

gorra [ˈgɒrːa] *v* put, place, set

gorsav [ˈgɒrsav] *g* **+ow** station

gorsedh [ˈgɒrseð] *b* **+ow** gorsedd

gorth [ˈgɒrθ] *hg* contrary

gorthter [ˈgɒrθter] *g* opposition

gorthugher [gɒrˈθyˈfier] *g* **+ow** evening

gorthugherweyth [gɔrθˌyˈfierˈweɪθ] *av* in the evening

gorthybi [gɔrˈθɪˈbi] *v* answer, reply

gorthyp [ˈgɔrθɪp] *g* **gorthybow** answer, reply, response

gortos [ˈgɔrtɔs] *v* wait for, remain

gorvarghas [gɔrˈvarxas] *b* **+ow** supermarket

gorwedha [gɔrˈweˈða] *v* lie down

gorwel [ˈgɔrwel] *b* **+yow** horizon

gorwisk [ˈgɔrwisk] *g* **+ow** overalls

goskes [ˈgɔˈskes] *g* **goskeusow** shelter

goskeusi [gɔˈskœˈzi] *v* shelter

goskotter [gɔsˈkɔtːer] *g* **+yow** shade

gossen [ˈgɔsːen] *b* **+yow** rust

gosseni [gɔsˈeˈni] *v* rust

gour [ˈguːr] *g* **gwer** husband, man

gourel [ˈguˈrel] *hg* masculine, virile

gov [ˈgɔːv] *g* **+yon** blacksmith

govenek [gɔvˈeˈnek] *g* **-egow** hope

gover [ˈgɔˈver] *g* **+ow** brook

governans [gɔvˈernans] *g* **+ow** government

govisyon [gɔˈviˈzjɔn] *g* care, worry

govynn [ˈgɔˈvɪn] *g* **+ow** question: *v* ask, question

gow [ˈgɔw] *g* **+yow** lie

gowek [ˈgɔʊek] *hg* lying: *g* **gowygyon** liar

gowir [ˈgɔˈwir] *hg* virtual

gowl [ˈgɔʊl] *b* **+ow** fork, bifurcation, Y-shape

gowlek [ˈgɔʊlek] *hg* **yn howlek** astride

gowleverel [ˌgɔʊlevˈeˈrel] *v* tell a lie

gradh [ˈgraːð] *g* **+ow** degree

graghell [ˈgraˈxel] *b* **+ow** heap

graghella [grafiˈelːa] *v* heap

graghellys [grafiˈelːɪs] *hg* in a heap

gramer ['graˑmer] *g* **+yow** grammar

gramm ['gramː] *g* **+ow** gram

grappa ['grapːa] *g* **grappys**; **grappow** grape

gras ['graːs] *g* **+ow** grace

grassa ['graˑtsa] *v* thank

grastal ['graˑstal] *g* **+yow** tip, gratuity

gravath ['graˑvaθ] *b* **+ow** stretcher (for carrying)

gravath-ros [ˌgraˑvaθˈroːz] *b* **gravathow-ros** wheel-barrow

gre ['greː] *b* **+ow** herd

grek ['greːk] *hg* Greek

Grek ['greːk] *g* **Grekys** Greek person

Greka ['greˑka] *g* Greek language

greun ['grœːn] *hk* **+enn** grain

greunji ['grœndʒi] *g* **+ow** granary

greunvoes ['grœnvɤs] *g* **+ow** cereal

grevons ['greˑvɔns] *g* **+ys** medical complaint

grogys ['grɔˑgɪs] *g* **+yow** belt

grommya ['grɔmːja] *v* growl

grommyans ['grɔmːjans] *g* **+ow** growl

gronn ['grɔnː] *g* **+ow** bunch

gronna ['grɔnːa] *v* amass

growan ['grɔʊan] *g* **-enyow** granite

grug ['gryːg] *g* **+ow** heather

gul ['gyːl] *v* do, make; **gul war-lergh** imitate

gusigenn [gyˈziˑgen] *b* **+ow** blister

gwag ['gwaːg] *hg* empty, vacant

gwall ['gwalː] *g* **+ow** defect

gwan ['gwaːn] *b* **+yow** piercing

gwana ['gwaˑna] *v* pierce

gwandra ['gwandra] *v* wander

gwaneth ['gwaˑneθ] *hk* **+enn** wheat

gwann ['gwanː] *hg* weak

gwannhe [gwan'hɛː] *v* weaken

gwanus ['gwa·nys] *hg* piercing

gwara ['gwa·ra] *hk* **gwarenn** commodities, goods

gwarak ['gwa·rak] *b* **-egow** bow, arc, arch, coat-hanger

gwari ['gwa·ri] *v* play: *g* **+ow** game, play; **gwari mildamm** jigsaw puzzle

gwariell [gwa'ri·el] *b* **+ow** toy

gwarier [gwa'ri·er] *g* **-oryon** player, actor

gwarila [gwa'ri·la] *g* **-leow** stage

gwariva [gwa'ri·va] *b* **+ow** theatre

gwarnya ['gwarnja] *v* warn

gwarnyans ['gwarnjans] *g* **+ow** warning

gwarr ['gwarː] *b* **+ow** nape

gwarthav ['gwarθav] *g* **-evyow** top

gwarthek ['gwarθek] *hk* horned cattle

gwas ['gwaːz] *g* **gwesyon** fellow

gwask ['gwaːsk] *b* **+ow** stress

gwaska ['gwa·ska] *v* press

gwaskogforn [gwas'kɔkfɔrn] *b* **+ow** pressure-cooker

gwastas ['gwa·stas] *hg* flat, smooth

gwav ['gwaːv] *g* **+ow** winter

gwavas ['gwa·vas] *g* **+ow** winter-time

gwaya ['gwaɪa] *v* move

gwayans ['gwaɪans] *g* **+ow** movement

gwayn ['gwaɪn] *g* **+yow** gain

gwaynya ['gwaɪnja] *v* gain, win

gwaytyas ['gwaɪtjas] *v* hope, expect

gweder ['gwe·der] *g* **gwedrow** glass

gweder-mires [ˌgwe·der'mi·res] *g* **gwedrow-mires** mirror

gwedh ['gwe·ð] *b* **+ow** phase

gwedhow ['gwe·ðɔw] *g* **+yon** widower

gwedhra ['gweðra] *v* wither

gwedhwes ['gweðwes] *b* **+ow** widow

gwedhyn ['gwe·ðɪn] *hg* flexible, supple

gwedrenn ['gwedren] *b* **+ow** drinking glass

¹gwel ['gweːl] *g* **+yow** field

²gwel ['gweːl] *b* **+yow** sight, vision

³gwel ['gweːl] *hk* **+enn** rods, wands

gwelenn ['gwe·len] *b* **gwelynni, gwel** *hk* rod, shaft

gwelenn-byskessa [,gwe·lenbɪsk'esːa] *b* **gwelynni-pyskessa** fishing-rod

gweles ['gwe·les] *v* see

gweli ['gwe·li] *g* **+ow** bed; **gweli ha hansel** bed and breakfast

gwell ['gweːl] *hg* better; **gwell yw genev** I prefer

gwella ['gwelːa] *hg* best

gwellhe [gwel'heː] *v* improve

gwels ['gwels] *hk* **+enn** grass

gwelsigow [gwel'zi·gɔw] *lp* scissors

gwelv ['gwelv] *b* **+ow** lip

Gwener ['gwe·ner] *b* Venus; **dy' Gwener** Friday, on Friday

gwennenn ['gwenːen] *b* **+ow** sore

gwenon ['gwe·nɔn] *g* **-enyow** poison, venom

gwenonek [gwe·nɔ·nek] *hg* poisonous

gwenton ['gwentɔn] *g* **-enyow** spring (season)

¹gweres ['gwe·res] *v* help, aid: *g* help

²gweres ['gwe·res] *g* **+ow** soil

gwerin ['gwe·rɪn] *b* folk, common people

gwerinek [gwe·ri·nek] *hg* popular

gweriniethor [gwer,ini'e·θɔr] *g* **+yon** democrat

gwerinor [gwe·ri·nɔr] *g* **+yon** peasant, pawn (in chess)

¹gwern ['gwern] *b* **+ow** mast

70

²gwern ['gwern] *hk* **+enn** alder-trees
gwerth ['gwerθ] *b* **+ow** sale
gwertha ['gwerθa] *v* sell
gwerther ['gwerθer] *g* **-oryon** salesman, seller
gwerthji ['gwerθtʃi] *g* shop
gwerthys ['gwerθɪs] *b* **+ow** shuttle
gweskel ['gweˑskel] *v* beat, hit, strike
gwester ['gweˑster] *g* **-oryon** guest
gwesti ['gweˑsti] *g* **+ow** hotel
gweth ['gweːθ] *hg* worse
gwethhe [gweθ'heː] *v* worsen, deteriorate
gwettha ['gweθːa] *hg* worst
¹gweyth ['gweɪθ] *b* **+yow** occasion, time
²gweyth ['gweɪθ] *g* **+yow** work
gweythor ['gweɪθɔr] *g* **+yon** worker
gweythow ['gweɪθɔʊ] *lp* works
gweythres ['gweɪθres] *g* **+ow** action
gweythva ['gweɪθfa] *b* **+ow** factory
gwia ['gwiˑa] *v* knit
gwiader [gwiˑa'der] *g* **-oryon** weaver
gwians ['gwiˑans] *g* knitting
gwias ['gwiˑas] *g* **+ow** tissue, web
gwiasva [gwiˑazva] *b* **+ow** web-site
gwibes ['gwiˑbes] *hk* **+enn** gnats
gwig ['gwiːg] *b* **+ow** village
gwikor ['gwiˑkɔr] *g* **+yon** trader, merchant
gwin ['gwiːn] *g* **+yow** wine
gwir ['gwiːr] *hg* true, real, right; **dhe wir** indeed: *g*
   +yow right, truth
gwirenn ['gwiˑren] *b* **+ow** fact
gwirvreus [ˌgwiˑr'vrœːz] *g* justice
gwiryon ['gwiˑrjɔn] *hg* genuine, sincere, truthful,
   veracious

gwiryonedh [gwɪr'jɔ·neð] *g* truth

gwisk ['gwiːsk] *g* dress, clothes

gwiska ['gwi·ska] *v* dress, wear

gwiskas ['gwi·skas] *g* **+ow** coat (e.g. of paint), coating

gwiskva ['gwi·skfa] *b* **+ow** cloakroom

gwith ['gwiːθ] *g* custody; **gwith chi** housekeeping

gwitha ['gwi·θa] *v* keep, preserve, protect from; **gwitha war** watch over

gwithti ['gwiθti] *g* **+ow** museum

gwithva ['gwi·θfa] *b* **+ow** store

gwithyas ['gwi·θjas] *g* **gwithysi** guard, guardian, keeper

gwithyas-kres [ˌgwiθjas'kreːz] *g* **gwithysi-gres** policeman

gwiver ['gwi·ver] *hk* **gwivrenn** wire

gwiw ['gwiw] *hg* fit, suitable

gwiwer ['gwiwer] *g* **-ow** squirrel

gwlan ['gwla·n] *hk* **+enn** wool

gwlanek ['gwla·nek] *g* **gwlanogow** jersey, jumper

gwlanenn ['gwla·nen] *b* **+ow** flannel

gwlas ['gwlaːz] *b* **+ow** country, land

gwlaskor ['gwla·skɔr] *b* **-kordhow** kingdom

gwledh ['gwleːð] *b* **+ow** banquet

gwlygh ['gwlɪːx] *g* damp

gwlygha ['gwlɪ·xa] *b* moisture

gwragh ['gwra·x] *b* **+es** witch

gwreg ['gwreːg] *b* **gwragedh** wife, married woman

gwregel ['gwre·geɪ] *hg* feminine

gwrekk ['gwrek] *g* **+ys** wreck

gwres ['gwreːz] *b* heat

gwrians ['gwri·ans] *g* **+ow** manufacture

gwrias ['gwri·as] *v* sew

72

gwrier ['gwri·er] *g* **-oryon** maker
gwruthyl ['gwry·θɪl] *v* create
gwrynya ['gwrɪ·nja] *v* wrestle, squeeze
gwrynyer ['gwrɪ·njer] *g* **-yoryon** wrestler
gwrythya ['gwrɪ·θja] *v* perform
gwydhek ['gwɪ·ðek] *b* **-egi** woodland
Gwydhelek [gwɪð'e·lek] *hg* Gaelic language
gwydhelek [gwɪð'e·lek] *g* Gaelic
gwydhyow ['gwɪ·ðjɔw] *g* **+yow** video
gwyls ['gwɪls] *hg* wild
gwynk ['gwɪnk] *g* **+ow** wink of eye
gwynkya ['gwɪnkja] *v* wink
gwynn ['gwɪn:] *hg* white
gwynnel ['gwɪn:el] *v* squirm, struggle
gwynnrudh ['gwɪnryð] *hg* pink
gwyns ['gwɪns] *g* **+ow** wind
gwynsek ['gwɪnzek] *hg* windy
gwyr' ['gwɪr] *hg* green
gwyrdh ['gwɪrð] *hg* green
gwyrghes ['gwɪrxes] *b* **+ow** virgin
gwythi ['gwɪ·θi] *hk* **+enn** veins
gyllys ['gɪl:ɪs] *hg* gone

H

ha [ha] *m* and
habadoellya [ˌhabad'ɤl:ja] *g* disturbance, uproar
hag [hag] *m* and, which (before a vowel)
ha'gan [hagan] and our
hager ['hager] *hg* ugly
hager-awel [ˌha·ge'rawel] *b* **+yow** bad weather

hal ['haːl] *b* **halow** moor

hanaf ['haˑnaf] *g* **+ow** cup

hanafik [haˑnaˈfɪk] *g* **-igow** goblet

hanas ['haˑnas] *g* **+ow** murmur

hanasa [haˑnaˈza] *v* murmur

haneth ['haˑneθ] *av* tonight, this evening

hanow ['hanɔw] *g* **henwyn** name, noun, surname;
   pyth yw dha hanow? what is your name?

hansel ['hansel] *g* **+yow** breakfast

hanter ['hanter] *g* **+yow** half

hanter-broder [ˌhanterˈbrɔˑder] *g* **hanter-breder**
   half-brother

hanter-dydh [ˌhanterˈdɪːð] *g* **+yow** midday, noon

hanter-hwoer [ˌhanterˈhwoːr] *b* **hanter-hwerydh**
   half-sister

hanter-kans ['hanterˈkans] *niv* **+ow** fifty

hanter-nos [ˌhanterˈnɔːz] *b* midnight

hanter-our [ˌhanterˈuːr] *g* **+yow** half-hour (duration)

harber ['harber] *g* **+ys** refuge

hardh ['harð] *hg* bold

harow! ['haˑrɔw] *esk* help!

harth ['harθ] *g* **+ow** bark (of an animal)

hartha ['harθa] *v* bark

has ['haːz] *hk* **+enn** seed

hasa ['haˑza] *v* sow

hatt ['hat] *g* **+ow**; **+ys** hat

hav ['haˑv] *g* **+ow** summer

haval ['haˑval] *hg* similar; **haval dhe** similar to

havas ['haˑvas] *g* **+ow** summer-time

havyas ['haˑvjas] *g* **-ysi** summer visitor, holiday-
   maker

hay ['haɪ] *esk* hey

heb [heb] *rg* without

hebask ['he·bask] *hg* calm, pacific
hebaskhe [hebask'he:] *v* calm
hedh ['he:ð] *g* **+ow** full-stop
hedhi ['he·ði] *v* stop (intrans.), cease, pause
hedhyw [he·ðɪw] *av* today
hedorr ['he·dɔr] *hg* fragile
hedre² [he·dre:] *m* while, as long as
hegar ['he·gar] *hg* lovely
¹hel ['he:l] *hg* generous, hospitable
²hel ['he:l] *b* **+yow** hall
helgh ['helx] *g* **+ow** hunt
helghya ['helxja] *v* hunt
helghyer ['helxjer] *g* **-oryon** hunter
Hellys ['hel:ɪs] *le* Helston
helyk ['he·lɪk] *hk* **-ygenn** willow
hembronk ['hembrɔnk] *v* lead, escort
hembrenkyas [hem'brenkjas] *g* **-ysi** leader
hemma ['hem:a] *rh* this one (m.)
hendas ['hendas] *g* **+ow** grandfather
henedh ['he·neð] *g* **+ow** generation (people in a
  family)
hengovek [hen'gɔ·vek] *hg* traditional
henhwedhel [hen'hweðel] *g* **-dhlow** legend, fable
henlavar [hen'la·var] *g* **+ow** saying
henna ['hen:a] *rh* that one (m.)
henvamm ['henvam] *b* **+ow** grandmother
henwel ['henwel] *v* name
henwys ['henwɪs] *hg* named
hepken [hep'ke:n] *av* only
hepkorr ['hepkɔr] *v* relinquish
herdhya ['herðja] *v* ram, push
herwydh ['herwɪð] *rg* according to
heskenn ['he·sken]; **+ow** saw (tool)

heskenna [hesk'enːa] *v* saw

heudh ['hœːð] *hg* merry, glad

hevelep [hev'e·lep] *hg* similar

hevelepter [ˌhevel'epter] *g* **+yow** image, likeness, similarity

heveli [hev'e·li] *v* seem

hevis ['he·vɪs] *g* **+yow** shirt (rough)

hevlyna [hev'lɪ·na] *av* this year

heyl ['heɪl] *g* **+yow** estuary

Heyl *le* Hayle

hi ['hiː] *rh* she, it, her (obj.)

hik ['hiːk] *g* **+ow** hiccup

hikas ['hi·kas] *v* hiccup

hil ['hiːl] *b* **+yow** race (ethnic)

hilgasydh ['hɪl'ga·zɪð] *g* **+yon** racist

hin ['hiːn] *b* **+yow** climate

hir ['hiːr] *hg* long, tall, lengthy

hirbedrek [hir'bedrek] *g* **hirbedrogow** rectangle

hirder ['hirder] *g* **+yow** length

hireth ['hi·reθ] *b* **+ow** longing

hirgorn ['hirgɔrn] *g* **hirgern** trumpet

hirgrennenn [hir'gren·en] *b* **+ow** cylinder

hirgylgh ['hirgɪlx] *g* **+yow** oval

hirgylghyek [hir'gɪlxjek] *hg* oval

hirhe [hir'heː] *v* lengthen

hoba ['hɔ·ba] *g* **+s** pony, hobby

hoelan ['ho·lan] *hk* **+enn** salt

hoelanek [hɤ'la·nek] *hg* salty

hogh ['hɔːx] *g* **-es** pig

hok ['hɔːk] *g* **+ys** hawk; **hok karyn** vulture

holya ['hɔ·lja] *v* follow

homma ['hɔmːa] *rh* this one (f.)

honan ['hɔ·nan] *g* self; **y honan** by himself; **agas**

honan yourselves

honna ['hɔnːa] *rh* that one (f.)

hora ['hɔːra] *b* **horys** whore, prostitute

hordh ['hɔrð] *g* **+es** ram

horn ['hɜrn] *g* **hern** iron (metal)

hornell ['hɔrnel] *b* **+ow** iron (appliance)

hornella [hɔrn'elːa] *v* iron

hos ['hɔːz] *g* **heyji** duck

hou! ['huː] *esk* hallo!

Howl ['hɔʊl] *g* Sun

howldrevel [hɔʊl'dreːvel] *g* **+yow** sunrise, orient

howllenn ['hɔʊlːen] *b* **+ow** parasol

howlleski [hɔʊl'leːski] *v* tan (sunburn)

howlsedhes [hɔʊl'seːðes] *g* **+ow** sunset, west, occident

hun ['hyːn] *g* **+yow** sleep

hungarek [hyn'gaːrek] *hg* Hungarian

Hungarek [hyn'gaːrek] *g* Hungarian language

Hungari [hyn'gaːri] *le* Hungary

huni ['hyːni] *r*; **an huni** the one

hunlev ['hyːnlev] *g* **+ow** nightmare

hunros ['hyːnrɔs] *g* **+ow** dream

hunrosa [hyn'rɔːza] *v* dream

hunrosyer [hyn'rɔːzjer] *g* **-yoryon** dreamer

hunva ['hynva] *b* **+ow** dormitory

hwaff ['hwafː] *g* **+ys** blow

hwannenn ['hwanːen] *b* **+ow** flea

hwans ['hwans] *g* **+ow** desire, longing, wish

hwar ['hwaːr] *hg* gentle

hware [hwaːr'eː] *av* at once

hwarth ['hwarθ] *g* **+ow** laugh, laughter

hwarthus ['hwarθys] *hg* funny, humorous

hwarvos ['hwarvɔs] *v* happen, occur

hwath ['hwaːθ] *av* yet, still

hwedhel ['hweðel] *g* **hwedhlow** story, tale

hweg ['hweːg] *hg* sweet, pleasant, nice

hweger ['hweˑger] *b* **hwegrow** mother-in-law

hwegh ['hweːx] *niv* six

hwegoll ['hweˑgɔl] *hg* darling

hwegrewi [hweg'rewi] *v* ice a cake

hwegron ['hwegrɔn] *g* **+yon** father-in-law

hwegynn ['hweˑgɪn] *g* **+ow** sweet

hwel ['hweːl] *g* **+yow** work

hwerow ['hwerɔw] *hg* bitter

hwerthin ['hwerθin] *v* laugh

hwesker ['hweˑsker] *hk* **+enn** insects

hwetek ['hweˑtek] *niv* sixteen

hwi² ['hwiː] *rh* you (plural)

hwibana [hwi'baˑna] *v* whistle (by mouth)

hwibon ['hwiˑbɔn] *g* **+es** stork

hwigenn ['hwiˑgen] *b* crumb of loaf

hwil ['hwiːl] *g* **+es** beetle

hwilas ['hwiˑlas] *v* seek, search for

hwil-tan ['hwiːl,taˑn] *g* **hwiles-tan** moped

hwithra ['hwiθra] *v* examine

hwithrans ['hwiθrans] *g* **+ow** research

hwoer ['hwoːr] *b* **hwerydh** sister; **hwoer dre lagha** sister-in-law

hwyja ['hwɪˑdʒa] *v* vomit

hwypp ['hwɪp] *g* **+ys** whip

hwyppya ['hwɪpːja] *v* whip

hwys ['hwɪːz] *g* **+ow** sweat

hwysa ['hwɪˑza] *v* sweat

hwystra ['hwɪstra] *v* whisper

hwystrenn ['hwɪstren] *b* **+ow** whisper

hwytha ['hwɪˑθa] *v* blow, blast, play a wind instrument

78

hwythenn ['hwɪ·θen] *b* **+ow** bubble
hwythfi ['hwɪθfi] *v* swell
hy³ [hɪ] *rh* her, its
hyga ['hɪ·ga] *v* cheat, tease
hyger ['hɪ·ger] *g* **-oryon** cheat
hyli ['hɪ·li] *g* **+ow** salt water
hymna ['hɪmna] *g* **hymnys** hymn
hyns ['hɪns] *g* **+yow** road, way, path
hyns-horn [ˌhɪns'hɔrn] *g* **hynsyow-horn** railway
hys ['hɪːz] *g* **+ow** length

I

i ['iː] *rh* they, them
idhyow [i'ðjɔw] *hk* **+enn** ivy
ifarn ['i·farn] *g* **+ow** hell
igeri [ig'e·ri] *v* open
igor ['i·gɔr] *hg* open
ilewydh [il'ewɪð] *g* **+yon** musician
ilow ['i·lɔw] *b* music
isel ['i·zel] *hg* low
Iseldiryow [ˌɪzel'di·rjɔw] *lp* Netherlands
iselgostek [ˌɪzel'gɔ·stek] *hg* cheap
iselhe [ɪzel'heː] *v* lower
iselheans [ɪzel'he·ans] *g* lowering
islavrek [ɪs'lavrek] *g* **-ogow** underpants, knickers
isleftenant [ɪslef'tenant] *g* **+s** sub-lieutenant, ensign (rank)
islinenna [ɪsli'en:a] *v* underline
issoedhek [ɪs'so·ðek] *g* **issoedhogyon** junior officer

79

istori [ˈɪstəri] *g* **+ow** history
italek [ɪˈtaˑlek] *hg* Italian
Italek [ɪˈtaˑlek] *g* Italian language
Itali [ɪˈtaˑli] *le* Italy
Iwerdhon [ɪˈwerðən] *le* Ireland
¹Iwerdhonek [ˌiwerˈðɔˑnek] *hg* Irish
²Iwerdhonek [ˌiwerˈðɔˑnek] *g* Irish language

J

jell [ˈdʒelː] *g* **+ow** gel
jerkynn [ˈdʒerkɪn] *g* **+ow** jacket
jiraf [dʒɪˈraːf] *g* **+es** giraffe
jornalyas [dʒɔrˈnaˑljas] *g* **-ysi** journalist
joy [ˈdʒɔɪ] *g* **joyys** joy
junya [ˈdʒyˑnja] *v* join, connect
jynn [ˈdʒɪnː] *g* **+ow**; **+ys** machine, engine, motor
jynn-amontya [ˌdʒɪnaˈmɔntja] *g* **jynnow-amontya** computer
jynn-ebron [ˌdʒɪnˈebrən] *g* **jynnow-ebron** aircraft, aeroplane, plane
jynn-skrifa [ˌdʒɪnˈskriˑfa] *g* **jynnow-skrifa** typewriter
jynn-tenna [ˌdʒɪnˈtenna] *g* **jynnow-tenna** tractor
jynnweythor [dʒɪnˈweɪθɔr] *g* **+yon** mechanic, engineer

K

kabel ['ka·bel] *g* blame, accusation, censure

kabla ['kabla] *v* blame, censure, incriminate

kablus ['kablʏs] *hg* guilty, blameworthy, culpable

kaboli [ka'bɔ·li] *v* stir, splash

kachya ['ka·tʃja] *v* catch, snatch, capture

kadon ['ka·dɔn] *b* **+yow** chain, bond

kador ['ka·dɔr] *b* **+yow** chair, seat

kador-dreth [ˌka·dɔr'dre:θ] *b* **kadoryow-treth** deck-chair

kador-herdhya [ˌka·dɔr'herðja] *b* **kadoryow-herdhya** push-chair

kador-ros [ˌka·dɔr'rɔːz] *b* **kadoryow-ros** wheel-chair

kador-vregh [ˌka·dɔr'vre:x] *b* **kadoryow-bregh** armchair

kaja ['ka·dʒa] *b* **kajow** daisy

kala' ['ka·la] *hk* **kalavenn** straw

kales ['ka·les] *hg* hard, difficult, arduous

kalesenn [ka'le·zen] *b* **+ow** marble (small sphere), callosity

kaletter [ka'let:er] *g* **+yow** difficulty, hardness

¹kalgh ['kalx] *b* **+yow** penis

²kalgh ['kalx] *g* lime (mineral)

kalkonieth [ˌkalkɔ'niˑeθ] *b* calculation as a science

kalkya ['kalkja] *v* calculate

kalkya ['kalkja] *v* caulk

kalkyans ['kalkjans] *g* **+ow** an individual calculation

kalmynsi [kal'mɪnzi] *g* calm, stillness, tranquillity

kals ['kals] *g* **+ow** heap, abundance

kalter ['kalter] *b* **+yow** kettle

kamera ['kamera] *g* **+s** camera

¹kamm ['kamː] *hg* bent, crooked, wrong: *g* **+ow** mistake

²kamm ['kamː] *g* **+ow** step, pace

kammas ['kamːas] *b* **+ow** bay (coastal indentation), bend

Kammbronn ['kambrɔn] *le* Camborne

kammdira [kam'diːra] *v* run aground

kammgemmeryans [ˌkamgeˈmeˑrjans] *g* **+ow** mistake

kammigell [kamˈiˑgel] *b* **+ow** zigzag

kammlagasek [ˌkamːlaˈgaˑzek] *hg* squint-eyed, cross-eyed

kammneves [ˌkamːˈneˑves] *b* **+ow** rainbow, spectrum

kammweyth ['kamweɪθ] *g* **+ow** error, misdeed, trespass

kammwul ['kamːwyl] *v* make a mistake, do ill, err

kamp ['kamp] *g* **+ow** camp, bivouac

kampoell ['kampɤl] *g* **+ow** mention, comment

kampoella [kam'pɤlːa] *v* mention, comment

kampva ['kampva] *b* **+ow** camp-site

kampya ['kampja] *v* camp, bivouac

kampyer ['kampjer] *g* **-oryon** champion

kan ['kaːn] *b* **+ow** song

kana ['kaˑna] *v* sing

Kanada ['kanada] *le* Canada

kanadek [kaˈnaˑdek] *hg* Canadian

kanel ['kaˑnel] *b* **kanolyow** channel, inlet of sea, television channel

kanell ['kaˑnel] *g* **+ow** plug

kaner ['kaˑner] *g* **-oryon** singer (male)

kangourou [kanguˈruː] *g* **+s** kangaroo

kanker ['kanker] *g* **kankres** crab, cancer; **An**

Kanker Cancer (star-sign)

kanna ['kanːa] *g* **kannow** can, tin

kanna ['kanːa] *v* bleach, wash clothes

kannas ['kanːas] *b* **+ow** ambassador, envoy, delegate

kanon ['kaˈnɔn] *g* **+yow** cannon

kanores [kaˈnɔˑres] *b* **+ow** singer (female)

kans ['kans]; **+ow** hundred

kansblydhen [kanzˈblɪˑðen] *b* **kansblydhynyow** century, hundred years

kansrann ['kanzran] *b* **+ow** percentage, per cent

kanstell ['kanstel] *b* **+ow** basket

kantol ['kantɔl] *b* **+yow** candle, spark-plug

kappa ['kapːa] *g* **kappow** cap

kapten ['kapten] *g* **+yon** captain

kar ['kaːr] *g* **kerens** relative, relation, parent, kinsman

kara ['kaˑra] *v* love, like, care for

karadow [kaˈraˑdɔw] *hg* beloved, loving, lovable

karavan ['karavan] *g* **+s** caravan

kardigan ['kardɪgan] *g* **+s** cardigan

karer ['kaˑrer] *g* **-oryon** boy-friend

kares ['kaˑres] *b* **+ow** girl-friend

karetys [karˈeˑtɪs] *hk* **+enn** carrots

karga ['karga] *v* charge (e.g. a battery)

Karibyas [kaˈribˑjas] *g* **-ysi** West Indian

karjel ['kardʒel] *g* **+yow** accordion

¹karn ['karn] *g* **+ow** rock-pile, tor, cairn

²karn ['karn] *g* **+ow** hoof

karores [kaˈrɔˑres] *b* **+ow** lover (female)

karow ['karɔw] *g* **kerwys** deer (male)

karr ['karː] *g* **kerri** car, cart, vehicle

karrek ['karːek] *b* **kerrek** rock

karrji [ˈkardʒi] *g* **+ow** garage

karr-klavji [ˌkarˈklavdʒi] *g* **kerri-klavji** ambulance

karr-slynk [ˌkarrˈslɪnk] *g* **kerri-slynk** sledge

kartenn [ˈkarten] *b* **+ow** card

kartenn-bost [ˌkartenˈbɔːst] *b* **kartennow-post** post-card

karyans [ˈkaˑrjans] *g* transport, carriage (act of carrying)

¹kas [ˈkaːs] *g* hate, hatred, hostility

²kas [ˈkaːs] *g* **+ys** case, instance

³kas [ˈkaːz] *b* **+ow** battle, fight

kasa [ˈkaˑsa] *v* hate, detest

kasadow [kaˑsaˑdɔw] *hg* hateful, detestable

kasek [ˈkaˑzek] *b* **kasegi** mare

kasel [ˈkaˑzel] *b* **+yow** arm-pit, aisle

kaslewydh *g* **+yon** marshal

kasor [ˈkaˑzɔr] *g* **+yon** warrior, fighter

kast [ˈkaːst] *g* **+ys** trick

kastell [ˈkaˑstel] *g* **kastylli; kestell** castle, fortress, hill-fort

katalunek [kataˑlyˑnek] *hg* Catalan

Katalunek [kataˑlyˑnek] *g* Catalan language

Kataluni [kataˑlyˑni] *le* Catalonia

kath [ˈkaːθ] *b* **kathes** cat

katholik [kaˑθɔˑlɪk] *hg* Catholic

kavoes [ˈkaˑvʀs] *v* get, find, acquire, have

kaws [ˈkaʊz] *g* **+ys** cause

kay [ˈkaɪ] *g* **kayow** quay, wharf, platform (of railway station)

¹ke [ˈkeː] *g* **keow** hedge, fence, low wall of earth and stone; **war an ke** abstaining in a vote

²ke [ˈkeː] *rv* go!

keber [ˈkeˑber] *b* **kebrow** beam (timber)

kedhla [ˈkeðla] *v* inform

kedhlor [ˈkeðlɔr] *g* **+yon** informer, informant

kedhlow [ˈkeðlɔw] *lp* information

kedrynn [keˈdrɪnː] *b* **+ow** trouble, quarrel, dispute

kedrynna [keˈdrɪnːa] *v* quarrel

keffrys [keˈfrɪːz] *av* also, too

keffrysyas [keˈfrɪˑzjas] *g* **-ysi** ally

kegin [ˈkeˑgɪn] *b* **+ow** kitchen

kegina [keˈgiˑna] *v* cook

keginer [keˈgiˑner] *g* **-oryon** cook

keginieth [ˌkegɪˈniˑeθ] *b* cookery, cuisine

keginys [keˈgiˑnɪs] *hg* cooked

kehaval [keˈhaˑval] *hg* similar, equal, corresponding

keher [ˈkeˑher] *hk* **+enn** muscle

keheveli [ˌkeheˈveˑli] *v* compare

kehysedh [keˈhɪˑzeð] *g* **+ow** equator

kekeffrys [kekeˈfrɪːz] *av* moreover

kekemmys [keˈkemˑɪs] *av* as many as, as much as

kel [ˈkeːl] *hg* hidden; **yn-dann gel** in secret, covertly

keles [ˈkeˑles] *v* hide, conceal, keep secret

kell [ˈkelː] *b* **+ow** cell (Biol.); **+ow, diwgell** *hd* testicles

kelli [ˈkelːi] *v* lose, forfeit

kelli [ˈkelːi] *b* **kelliow** grove, copse

kelmi [ˈkelmi] *v* tie, bind, lash, knot

kelorn [ˈkeˑlɔrn] *g* **kelern** bucket, pail

Kelt [ˈkelt] *g* **+yon** Celt

keltek [ˈkeltek] *hg* Celtic

Keltek [ˈkeltek] *g* Celtic language

kelynn [ˈkeˑlɪn] *hk* **+enn** holly, holly-trees

kelyon [ˈkeˑljɔn] *hk* **+enn** flies

Kembra [ˈkembra] *le* Wales

85

kembrek ['kembrek] *hg* Welsh

Kembrek ['kembrek] *g* Welsh language

Kembro ['kembrɔ] *g* **+yon** Welshman

Kembroes [kembr'ɔ:es] *b* **+ow** Welshwoman

kemmeres [ke'me·res] *v* take, receive

kemmeryans [ke'me·rjans] *g* **+ow** reception

kemmyn ['kem:ɪn] *hg* common

kemmynna [ke'mɪn:a] *v* bequeath

kemmys ['kem:ɪs] *hg* so much, as much as, as many as; **kemmys y'th karav** I love you so

kemmysk ['kem:ɪsk] *g* **+ow** mixture, blend, alloy, miscellany

kemmyska [ke'mɪ·ska] *v* mix, mingle, blend, confuse

kempenn ['kempen] *hg* tidy, neat, orderly

kempenna [kem'pen:a] *v* tidy, set in order

kempennyades [ˌkempen'ja·des] *b* **+ow**; **kempennyades gols** hairdresser

kempennyas [kem'pen:jas] *g* **-ysi**; **kempennyas gols** hairdresser

kemusur [ke'my·zyr] *g* **+yow** symmetry, proportion

¹ken ['ke:n] *hg* other: *av* otherwise, else

²ken ['ke:n] *g* **+yow** reason

kenderow ['kenderɔw] *g* **kenderwi** cousin (male)

kendon ['kendɔn] *b* **+ow** debt, liability; **ri kendon** lend; **ri neppyth yn kendon dhe nebonan** lend something to someone

kenedhel ['keneðel] *b* **-dhlow** nation

kenedhlek ['keneðlek] *hg* national

keniterow [ˌke'niterɔw] *b* **keniterwi** cousin (female)

keniver [ke'ni·ver] *hg* as many

kenn ['ken:] *g* **+ow** skin, hide, peel

kennertha [ke'nerθa] *v* encourage, motivate

kennin ['ken:ɪn] *hk* **+enn** garlic

kenter ['kenter] *b* **kentrow** nail, spike

kentevynn [ken'te·vɪn] *g* **+ow** concrete

kentra ['kentra] *v* nail

kentrevek [ken'tre·vek] *g* **-ogyon** neighbour (male)

kentreveth [ken'tre·veθ] *b* **+ow** neighbourhood

kentrevoges [ˌkentre'vɔ·ges] *b* **+ow** neighbour (female)

kenwerth ['kenwerθ] *g* **+ow** commerce, trade

kenwertha [ken'werθa] *v* trade

kenwoestel [ken'wo·stel] *g* **kenwoestlow** bet, wager

kenwoestla [ken'wʏstla] *v* bet

kenys ['ke·nɪs] *g* singing, crowing of cock

kepar [ke'pa:r] *av* like; **kepar ha** such as

¹**ker** ['ke:r] *hg* dear, costly, expensive

²**ker** ['ke:r] *b* **+yow** fort, camp, earthwork, hill-fort

kerdh ['kerð] *g* **+ow** walk, journey

kerdher ['kerðer] *g* **-oryon** pedestrian, walker

kerdhes ['kerðes] *v* walk

keredh [ke'reð] *b* **+yow** rebuke, reproach, reproof, scolding

keredhi [ke're·ði] *v* rebuke, reproach, reprove, tell off

kerens ['ke·rens] *lp* parents, kinsmen

kerensa [ke'renza] *b* love, affection

keres ['ke·res] *hk* **+enn** cherries

keresik [ke're·zɪk] *g* **-igyon** sweetheart, darling

kernewek [ker'neʋek] *hg* Cornish

Kernewek [ker'neʋek] *g* Cornish language

Kernewes [ker'neʋes] *b* **+ow** Cornishwoman

Kernow ['kernɔw] *le* Cornwall: *g* **+yon** Cornishman; **Kernow bys vykken!** Cornwall for ever!

kert ['kert] *g* **+ow**; **+ys** lorry, cart; **kert pedrosek** waggon

kertik ['kertɪk] *g* **-igow** van

kervya ['kervja] *v* carve

keschanj ['kestʃandʒ] *g* **+yow** exchange

keschanjya [kes'tʃandʒja] *v* exchange

keser ['keˑzer] *hk* **+enn** hail (weather)

keskerðhes [kes'kerðes] *v* process (walk)

keskewsel [kes'keʊzel] *v* converse (speech)

keski ['keˑski] *v* admonish, tell off

keskorra [kes'kɔːra] *v* assemble (trans.)

keskowalhe [kes,kɔwal'heː] *v* complement

keskows ['keˑskɔʊs] *g* **+ow** conversation

kesoberi [kezɔ'beˑri] *v* co-operate, collaborate

kespar ['keˑspar] *g* **+ow** partner

kespareth [kes'paˑreθ] *b* **+ow** partnership

kesstrif ['kestrif] *g* **+ow** competition

kesstrivor [ke'striˑvɔr] *g* **+yon** competitor

kessydhya [kes'sɪˑðja] *v* punish

kessydhyans [kes'sɪˑðjans] *g* **+ow** punishment, sanction, retribution

kestav ['keˑstav] *g* **+ow** contact

kestava [kes'taˑva] *v* contact

kesten ['keˑsten] *hk* **+enn** chestnuts

kesva ['kezva] *b* **+ow** board (group of people), assembly; **Kesva an Taves Kernewek** Cornish Language Board

kesvywa [kez'vɪwa] *v* live together, cohabit

keswlasek [kez'wlaˑzek] *hg* international

¹keth ['keˑθ] *hg* same, identical; **an keth tra** the same thing; **an keth ha** the same as

²keth ['keːθ] *hg* servile, subject, captive

kethreydhek [keθ'reɪðek] *g* **-ogyon**

88

kethreydhel [keθ'reɪðek] *hg* homosexual

kettell² ['ket:el] *av* as soon as

kettep ['ket:ep] *hg* each, every; **yn kettep penn** everyone, everybody

keudh ['kœ:ð] *g* **+ow** sorrow, grief, travail

keudhesik [kœ'ðe·zɪk] *hg* sorry, contrite, repentant

keunegenn [kœ'ne·gen] *b* **+ow** bog, reed-bed

keunys ['kœ·nɪs] *hk* **+enn** firewood, fuel

keus ['kœ:z] *g* **+yow** cheese

kevambos [kev'ambɔs] *g* **+ow** agreement, contract, covenant, treaty

kevammok [kev'am:ɔk] *g* **-ogow** battle, fight

kevannedhi [ˌkeva'ne·ði] *v* occupy

kevarwoedha [ˌkevar'wo·ða] *v* guide

kevarwoedher [ˌkevar'wo·ðer] *g* **+yon** guide

kever ['ke·ver] *g* **yn kever** about, concerning, with respect to; **y'th kever** about you

keveylya [ke'veɪlja] *v* accompany

kevnis ['kevnɪs] *hk* **+enn** spiders

kevoes ['ke·vɤs] *hg* contemporary

kevradh ['kevráð] *g* **+ow** rate

kevrenn ['kevren] *b* **+ow** share, dividend, fastening, link, conjunction

kevrenna [kev'ren:a] *v* share, divide

kevrenner [kev'ren:er] *g* **-oryon** participant

kevrin ['kevrin] *g* **+yow** mystery, secret

kevrinek [kev'ri·nek] *hg* secret, mysterious, occult

kevyl ['ke·vɪl] *g* mount (horse)

kevywi [ke'vɪwi] *g* **+ow** party, feast

kew ['kew] *b* **+yow** enclosure

kewar [ke'wa:r] *hg* correct, exact, precise

kewask [ke'wa:sk] *hg* compact

kewer ['keʋer] *b* **+yow** weather

kewsel ['keʊzel] *v* speak, talk, converse; **kewsel orth** speak to

keyn ['keɪn] *g* **+ow** back, ridge, keel

keynvor ['keɪnvər] *g* **+yow** ocean; **Keynvor Atlantek** Atlantic Ocean; **Keynvor Eyndek** Indian Ocean; **Keynvor Hebask** Pacific Ocean

ki ['kiː] *g* **keun** dog, hound

kibell ['kiˑbel] *b* **+ow** bath, tub

kibya ['kiˑbja] *v* snatch

kig ['kiːg] *g* **+yow** meat, flesh; **kig an dyns** gums

kiger ['kiˑger] *g* **-oryon** butcher; **kiger mogh** pork butcher

kigereth [kiˑgeˑreθ] *b* butchery (trade)

kiji ['kiˑdʒi] *g* **+ow** kennel for one dog

kila ['kiˑla] *g* **y gila** the other (m.); **an eyl ... y gila** the one ... the other

kildenna [kilˈdenˑa] *v* pull back, retreat, recoil, withdraw, reverse, move back

kilogramm [ˌkiləˈgramː] *g* **+ow** kilogram

kilometer [ˌkiləˈmeˑter] *g* **+metrow** kilometre

kinyow ['kiˑnjəw] *g* **kinyewow** dinner

kist ['kiːst] *b* **+yow** box (container)

kisya ['kiˑzja] *v* destroy, damage

kisyans ['kiˑzjans] *g* damage

kisys ['kiˑzɪs] *hg* damaged

klamder ['klamder] *g* **+yow** faint

klamdera [klamˈdeˑra] *v* faint, lose consciousness

klapp ['klap] *g* chatter, gabble, babble

klappkodh ['klapkəð] *b* **+ow** mobile telephone

klappya ['klapːja] *v* chatter, gabble, babble, jabber

klass ['klas] *g* **+ys**; **+ow** class, category

klassans ['klasːans] *g* **+ow** classification

klassek ['klasːek] *hg* classical

klattra ['klatra] *v* chatter, talk noisily, clatter

klav ['klaːv] *hg* sick, ill

klavji ['klavdʒi] *g* **+ow** hospital

klavjior [klav'dʒiˑɔr] *g* **+yon** nurse (male)

klavjiores [ˌklavdʒiˑɔˑres] *b* **+ow** nurse (female)

kledh ['kleːð] *hg* left (opposite of right)

kledha ['kleˑða] *g* **kledhedhyow** sword

kledhbarth [ˌkleˑðˈbarθ] *b* **+ow** north, northern side

kledhek ['kleˑðek] *hg* left-handed: *g* **-ogyon** left-hander

kleger ['kleˑger] *g* **+yow** precipice, cliff, crag

kleghti ['klexti] *g* **+ow** belfry

kler ['kleːr] *hg* clear, evident

klerhe [kler'heː] *v* clear, brighten, clarify

klerji ['klerdʒi] *k* the learned, clergy

kleudh ['klœːð] *g* **+yow** ditch, trench, excavation

kleudhya ['klœˑðja] *v* dig a trench

kleves ['kleˑves] *g* **+ow** illness, sickness, malady

klewes ['klewes] *v* hear, feel

klewwelyek [kleuˈweˑljek] *hg* audio-visual

kleys ['kleiz] *g* **+yow** ditch

kliens ['kliˑens] *g* **+ow** client

kloes ['kloːz] *b* **+yow** fence, rack

kloes-dhiwvronn [ˌkloˑzðiʊˈvrɔnː] *b* **kloesyow-d.** rib-cage, thorax

klof ['klɔːf] *hg* lame

klogh ['klɔːx] *g* **klegh** bell; **klogh an marow** death knell; **klogh daras** door-bell

klokk ['klɔk] *g* **+ow** clock

klopenn ['klɔˑpen] *g* **+ow** skull, numskull

klor ['klɔːr] *hg* mild

klos ['klɔːz] *hg* enclosed, closed: *g* **+yow** enclosure, close, precinct

klow [ˈklɔw] *g* **+yow** lock of door

klus [ˈklyːz] *g* **+yow** roost, perch

klusya [ˈklyˑzja] *v* roost, perch

klykkya [ˈklɪkˑja] *v* click

klysa [ˈklɪˑza] *v* make snug, shelter

knias [ˈkniˑas] *v* gnaw, chew, corrode

knouk [ˈknuːk] *g* **-ys** knock

knoukya [ˈknuˑkja] *v* knock

know [ˈknɔw] *hk* **+enn** nuts; **knowenn frynk** walnut; **knowenn goll** hazelnut

knowwydh [ˈknɔuwɪð] *b* **+enn** nut-trees

kober [ˈkɔˑber] *g* copper

Kobrynys [kɔˈbrɪˑnɪs] *le* Cyprus

Kobrynyser [kɔbrɪˈnɪˑzer] *g* **-oryon** Cypriot

kocha [ˈkɔˑtʃa] *g* **kochow**; **kochys** coach, stage-coach, carriage of train

kodenn [ˈkɔˑden] *b* **+ow** code

koedh [ˈkɔːð] *g* **+ow** fall

koedha [ˈkɔˑða] *v* fall, happen, befall; **y koedh dhymm mos** I ought to go

koeg [ˈkɔːg] *hg* empty, worthless, vain

koen [ˈkɔːn] *b* **+yow** late dinner, supper

koena [ˈkɔˑna] *v* eat late dinner

koer [ˈkɔːr] *hk* **+enn** wax

koera [ˈkɔˑra] *v* wax

koerenn [ˈkɔˑren] *b* **+ow**, **koer** *hk* cake of wax

koes [ˈkɔːz] *g* **+ow** wood (trees)

koeswik [ˈkɔˑzwɪk] *b* **-igow** forest

koeth [ˈkɔːθ] *hg* excellent

koffi [ˈkɔfˑiː] *g* **+ow** coffee

koffiji [kɔˈfiˑdʒi] *g* **+ow** cafe, coffee-house

kofrynn [ˈkɔfrɪn] *g* **+ow** casket

kog [ˈkɔːg] *g* **+ow** cook (male)

koges ['kɔ·ges] *b* **+ow** cook (female)

kogforn ['kɔgfɔrn] *b* **+ow** cooker, cooking-stove

¹kogh ['kɔːx] *g* **+ow** hood, bonnet, hull

²kogh ['kɔːx] *hg* blood-red, scarlet

kok ['kɔːk] *g* **kokow** fishing boat

kolghes ['kɔlxes] *b* **+ow** quilt, bedspread, duvet

¹koll ['kɔlː] *g* **+ow** loss, perdition

²koll ['kɔlː] *hk* **+enn** hazel-trees

kollell ['kɔlːel] *b* **kellylli** knife

kollji ['kɔldʒi] *g* **+ow** college, chapter of cathedral

kollwydh ['kɔlwɪð] *hk* **+enn** hazel-trees

kolm ['kɔlm] *g* **+ow** knot, tie, node

kolmedh ['kɔlmeð] *g* **+ow** league (e.g. football)

kolodhyon [kɔ'lɔðjɔn] *hk* **+enn** bowels, guts, intestines

kolomm ['kɔlɔm] *b* **kelemmi** dove, pigeon

kolommenn [kɔ'lɔmːen] *b* **+ow, kelemmi** *hk* pigeon

kolonn [kɔ·lɔn] *b* **+ow** heart

kolonnek [kɔ'lɔnːek] *hg* hearty, bold, brave

kolonnekter [ˌkɔlɔ'nekter] *g* bravery, courage, boldness

kolorenn [kɔ'lɔ·ren] *b* **+ow** collar

koloven [kɔ'lɔ·ven] *b* **+yow** column

kommendya [kɔ'mendja] *v* recommend, commend, introduce, present

kommendyas [kɔ'mendjas] *g* **-ysi** presenter

kommol ['kɔmːɔl] *hk* **+enn** cloud

kommolek [kɔ'mɔ·lek] *hg* cloudy

kompella [kɔm'pelːa] *v* compel

kompes ['kɔmpes] *hg* even, level, calm (of sea)

komplek ['kɔmplek] *hg* complicated

konfort ['kɔnfɔrt] *g* **+s** spiritual comfort, consolation,

93

encouragement

konfortya [kɔnˈfɔrtja] *v* console, comfort

konin [ˈkɔːnɪn] *g* **+es** rabbit

konna [ˈkɔnːa] *g* **+ow** neck, narrow strip of land

konna-bregh [ˌkɔnːaˈbreːx] *g* **konnaow-bregh** wrist

konnar [ˈkɔnːar] *b* fury, rabies, rage

konneryek [kɔˈnerˑjek] *hg* rabid, furious, manic

konnyk [ˈkɔnːɪk] *hg* clever

¹**kons** [ˈkɔns] *g* **+ow** pavement, causeway

²**kons** [ˈkɔns] *b* **+yow** vagina

konsel [ˈkɔnsel] *g* **+yow** council

konsevya [kɔnˈseˑvja] *v* conceive

konter [ˈkɔnter] *hg* contrary, opposite: *g* **+s** opposite

konvedhes [kɔnˈveˑðes] *v* understand, perceive, realize, comprehend: *g* understanding

kopel [ˈkɔpel] *g* **koplow** couple, pair

kopla [ˈkɔpla] *v* couple

kordenn [ˈkɔrden] *b* **kerdyn** string, cord

korev [kɔˈrev] *g* **+ow** beer, ale

korf [ˈkɔrf] *g* **+ow** body, corpse; **korf eskern** skeleton

korflann [ˈkɔrflan] *b* **+ow** churchyard, cemetery

korkynn [ˈkɔrkɪn] *g* **+ow** cork, stopper, bung

¹**korn** [ˈkɔrn] *g* **kern** musical horn, **dewgorn** *hd* horn of animal

²**korn** [ˈkɔrn] *g* **kernow** corner

kornell [ˈkɔrnel] *b* **+ow** corner, nook

korporal [ˈkɔrpɔral] *g* **+s** corporal

korr [ˈkɔrː] *g* **+yon** dwarf

korrbryv [ˈkɔrbrɪv] *g* **+es** microbe, germ

korrgowsell [kɔrˈgɔuzel] *b* **+ow** microphone

korrigan [kɔˈriˑgan] *g* **+es** elf

korrstyr [ˈkɔrstɪr] *g* **+yow** nuance

korsek [ˈkɔrsek] *hg* Corsican

Korsek [ˈkɔrsek] *g* Corsican language

Korsika [ˈkɔrsɪka] *le* Corsica

kortes [ˈkɔrtes] *hg* polite, courteous

kortesi [ˈkɔrtesi] *g* **+s** politeness

kosa [ˈkɔˑza] *v* tickle, itch, tingle

kosel [ˈkɔˑzel] *hg* quiet, still, tranquil

¹kosk [ˈkɔːsk] *g* sleep, mould, fungus, rot in timber

²kosk [ˈkɔːsk] *b* **+ow** admonishment

koska [ˈkɔˑska] *v* sleep, go mouldy, get dry rot

kosoleth [kɔˈzɔˑleθ] *b* quiet, quietness, stillness, tranquillity

kost [ˈkɔːst] *g* **+ow** cost, expense, charge

kostek [ˈkɔˑstek] *hg* costly, expensive, pricey

kostenn [ˈkɔˑsten] *b* **+ow** target, large shallow straw basket

kostya [ˈkɔˑstja] *v* cost

kota [ˈkɔˑta] *g* **kotow** coat

koth [ˈkɔːθ] *hg* old, ancient; **an re goth** the old

kothhe [kɔθˈheː] *v* grow old

kothman [ˈkɔθman] *g* **+s** comrade, friend

kothni [ˈkɔθni] *b* old age

koton [ˈkɔˑtɔn] *g* **-enyow** cotton

kottha [ˈkɔθːa] *hg* older

kov [ˈkɔːv] *g* **+yow** memory, recollection, recall

kovadh [ˈkɔˑvað] *g* **+ow** remembrance, record

kovhe [kɔvˈheː] *v* remind, remember, commemorate

kovlyver [kɔvˈlɪˑver] *g* **-lyvrow** register

kovskrifa [kɔvˈskriˑfa] *v* register

kovskrifenn [kɔvˈskriˑfen] *b* **+ow** archive

kow [ˈkɔw] *hg* hollow: *b* **+yow** hollow

kowal [ˈkɔwal] *hg* complete, entire, whole, thorough: *av* totally

kowalder [kɔ'walder] *g* totality

kowann ['kɔuan] *b* **+ow** owl

kowas ['kɔuas] *b* **kowasow** shower, rainstorm

kowasell [kɔ'wa·zel] *b* **+ow** domestic shower

kowbal ['kɔubal] *g* **+yow** ferry

kowell ['kɔ·wel] *g* **+ow** cage

koweth ['kɔweθ] *g* **+a** companion (male), friend (male)

kowethas [kɔ'we·θas] *g* **+ow** company, society, association

kowethes [kɔu'e·θes] *b* **+ow** companion (female), friend (female)

kowethlyver [kɔue θ'lɪ·ver] *g* **-lyvrow** manual, handbook, guide-book

kowethyans [kɔu'e·θjans] *g* **+ow** fellowship, association, company

kowfordh ['kɔufɔrð] *b* **+ow** tunnel

kowgans ['kɔugans] *hg* certain, sure

kowganseth [kɔu'ganzeθ] *b* **+ow** certainty

¹**kowl** ['kɔul] *hk* **+enn** cabbage

²**kowl** ['kɔul] *g* **+ow** soup, broth, pottage

kowlvleujenn [kɔul'vlœ·dʒen] *b* **+ow** cauliflower, broccoli

kowlwul ['kɔulwyl] *v* complete, accomplish, finish doing

kowr ['kɔur] *g* **kewri** giant, ogre

kowrvargh ['kɔurvarx] *g* **-vergh** camel

kows ['kɔuz] *g* **+ow** speech, talk

koynt ['kɔint] *hg* strange, extraordinary, unusual, odd, eccentric

kragh ['kraːx] *hg* scurvy, scabby

krakk ['krak] *g* **+ys** crack, snap

krakkya ['krakːja] *v* crack, snap

krambla [ˈkrambla] *v* climb

krampoeth [ˈkrampχθ] *hk* **+enn** pancakes, crepes

kramya [ˈkraˑmja] *v* crawl, creep

kras [ˈkraːz] *hg* parched, toasted: *k* **+enn** toast (food)

krasa [ˈkraˑza] *v* toast

kravas [ˈkraˑvas] *v* scrape, scratch: *g* **+ow** scratch

kravlost [ˈkravlɔst] *g* **+ow** goblin

krefter [ˈkrefter] *g* **-oryon** craftsman, artisan

kreg [ˈkreːg] *hg* hoarse

kregi [ˈkreˑgi] *v* hang, suspend; **kregi war** depend on

kren [ˈkreːn] *g* **+yow** quake

krena [ˈkreˑna] *v* shake, tremble

krenn [ˈkrenː] *hg* round, circular

krennhys [ˈkrenhɪs] *g* circumference

¹kres [ˈkreːz] *g* peace

²kres [ˈkreːz] *b* faith

³kres [ˈkreːz] *hg* middle, intermediate: *g* **+yow** centre, middle, waist

kresek [ˈkreˑzek] *hg* average, mediocre: *g* **kresogow** average

kresenn [ˈkreˑzen] *b* **+ow** centre (building)

kresenni [kreˈzenːi] *v* centralize, centre

kreslu [ˈkrezly] *g* **+yow** constabulary, police force

kressya [ˈkresːja] *v* increase, multiply, extend

kresva [ˈkresfa] *b* **+ow** centre (building)

kreswas [ˈkrezwas] *g* **-wesyon** centre (in rugby), middleman

kreswedhek [krezˈweˑðek] *hg* medium

kreuni [ˈkrœˑni] *v* accumulate

krev [ˈkreːv] *hg* strong, mighty, vigorous

krevder [ˈkrevder] *g* **+yow** strength, might

krevenn [ˈkreˑven] *b* **+ow** scab

97

krevhe [kref'he:] *v* strengthen, reinforce

krey ['kreɪ] *g* **+ow** chalk

kreyth ['kreɪθ] *hk* **+enn** scars

kri ['kri:] *g* **+ow** cry

kria ['kri·a] *v* cry (call)

krib ['kri:b] *b* **+ow** comb, crest, reef of rocks

kribas ['kri·bas] *v* comb

kribenn ['kri·ben] *b* **+ow**; **kribenn vel** honeycomb

Krist ['kri:st] *hp* Christ

Kristonedh [krɪs'tɔ·neð] *g* Christianity

Kristyon ['kri·stjɔn] *hg* Christian: *g* **Kristonyon** Christian

Kristyoneth [krɪs'tjɔ·neθ] *b* Christendom

kriv ['kri:v] *hg* raw, uncooked, unripe

Kroat ['krɔ·at] *g* **+yon** Croat

kroatek [krɔ·a'tek] *hg* Croatian

Kroatek [krɔ·a'tek] *g* Croatian language

Kroati [krɔ·a'ti] *le* Croatia

kroch ['krɔːtʃ] *g* **+ow, dewgroch** *hd* crutch

krodhvol ['krɔðvɔl] *g* **+yow** complaint, grumble

krodhvolas [krɔð'vɔ·las] *v* complain, grumble

krogen ['krɔ·gen] *b* **kregyn** shell, carapace

kroghen ['krɔ·xen] *b* **kreghyn** skin; **kroghen an lagas** eyelid

kroghena [krɔ'fie·na] *v* skin, flay

kroghendanow [ˌkrɔ·xen'da·nɔw] *hg* sensitive

kroglenn ['krɔglen] *b* **+ow** curtain, hanging

krokodil ['krɔkɔdɪl] *g* **+es** crocodile

kromm ['krɔm:] *hg* curved, crooked, bent

kromman ['krɔm:an] *b* **+ow** sickle

krommgenter [krɔm'genter] *b* **-gentrow** staple

krommgentra [krɔm'gentra] *v* staple

krommgentrell [krɔm'gentrel] *b* **+ow** stapler

kronk ['krɔnk] *g* **+ys** thump

kronkya ['krɔnkja] *v* thump

kroust ['kruːst] *g* **+yow** picnic lunch, meal taken to work, snack

¹**krow** ['krɔw] g bloodshed

²**krow** ['krɔw] *g* **+yow** hut, shed, shack

krowji ['krɔwdʒi] *g* **+ow** one-roomed cottage, cabin

krows ['krɔwz] *b* **+yow** cross, rood

krowsfordh ['krɔwsfɔrð] *b* **+ow** crossroads

krowsvyaj [krɔwsˈfɪˈadʒ] *g* **+yow** cruise

krugya ['kryˈgja] *v* put in a heap

krullys ['krylˈɪs] *hg* curly

krygell ['krɪˈgel] *b* **+ow** spider-crab

krygh ['krɪːx] *g* **+yow** wrinkle, ripple, crinkle

kryghias [krɪˈfiˈaz] *v* whinny

kryghlamm ['krɪxlam] *g* **+ow** somersault

kryjyans ['krɪˈdʒjans] *g* **+ow** belief, faith, creed, religion

kryjyk ['krɪˈdʒɪk] *hg* religious

krys ['krɪːz] *g* **+yow** shirt, chemise; **krys T** tee-shirt

krysi ['krɪˈzi] *v* believe, have faith in

kryspows ['krɪˈspɔws] *b* **+yow** jacket, waistcoat

krysya ['krɪˈzja] *v* quake

kub ['kyːb] *g* **+ow** cube; **kub rew** ice cube

kudh ['kyːð] *hg* hidden, concealed, covert

kudha ['kyˈða] *v* hide, conceal

kudhlenn ['kyðlen] *b* **+ow** veil, cover of a book

kudynn ['kyˈdɪn] *g* **+ow** problem, lock of hair, skein; **kudynn vyth** no problem

kuhudha [kyˈhyˈða] *v* accuse, denounce, tell tales about

kuhudhans [kyˈhyˈðans] *g* **+ow** accusation, indictment

kul ['ky:l] *hg* narrow

kulyek ['ky·ljek] *g* **+es**; **-ogyon** cock, cockerel, male bird

kummyas ['kym:jas] *g* **+ow** permission, leave, licence, permit, sanction; **ri kummyas** sanction

kuntell ['kyntel] *v* gather, pick, collect (trans.): *g* **+ow** collection

kuntellek [kyn'tel:ek] *hg* collective

kuntelles [kyn'tel:es] *g* **+ow** gathering, meeting, assembly, congress

kur ['ky:r] *g* **+yow** care, cure, remedy

kurun ['ky·ryn] *b* **+yow** crown

kuruna [ky'ry·na] *v* crown

kusul ['ky·syl] *b* **+yow** advice, counsel, opinion

kusulya [ky'sy·lja] *v* advise, counsel

kusulyer [ky'sy·ljer] *g* **-oryon** counsellor

kuv ['ky:v] *hg* dear, kind, loving: *g* **+yon**; **kuv kolonn** sweetheart

kwarel ['kwa·rel] *g* **+s** pane of glass

kwarter ['kwarter] *g* **kwartrys** quarter (geog.), quarter (fraction)

kwartron ['kwartrɔn] *g* **+ys** quarter (fraction), quarter (geog.)

kweth ['kwe:θ] *b* **+ow** cloth

kwethynn ['kwe·θɪn] *g* **+ow** napkin

kwilkyn ['kwɪlkɪn] *g* **+yow** frog

kyf ['kɪ:f] *g* **+yon** tree-trunk

kyfeyth ['kɪ·feɪθ] *g* **+yow** preserve, jam, confection

kyfyans ['kɪ·fjans] *g* confidence, trust, reliance

kyhwedhel [kɪ'hwe·ðel] *g* **kyhwedhlow** tale, rumour, hearsay

kylgh ['kɪlx] *g* **+yow** circle, round, ring

kylghfordh ['kɪlxfɔrð] *b* roundabout

kylghyek ['kɪlxjek] *hg* round
kylghynn ['kɪlxɪn] *g* **+ow** hoop
kyllas ['kɪlːas] *hk* **+enn** shale, slate
kymygenn [kɪ'mɪ·gen] *b* **+ow** chemical
kymygieth [ˌkɪmɪ·gi·eθ] *b* chemistry
kymyk ['kɪ·mɪk] *hg* chemical
kyn[5] [kɪn] *m* though, although
kyni ['kɪ·ni] *v* lament, mourn, wail, bemoan
kynnik ['kɪnːɪk] *g* **-igow** offer, proposition
kyns ['kɪns] *rg* before: *av* formerly, sooner, rather,
    previously: *hg* former
kynsa ['kɪnza] *hg* first
kynth [kɪnθ] *m* though, although
kynvann ['kɪnvan] *g* **+ow** lamentation, mourning
kynyav ['kɪ·njav] *g* **+ow** autumn
kyrghes ['kɪrxes] *v* fetch, bring, get
kyrghynn ['kɪrxɪn] *g* **+ow** surroundings; **yn
    kyrghynn** around
kyrghynna [kɪr'fɪnːa] *v* surround
kyrghynnedh [kɪr'fɪnːeð] *g* **+ow** environment
kyttrin [kɪt'triːn] *g* **+yow** bus
kywni ['kɪʊni] *hk* **+enn** moss

L

lader ['lader] *g* **ladron** thief
ladha ['la·ða] *v* kill, slay, slaughter, switch off
ladhva ['la·ðva] *b* **+ow** slaughter
ladra ['la·dra] *v* steal, rob
ladrans ['ladrans] *g* **+ow** robbery (individual crime),
    theft (individual crime)

ladres ['ladres] *b* **+ow** sluice

ladrynsi [la'drɪnzi] *g* robbery (in general), theft (in general)

lagas ['laːgas] *g* **lagasow, dewlagas** *hd* eye

lagenn ['laːgen] *b* **+ow** puddle, pond

lagenna [la'genːa] *v* splash

lagha ['laːxa] *b* **laghys** law, dogma

lakka ['lakːa] *hg* worse

lamm ['lamː] *g* **+ow** leap, jump, bound

lamma ['lamːa] *v* leap, jump, bound

lammlenn ['lamlen] *b* **+ow** parachute

lammleur ['lamlen] *g* **+yow** trampoline

lanketh ['lankeθ] *b* adolescence

lann ['lanː] *b* **+ow** church-land, monastic close

Lannstevan [lan'steːvan] *le* Launceston

lanow ['lanɔw] *g* **+yow** high tide, fullness

lappieth [lap'iˑeθ] *b* gymnastics

lapya ['laːpja] *v* lick, lap

las ['laːz] *g* **+ow** dram, liquor, alcohol

lasya ['laˑsja] *v* lace

lath ['laːθ] *b* **+ow** rod, yard (measure), stick

latimer ['laˑtɪmer] *g* **+s** interpreter

Latvi ['latvi] *le* Latvia

lavar ['laˑvar] *g* **+ow** sentence, saying, utterance; **lavar koth** proverb

lavasos [la'vaˑzɔs] *v* venture, dare

lavrek ['lavrek] *g* **lavrogow** trousers, breeches

lavur ['laˑvyr] *g* **+yow** labour, toil, work

lavurya [la'vyˑrja] *v* labour, toil, work, travel

¹le ['leː] *g* **leow** place, situation, spot, site; **yn le** instead; **yn y le** instead of him

²le ['leː] *hg* less

ledan ['leˑdan] *hg* wide, broad

102

leder ['le·der] *b* **ledrow** slope
ledher ['le·ðer] *g* **+ow** leather
ledya ['le·dja] *v* lead
ledyer ['le·djer] *g* **ledyoryon** leader
leftenant [lef'te·nant] *g* **+s** lieutenant
legest ['le·gest] *g* **+i** lobster
legh ['le:x] *b* **+yon** slab
leghenn ['le·xen] *b* **+ow** slate, thin flat stone
lel ['le:l] *hg* loyal, faithful, trusty
lemmel ['lem:el] *v* spring, jump
lemmyn ['lem:ɪn] *av* now, at present
lenna ['len:a] *v* read aloud
lenner ['len:er] *g* **-oryon** reader
lent ['lent] *hg* slow; **yn lent** slowly
lentrus *hg* shiny
lenwel ['lenwel] *v* fill, endue
lergh ['lerx] *g* **+ow** track
¹les ['le:z] *g* **+yow** plant
²les ['le:z] *g* profit, advantage, benefit, usefulness;
dhe les useful, interesting
³les ['le:z] *g* **+yow** width, breadth
lesa ['le·za] *v* spread, unfold, expand
lesk ['le:sk] *g* **+ow** swing, oscillation, cradle
leska ['le·ska] *v* swing, rock
leski ['le·ski] *v* burn
lesranna [lez'ran:a] *v* distribute
lesta ['le·sta] *v* prevent, hinder
lester ['le·ster] *g* **lestri** vessel (container or ship),
vase
lester-sedhi [ˌle·ster'se·ði] *g* **lestri-sedhi** submarine
lesus ['le·zys] *hg* advantageous
leswedh ['le·zweð] *g* **+ow** frying-pan
leth ['le:θ] *g* **+ow** milk

le'ti [ˈleˑti] *g* **+ow** dairy

lett [ˈlet] *g* **+ow**; **+ys** hindrance, blockage, barrier, impediment, obstacle; **heb lett** incessantly

lettya [ˈletˑja] *v* hinder, impede, prevent, block, obstruct

letus [ˈleˑtys] *hk* **+enn** lettuce

leugh [ˈlœːx] *g* **+i** calf

leun [ˈlœːn] *hg* full

leur [ˈlœːr] *g* **+yow** floor, ground, storey

leurlenn [ˈlœrlen] *b* **+ow** carpet

leuv [ˈlœːv] *b* **+yow, diwla, diwleuv** *hd* hand (in general)

leuvbann [ˈlœvban] *g* **+ow** felt (material)

leuvtoesa [lœfˈtoˑza] *v* massage

leuvtoesans [lœfˈtoˑzans] *g* **+ow** massage

leuvvedhek [lœvˈveˑðek] *g* **-ogyon** surgeon

lev [ˈleːv] *g* **+ow** voice, cry

leven [ˈleven] *hg* smooth, even, level

levena [leˈveˑna] *v* smooth

leverel [leˈveˑrel] *v* say, tell, relate, utter

leveryans [leˈveˑrjans] *g* **+ow** pronunciation

¹lew [ˈlew] *g* **+yon** lion

²lew [ˈlew] *b* **+yow** league (3 miles)

³lew [ˈlew] *g* **+yow** rudder

lewya [ˈleʊja] *v* drive, steer

lewyader [leʊˈjaˑder] *g* **-oryon** steersman, helmsman

lewyas [ˈleʊjas] *g* **+ysi** chauffeur

lewydh [ˈlewıð] *g* **+yon** director, president

lewyer [ˈleʊjer] *g* **-yoryon** driver, pilot

leys [ˈleız] *g* **+yow** mud, slime, alluvium

leyth [ˈleıθ] *hg* moist

li [ˈliː] *b* **livyow** lunch(eon)

libel [ˈliˑbel] *g* **+s** label

lien ['li·en] *g* **+yow** napkin; **lien dorn** handkerchief; **lien diwla** serviette; **lien konna** scarf; **lien gweli** sheet for a bed

lies ['li·es] *rh* many; *hg* many; **lies chi** many houses, a lot of houses

liesek ['li·ezek] *hg* multiple, various

liesliw [,lies'liw] *hg* multicoloured

liesplek ['liesplek] *hg* **-egow** plural

liesskrifa [,lies'skri·fa] *v* photocopy, make copies of a document

Liger ['li·ger] *le* Loire

lili ['li·li] *b* **+s**; **lili Gorawys** daffodil

lim ['li:m] *g* **+yow** lime (mineral)

lin ['li:n] *hk* **+enn** linen, flax

linas ['li·nas] *hk* **+enn** nettles

linenn ['li·nen] *b* **+ow** line, streak

linenna [li'nen:a] *v* outline, sketch, draw lines

linennans [li'nen:ans] *g* **+ow** sketch

Lithuani [lɪθy'a·ni] *le* Lithuania

liv ['li:v] *g* **+ow** flood

liva ['li·va] *v* flood

livra ['livra] *v* liberate, set free, release

livreson [liv're·sɔn] *g* delivery

livya ['li·vja] *v* eat, have lunch

liw ['liw] *g* **liwyow** colour, hue

liwa ['liwa] *v* colour, dye

lo ['lɔ:] *b* **loyow** spoon

loder ['lɔder] *g* **lodrow** stocking

lodrik ['lɔdrɪk] *g* **-igow** sock

Loer ['lɔ:r] *b* **+yow** Moon

loerell ['lo·rel] *b* **+ow** artificial satellite

loergann ['lo·rgan] *g* moonlight, Full Moon

loes ['lɔ:z] *hg* grey, mouldy

Logh [ˈlɔːx] *le* Looe

logos [ˈlɔˑgɔs] *hk* **+enn** mice

lo-ledan [ˌlɔˑˈleˑdan] *b* **loyow-ledan** ladle

¹lomm [ˈlɔmː] *hg* bare

²lomm [ˈlɔmː] *g* **+ow** drop

londer [ˈlɔnder] *g* **+yow** gutter

loneth [ˈlɔˑneθ] *b* **-i, diwloneth** *hd* kidney

loskvenydh [lɔskˈveˑnɪð] *g* **+yow** volcano

losow [ˈlɔˑzɔw] *hk* herbs, vegetables

losowenn [lɔˈzɔʊen] *b* **+ow, losow** *hk* herb;
   losowenn an hav lily of the valley

lost [ˈlɔːst] *g* **+ow** tail, queue

lostenn [ˈlɔˑsten] *b* **+ow** skirt

Lostwydhyel [ˌlɔˑstˈwɪˈðjel] *le* Lostwithiel

Loundres [ˈlundres] *le* London

lovan [ˈlɔˑvan] *b* **lovonow** rope

low [ˈlɔw] *hk* **lowenn** lice

lowarn [ˈlɔʊarn] *g* **lewern** fox

lowarth [ˈlɔʊarθ] *g* **+yow** garden

lowarther [lɔˈwarθer] *g* **-oryon** gardener

lowen [ˈlɔʊen] *hg* joyful, happy, glad

lowena [lɔˈweˑna] *b* joy, bliss, happiness

lowender [lɔˈwender] *g* mirth, jollity

lowenek [lɔˈweˑnek] *hg* merry, glad, jolly

lower [ˈlɔʊer] *hg* several

lown [ˈlɔʊn] *g* **+yow** blade

lownya [ˈlɔʊnja] *v* slice

lownyans [ˈlɔʊnjans] *g* **+ow** slice, veneer

lowr [ˈlɔʊr] *hg* enough: *av* quite; **da lowr** O.K.; **ker
   lowr** quite expensive

lows [ˈlɔʊs] *hg* loose, slack, careless

lu [ˈlyː] *g* **+yow** army, crowd, host

lugarn [ˈlyˑgarn] *g* **lugern** lamp, lantern

lughes ['ly·xes] *hk* **+enn** lightning
Luksemburg ['lyksembyrg] *le* Luxembourg
Lulynn ['ly·lɪn] *le* Newlyn
lusu ['ly·zy] *hk* **+enn** ashes, embers
lyenn ['lɪ·en] *g* **+ow** literature
lyfans ['lɪ·fans] *g* **+es** toad
lyg ['lɪːg] *hg* obscene
lyha ['lɪ·ha] *hg* least
lymm ['lɪm:] *hg* sharp, keen, acute
lymna ['lɪmna] *v* paint (a picture), illustrate
lymnans ['lɪmnans] *g* **+ow** painting, picture, illustration
lymner ['lɪmner] *g* **-oryon** artist, illustrator
lymon ['lɪ·mɔn] *g* **+ys** lemon
lynn ['lɪn:] *b* **+yn** lake, pond
lys ['lɪːz] *b* **+yow** court
Lyskerrys [lɪs'ker:ɪs] *le* Liskeard
lystenn ['lɪsten] *b* **+ow** bandage
lystenna [lɪs'ten:a] *v* bandage
lyther ['lɪ·θer] *g* **+ow** letter (epistle)
lytherenn [lɪ'θe·ren] *b* **+ow** letter (of alphabet)
lytherennek [ˌlɪθe'ren:ek] *b* **-egi** alphabet
lytherva [lɪ'θerva] *b* **+ow** post-office
lythervaghteth [ˌlɪ·θer'vaxteθ] *b* **-veghtythyon** postwoman
lytherwas [lɪ'θerwas] *g* **-wesyon** postman
lyvenn ['lɪ·ven] *b* **+ow** leaf of paper, page of book
lyver ['lɪ·ver] *g* **lyvrow** book; **lyver notennow** notebook
lyver-dydhyow [ˌlɪ·ver'dɪ·ðjɔw] *g* **lyvrow-dydhyow** calendar
lyverji [lɪ'verdʒi] *g* **+ow** bookshop
lyver-termyn [ˌlɪ·ver'termɪn] *g* **lyvrow-termyn**

periodical, magazine

lyverva [lɪˈverva] *b* **+ow** library

lyveryas [lɪˈveˑrjas] *g* **-ysi** librarian

M

¹ma [ma] *rh* this; **an chi ma** this house

²ma [ma] *m* so that; **ma na** so that (neg.)

mab [ˈmaːb] *g* **mebyon** son, boy

mab-den [ˌmaˑbˈdeːn] *g* mankind, man

mab-wynn [ˌmaˑbˈwɪnː] *g* **mebyon-wynn** grandson

madama [maˈdaˑma] *b* **madamys** madam, lady, ma'am, milady

¹maga [ˈmaˑga] *v* feed, nourish, rear, bring up

²maga⁴ [ˈmaˑga] *m* as; **maga feri avel hok** as high as a kite

maghteth [ˈmaxteθ] *b* **+yon** maid, maiden, maidservant

magor [ˈmaˑgɔr] *b* **+yow** ruin

magores [maˈgɔˑres] *b* **+ow** nanny

mall [ˈmalː] *g* **+ow** haste, eagerness, urgency; **mall yw genev** I am in a hurry

Malta [ˈmalta] *le* Malta

maltek [ˈmaltek] *hg* Maltese

Maltek [ˈmaltek] *g* Maltese language

mamm [ˈmamː] *b* **+ow** mother

mammik [ˈmamːɪk] *b* **-igow** mum

mamm-vesydh [ˌmamˈveˑzɪð] *b* **mammow-besydh** godmother

mamm-wynn [ˌmamˈwɪnː] *b* **mammow-gwynn** grandmother

mammyeth ['mamːjeθ] *b* **+ow** mother-tongue

managh ['maˑnax] *g* **menegh** monk

manek ['maˑnek] *b* **manegow** glove

maner ['maˑner] *b* **+ow** manner, custom, way, manner

mann ['manː] *g* nothing, nil: *niv* zero

mannvrywi [man'vrɪwi] *v* pulverize

Manow ['maˑnɔw] *le* Man; **Ynys Vanow** Isle of Man

mantell ['mantel] *b* **mantelli** cloak

mantell-law ; mantelli-glaw raincoat

mantol ['mantɔl] *b* **+yow** balance, scales; **An Vantol** Libra

mantola [man'tɔˑla] *v* balance

manylyon [ma'nɪˑlʲɔn] *lp* details

mappa ['mapːa] *g* **mappow** map

¹mar⁴ [mar] *m* if: *g* doubt; **mar pleg** please; **heb mar** without doubt

²mar² [mar] *av* so; **mar goth** so old

marchont ['martʃont] *g* **-ons** merchant, trader, dealer

margh ['marx] *g* **mergh** horse

marghador [mar'fiaˑdɔr] *g* **+yon** marketeer, merchant

marghas ['marxas] *b* **+ow** market

marghek ['marxek] *g* **-ogyon** horseman, knight, cavalier

marghogeth [mar'fiɔˑgeθ] *v* ride

marghti ['marxti] *g* **+ow** stable

marnas ['marnas] *m* unless, except, save

marner ['marner] *g* **marners** sailor, mariner

marow ['marɔw] *hg* dead, out (of fire)

marowvor ['marɔwvor] *g* **+yow** neap tide

martesen [mar'teˑsen] *av* perhaps, perchance, maybe

marth ['marθ] *g* **+ow** wonder, astonishment, surprise

marthus ['marθys] *g* **+yon** marvel, miracle, wonder

mas ['maːz] *hg* morally good, virtuous

mason ['maˑsɔn] *g* **+s** mason

mata ['maˑta] *g* **matys** mate, pal, comrade, companion

mater ['maˑter] *g* **+yow** matter, subject; **mater tykkli** delicate matter

maw ['maw] *g* boy, lad, youth

may[5] [maɪ] *m* so that

maylya ['maɪlja] *v* wrap, bind, swathe, envelop

maylyer ['maɪljer] *g* **+s** envelope

mayn ['maɪn] *hg* mean, average: *g* **+ys** means, agency

mayni ['maɪni] *g* **+ow** household, crew, staff

maynorieth [maɪnɔrˈiˑeθ] *b* mediation

maystri ['maɪstri] *g* mastery, domination, control

mayth [maɪθ] *m* so that

mebel ['meˑbel] *g* furniture

medh ['meːð] *g* mead (drink), hydromel

medhador [meˑðaˑdɔr] *g* **+yon** mediator

medhegieth [meðeˈgiˑeθ] *b* medicine as science

medhegneth [meˈðegneθ] *b* **+ow** medicine as remedy

medhegva [meˈðegva] *b* **+ow** clinic, surgery, medical centre

medhek ['meˑðek] *g* **medhogyon** doctor, physician

medhel ['meˑðel] *hg* soft, delicate

medhelweyth [ˌmeðelˈweɪθ] *g* software

medhes ['meˑðes] *v*; **yn-medh ev** he says/said

medhow ['meˑðɔw] *hg* drunk, intoxicated

medras ['medras] *g* **+ow** aim, aspiration

meghin ['meˑxin] *g* **+yow** bacon

megi ['meˑgi] *v* smoke, smother, stifle; **megi a dhifenner** no smoking

megyans ['meˑgjans] *g* **+ow** culture, diet

mel ['me:l] *g* **+yow** honey

melhwenn ['melhwen] *b* **+ow** slug

melhwes ['melhwes] *hk* **+enn** snails

melhwyoges [ˌmelhwɪˈɔˑges] *b* **+ow** tortoise

melin ['meˑlɪn] *b* **+yow** mill

mell ['mel:] *g* **+ow** joint

mellyon ['mel:jɔn] *hk* **+enn** clover, violets

melon ['meˑlɔn] *g* **+yow** melon

melyn ['meˑlɪn] *hg* yellow, blond

melyseth [meˈlɪˑzeθ] *b* **+ow** perfume

melyssand [meˈlɪsːand] *g* **+ys** dessert

men ['me:n] *g* **meyn** stone

meneghi [meˈneˑxi] *g* **+ow** sanctuary, refuge, place of asylum

menegva [meˈnegva] *b* **+ow** index of a book

mengleudh ['menglœð] *g* **+yow** quarry, stone-pit

menhir [menˈhiˑr] *g* **+yon** long-stone, standing stone

menowgh ['meˑnɔʊx] *hg* frequent: *av* often, frequently

menoyl ['meˑnɔɪl] *g* **+ys** petrol

men-pobas [ˌmeˑnˈpɔˑbas] *g* **meyn-pobas** bakestone, griddle

menta ['menta] *b* mint (plant)

mentena [menˈteˑna] *v* maintain, uphold

menydh ['meˑnɪð] *g* **+yow** mountain, hill

menyster ['meˑnɪster] *g* **-trys** minister

menystrans [meˈnɪˑstrans] *g* **+ow** administration, ministry

mer ['meˑr] *g* **+yon** mayor

Mergher ['merxer] *g* Mercury; **dy' Mergher** Wednesday, on Wednesday

merk ['merk] *g* **+yow** mark, brand

merkya ['merkja] *v* mark, perceive

mernans ['mernans] *g* **+ow** death

merther ['merθer] *g* **+yon** martyr

mertherynsi [ˌmerθeˈrınzi] *b* martyrdom

merwel ['merwel] *v* die, perish, expire

¹mes ['meːz] *g* **+yow** open field, open country: *av* out

²mes ['meːz] *hk* **+enn** acorns

³mes ['mes] *m* but

meskel ['meˈskel] *hk* **mesklenn** mussels

mesporth ['mespɔrθ] *g* **+ow** exit

messejer ['mesːedʒer] *g* **+s** messenger

mester ['meˈster] *g* **mestrysi** master

mestres ['meˈstres] *b* **+ow** mistress

mestrev ['meˈstrev] *b* **+ow** suburb

meter ['meˈter] *g* **metrow** metre (unit)

¹meth ['meːθ] *b* **+ow** shame; **meth a'm beus** I am ashamed

²meth ['meːθ] *g* nurture, nourishing

methek ['meˈθek] *hg* ashamed

methus ['meˈθys] *hg* shameful

metya ['meˈtja] *v* meet, encounter

meur ['mœːr] *hg* great, large, much; **meur a jiow** a lot of houses, many houses; **meur ras** thank you

meurgerys [mœrˈgeˈrıs] *hg* beloved, popular

Meurth ['mœrθ] *g* Mars; **dy' Meurth** Tuesday, on Tuesday

meus ['mœːz] *g* **+i** thumb

meusva ['mœzva] *b* **meusvedhi** inch

mewgh ['meʊx] *g* **+yow** bail, guarantee, warranty

mewghya ['meʊxja] *v* guarantee

meythrinva [meıˈθrinva] *b* **+ow** nursery, creche

¹mil² ['miːl] *g* **+yow** thousand

²mil ['miːl] *g* **+es** animal, wild beast

mildir [mılˈdiːr] *g* **+yow** mile

milva ['milva] *b* **milvaow** zoo

milvedhek [mɪl'veˑðek] *g* **-ogyon** vet

milvil² ['milvɪl] *g* **+yow** million

minhwarth ['minhwarθ] *g* **+ow** smile

minhwerthin [mɪn'hwerθin] *v* smile

minvlew ['minvlew] *hk* **+enn** whiskers, moustache

minyek ['miˑnjek] *hg* pointed

miowal [mɪ'ɔʊal] *v* mew

mirer ['miˑrer] *g* **-oryon** spectator, observer, onlooker

mires ['miˑres] *v* look, behold, observe; **mires orth** look at

mis ['miːz] *g* **misyow** month

mis-Du [ˌmiˑs'tyː] *g* **misyow-Du** November

mis-Ebrel [ˌmiˑz'ebrel] *g* **misyow-E.** April

mis-Est [ˌmiˑz'eːst] *g* **misyow-Est** August

mis-Genver [ˌmiˑs'kenver] *g* **misyow-G.** January

mis-Gortheren [ˌmiˑskɔr'θeˑren] *g* **misyow-G.** July

mis-Gwynngala [ˌmiˑskwɪn'gaˑla] *g* **misyow-G.** September

mis-Hedra [ˌmiˑs'hedra] *g* **misyow-H.** October

mis-Hwevrer [ˌmiˑs'hwevrer] *g* **misyow-H.** February

mis-Kevardhu [ˌmiˑskevar'ðyː] *g* **misyow-K.** December

miskweyth ['miˑskwɪθ] *g* **+ow** period of a month

mis-Me [ˌmiˑs'meː] *g* **misyow-Me** May

mis-Metheven [ˌmiˑsme'θeˑren] *g* **misyow-M.** June

mis-Meurth [ˌmiˑs'mœrθ] *g* **misyow-Meurth** March

misyek ['miˑsjek] *hg* monthly

mo ['mɔː] *g* **+yow** hour before dawn, dusk, twilight

modrep ['mɔdrep] *b* **modrebedh** aunt

moel ['mɔːl] *hg* bald, bare

¹moen ['mɔːn] *hg* slender, thin, slim

²moen ['mɔːn] *g* **+ow** ore, mineral

113

moes ['moːz] *b* **+ow** table

moesenn ['moˑzen] *b* **+ow** statistical table

moesik ['moˑzɪk] *b* **-igow** tablet

mog ['moːg] *g* smoke, fume, reek

moga ['moˑga] *v* choke

moggha ['moxːa] *hg* most

mogh ['moːx] *lp* pigs, swine

moghweder [mox'weˑder] *g* **-wedrow** magnifying-glass

molgh ['molx] *b* **+i** thrush

molgh-dhu [molˌfiˑðyː] *b* **molghi-du** blackbird

mona ['moˑna] *k* cash, money, change; **mona munys** small change

mor ['moːr] *g* **+yow** sea; **war vor** at sea; **mor a bobel** a sea of people

mordhos ['morðos] *b* **-ow, diwvordhos** *hd* thigh; **mordhos hogh** ham

mordid [ˌmor'diːd] *g* **+ys** tide

mordrik ['mordrɪk] *g* **-igow** low tide

morhogh ['morhox] *g* **+es** porpoise

morlann ['morlan] *b* **+ow** shore, strand

morlanow [mor'laˑnow] *g* **+yow** high tide

morlenwel [mor'lenwel] *v* rise of tide

morlu ['morly] *g* **+yow** navy

morrep ['morˑep] *g* **-ebow** sea-shore, seaside

morthol ['morθol] *g* **+ow** hammer

mortholya [mor'θoˑlja] *v* hammer

morvil ['morvɪl] *g* **+es** whale

morvleydh ['morvleɪð] *g* **+i** shark

morvran ['morvran] *b* **-vrini** cormorant

moryon ['morjon] *hk* **+enn** ants

mos ['moːz] *v* go; **mos yn-mes** go out; **mos dheves** go away; **mos tre** go home; **mos war benn-**

dewlin kneel (on both knees)

mosek ['mɔ·zek] *hg* pungent

mostedhes [mɔs'te·ðes] *g* filth, dirt, defilement

mostenn ['mɔ·sten] *b* **+ow** stain

mostya ['mɔ·stja] *v* soil, dirty, contaminate

moutya ['mu·tja] *v* sulk, mope

movya ['mɔ·vja] *v* move spiritually

movyans ['mɔ·vjans] *g* **+ow** emotional movement, motivation

mowes ['mɔʋes] *b* **mowesi** girl

moy ['mɔɪ] *hg* more; **moy ha moy** more and more; **moy po le** mor or less

moyha ['mɔɪha] *hg* most, maximum

Mr ['me·ster] *g* Mr (= Mister)

Mres ['me·stres] *b* Mrs

munys ['my·nɪs] *hg* tiny, small; **glaw munys** light rain; **sugra munys** fine sugar

mus ['my:z] *hg* mad

musur ['my·zyr] *g* **+yow** measure

musura [my·zy·ra] *v* measure, moderate

musurans [my·zy·rans] *g* **+ow** measurement

my ['mi:] *rh* I, me

myghtern [mɪfi'tern] *g* **+edh** king, sovereign, monarch

myghternes [mɪfi'ternes] *b* **+ow** queen

mygyl ['mɪ·gɪl] *hg* lukewarm, tepid

mynnas ['mɪn:as] *g* **+ow** wish, purpose, intention

mynnes ['mɪn:es] *v* wish, want, intend

myns ['mɪns] *g* **+ow** size, amount, dimension, quantity

mynysenn [mɪ'nɪ·zen] *b* **+ow** minute of time

myrgh ['mɪrx] *b* **myrghes** daughter, girl, young woman

myrgh-wynn [ˌmɪrx'wɪn:] *b* **myrghes-gwynn** granddaughter

myrtwydh ['mɪrtwɪð] *b* **+enn** myrtle-trees

mysi ['mɪ·zi] *v* reap

mysk ['mɪ:sk] *g* middle; **yn mysk** among

mysterlu [ˌmɪ·ster'ly:] *g* **+yow** trade union

myttin ['mɪt:in] *g* **+yow** morning; **myttin da!** good morning!

myttinweyth [mɪ'tinweɪθ], forenoon, duration of the morning

N

'n *rh* him, it

¹na [na] *av*; **an chi na** that house; **an chi bras na** that big house

²na² [na] *m*; **na res!** do not run!; **an huni na gows** the one who does not speak

³na [na] *m* nor; **na ... na** neither ... nor

Nadelik [na·de·'lɪk] *g* **-igow** Christmas; **Nadelik Lowen!** Merry Christmas!

nader ['na·der] *b* **nadres** viper, adder

nag [nag] *m* nor

nagh ['na:x] *g* **+ow** denial, refusal

nagha ['na·xa] *v* deny, refuse, renounce, decline

nahen [na'he:n], any other

nameur [na'mœ:r] *av* not much

namm ['nam:] *g* **+ow** defect, flaw, blot, spot, blemish

namma ['nam·a] *v* stain

nammna² ['namna] *av* almost, nearly; **nammna goedhis** I nearly fell

nammnag [ˈnamnag] *av* almost, nearly

nammnygen [namnɪˈgeːn] *av* just now

namoy [naˈmɔɪ] *hg* any more

naneyl [naˈneɪl] *m* neither

nans [ˈnans] *g* **+ow** valley, dale

nans [ˈnanz] *pv*; **nans yw** ago; **nans yw pell** long ago

naswydh [ˈnaˑzwɪð] *b* **+yow** needle, hand of clock; **gweyth nasweyth** needlework

nath [ˈnaːθ] *g* **+es** puffin

natur [ˈnaˑtyr] *b* **+yow** nature, character

naturel [naˈtyˑrel] *hg* natural

naw [ˈnaw] *niv* nine

neb [ˈneːb] *rh* some; **yn neb toll fiyn dhe'n fo** let us flee into some hole: *av* any: *m* who

nebes [ˈneˑbes] *g* few, some; **my a garsa eva nebes leth** I would like to drink some milk: *hg* few: *av* somewhat

nebonan [nebˈɔˑnan] *rh* someone, anyone, somebody, anybody

nedha [ˈneˑða] *v* twist (of yarn)

nedhans [ˈneˑðans] *g* **+ow** twist (of yarn)

nedhys [ˈneˑðɪs] *hg* twisted

negedhek [neˈgeˑðek] *hg* negative

negys [ˈneˑgɪs] *g* **+yow** business, transaction, affair, errand

nen [ˈneːn] *g* **+yow** ceiling

nep-pell [nepˈpel] *av* at some distance

nep-prys [nepˈpriːz] *av* sometime

neppyth [ˈneˑpɪθ] *g* something, anything

neptra [ˈneptra] *rh* anything

nep-tu [nepˈtyː] *av* somewhere, anywhere

Neptun [ˈneptyn] *le* Neptune

nerth ['nerθ] *g* **+ow** power, might, strength, energy

nerthek ['nerθek] *hg* powerful, mighty, potent, robust

nervenn ['nerven] *b* **+ow, nerv** *hk* nerve

nervus ['nervys] *hg* nervous

nes ['neːz] *hg* near

neshe [nes'heː] *v* approach

neskar ['ne·skar] *g* **neskerens** near relative

nessa ['nes·a] *hg* next: second; **dy' Lun nessa** next Monday

neus ['nœːz] *k* **+enn** thread

neusenn ['nœ·zen] *b* **+ow, neus** *hk* individual thread

neuvwisk ['nœvwisk] *g* swimwear

neuvya ['nœ·vja] *v* swim

nev ['neːv] *g* **+ow** heaven

nevra ['nevra] *av* never (in neg. phrases); **nevra namoy** nevermore

new ['new] *b* **+yow** trough, sink, wash-basin

neyth ['neιθ] *g* **+ow** nest

ni ['niː] *rh* we, us

Nihon ['ni·hɔn] *le* Japan

nihonek [nι'hɔ·nek] *hg* Japanese

Nihonek [nι'hɔ·nek] *g* Japanese language

nij ['niːdʒ] *g* **+ow** flight (in air)

nija ['ni·dʒa] *v* fly

nivel ['ni·vel] *g* **+yow** level, standard

niver ['ni·ver] *g* **+ow** number

nivera [nι'veˑra] *v* count, reckon, number

niverenn [nι'veˑren] *b* **+ow** numeral, number (e.g. of house)

niveronieth [nιverɔ'ni·eθ] *b* **+ow** arithmetic

niverus [nι'veˑrys] *hg* numerous

niveryans [nι'veˑrjans] *g* **+ow** counting, census,

118

enumeration

niwl ['niʊl] *g* **+ow** mist, fog

niwlek ['niʊlek] *hg* misty, foggy

niwllaw ['niʊlːaw] *g* drizzle

nobyl ['nɔˑbɪl] *hg* noble

noeth ['noːθ] *hg* naked, nude

nor ['nɔːr] *g* world

Norgagh ['nɔrgax] *le* Norway

norgaghek [nɔrˈgaˑxek] *hg* Norwegian

Norgaghek [nɔrˈgaˑxek] *g* Norwegian language

north ['nɔrθ] *g* north

north-est [ˌnɔrθˈeːst] *g* north-east

north-west [ˌnɔrθˈweːst] *g* north-west

norvys [nɔrˈviːz] *g* world

¹nos ['nɔːz] *b* **+ow** night; **nos dha!** goodnight!

²nos ['nɔːs] *av* yonder; **an chi nos** yonder house

nosweyth ['nɔsweıθ] *av: b* **+yow** night-time, night (duration)

notenn ['nɔˑten] *b* **+ow** note

notya ['nɔˑtja] *v* note

nown ['nɔʊn] *g* hunger, starvation

nownek ['nɔʊnek] *hg* hungry

nownsek ['nɔʊnzek] *niv* nineteen

nowodhow [nɔˈwɔˑðɔw] *lp* news

nowydh ['nɔwıð] *hg* new

noy ['nɔı] *g* **+ens** nephew

ny² [nı] *pv* not

nyhewer [nıˈhewer] *av* last night

nyns [nınz] *pv* not (before vowels in **bos** and **mos**)

O

obaya [ɔ'baɪa] *v* obey, submit

ober ['ɔ'ber] *g* **+ow** work, act, deed

oberenn [ɔ'be·ren] *b* **+ow** job, task, exercise (e.g. in school), work, opus

oberi [ɔ'be·ri] *v* work, do, operate

oberwas [ɔ'berwas] *g* **-wesyon** workman

oberyans [ɔ'be·rjans] *g* **+ow** operation

obisow [ɔ'bi·zɔʊ] *lp* funeral

oela ['o·la] *v* weep, cry, lament

oeles ['o·les] *b* **+ow** hearth, fireplace

oen ['oːn] *g* **eyn** lamb

oer ['oːr] *hg* excessively cold, freezing, frigid

oes ['oːz] *g* **+ow** age, period of time

oesweyth ['oːzweɪθ] *b* **+yow** epoch, period of time, era

oferenn [ɔ'fe·ren] *b* **+ow** mass (church service), eucharist, religious service

offra ['ɔf:ra] *v* offer

ogas ['ɔ·gas] *hg* near, close, adjoining: *av* nearly, almost: *hg* **yn ogas** nearby

ogh *esk* oh

oghanas [ɔ'fia·nas] *g* **+ow** moan

ojyon ['ɔ·dʒjɔn] *g* **oghen** ox

Oksitanek [ɔksi'ta·nek] *g* Occitan language

Oksitani [ɔksi'ta·ni] *le* Occitania

ol ['ɔːl] *g* **+ow** track, print (e.g. of foot), trail

olifans [ɔ'li·fans] *g* **-es** elephant

oliv ['ɔ·liv]; **+yow** olive-tree

oll ['ɔl:] *hg* all, every

ollgalloesek [,ɔlga'lo·zek] *hg* almighty

ollgemmyn [ɔl'gem:ɪn] *hg* general

Ollsyns ['ɔlsɪns] *lp* All Saints
ollvys ['ɔlvɪs] *g* **+ow** universe
ombellhe [əmbel'he:] *v* move away
omblegya [əm'ble·gja] *v* submit, bow
ombrederi [ˌɔmbre'de·ri] *v* reflect, ponder
ombrofyer [əm'brɔ·fjer] *g* **-oryon** candidate
omdenna [əm'den:a] *v* retire
omdennans [əm'den:ans] *g* **+ow** retirement
omdennys [əm'den:ɪs] *hg* retired from work
omdewlel [əm'deʋlel] *v* wrestle
omdhiserri [ˌɔmðɪ'ser:i] *v* calm down
omdhiskwedhes [ˌɔmðɪs'kwe·ðes] *v* appear
omdhisoedha [ˌɔmðɪ'so·ða] *v* resign
omdhisoedhans [ˌɔmðɪ'so·ðans] *g* **+ow** resignation
omdhivarva [ˌɔmðɪ'varva] *v* shave oneself
omdhivas [əm'ði·vas] *g* **+ow** orphan (male)
omdhivases [ˌɔmðɪ'va·zes] *b* **+ow** orphan (female)
omdowl ['ɔmdɔʋl] *g* **+ow** wrestling
omdowler [əm'dɔʋler] *g* **-oryon** wrestler
omgemmeryans [ˌɔmge'me·rjans] *g* **+ow** responsibility
omgemmeryek [ˌɔmge'me·rjek] *hg* responsible
omglewans [əm'glewans] *g* **+ow** feeling, sensation
omguntell [əm'gyntel] *v* collect (intrans.), assemble (intrans.)
omladh ['ɔmlað] *g* **+ow** fight
omladhans [əm'la·ðans] *g* **+ow** suicide
omlesa [əm'le·za] *v* spread (intrans.)
omlowenhe [əmlɔʋen'he:] *v* rejoice, enjoy oneself
omma ['ɔm:a] *av* here
omserri [əm'ser:i] *v* become angry
omsettyans [əm'set:jans] *g* **+ow** attack, raid
omsettyer [əm'set:jer] *g* **-yoryon** assailant

omwellhe [əmwel'heː] *v* get better

omwolghi [əm'wɔlxi] *v* wash oneself

omwul [əm'wyːl] *v* pretend

onan [ɔ'nan] one; **onan arall** another one

onest ['ɔ'nest] *hg* proper, decent, honest

onester [ɔ'neˈster] *g* propriety, decency, decorum, honesty

onn ['ɔːn] *hk* **+enn** ash-trees

onyonenn [ɔn'jɔ·nen] *b* **+ow, onyon** *hk* onion

or ['ɔːr] *b* **+yon** border, edge, boundary

ordena [ɔr'de·na] *v* put in order, arrange, appoint, organize

ordenans ['ɔrdənans] *g* **+ow** ordinance, decree

organ ['ɔrgan] *g* **+s** organ (Mus.)

ors ['ɔrs] *g* **+es** bear

orth ['ɔrθ] *rg* at, by

ost ['ɔːst] *g* **+ys** innkeeper, landlord

ostel ['ɔ·stel] *b* **+yow** lodging, hostel, hotel

ostes ['ɔ·stes] *b* **+ow** hostess

ostralek [ɔs'tra·lek] *hg* Australian

Ostrali [ɔs'tra·li] *le* Australia

ostrek ['ɔ·strek] *hg* Austrian

Ostri ['ɔ·stri] *le* Austria

ostya ['ɔ·stja] *v* lodge, stay (at a hotel, etc.)

ott ['ɔt] *esk* see

ottomma [ɔt'ɔmːa] *esk* look here, here is, here are, this is

oula ['u·la] *g* **oulys** owl

oulya ['u·lja] *v* howl

our ['uːr] *g* **+ys** duration of an hour

¹ow³ [ɔw] *hg* my

²ow⁴ [ɔw] *rv* -ing (indicating present participle)

own ['ɔun] *g* fear, dread, fright; **na borth own** don't

122

be afraid

ownek [ˈɔʊnek] *hg* afraid, timid: *g* **ownogyon** coward

ownekhe [ɔʊnekˈheː] *v* frighten, intimidate

ownus [ˈɔʊnʏs] *hg* timorous

owr [ˈɔʊr] *g* gold

owraval [ɔʊˈraːval] *g* **+ow** orange (fruit)

owrek [ˈɔʊrek] *hg* golden

owrer [ˈɔʊrer] *g* **-oryon** goldsmith

owrlin [ˈɔʊrlɪn] *g* **+yow** silk

oy [ˈɔɪ] *g* **+ow** egg **ny dal oy** it's absolutely worthless; **ny rov oy** I don't care a bit

oyl [ˈɔɪl] *g* **oylys** oil

P

pab [ˈpaːb] *g* **+ow** pope

padell [ˈpaˈdel] *b* **+ow** pan

padell-dhorn [ˌpaˈdelˈðɔrn] *b* **padellow-dorn** saucepan

padellik [paˈdelːɪk] *b* **-igow** saucer

pal [ˈpaːl] *b* **+yow** spade, shovel

palas [ˈpaˈlas] *v* dig, excavate

pali [ˈpaˈli] *g* velvet, brocade; **pali fals** plush

pallenn [ˈpalːen] *b* **+ow** blanket, covering

palores [paˈlɔˈres] *b* **+ow** chough

pals [ˈpals] *hg* plentiful, numerous, copious

palsya [ˈpalzja] *v* paralyse

palv [ˈpalv] *b* **+ow** palm of hand

palva [ˈpalva] *v* caress, stroke

palys [ˈpaˈlɪs] *g* **palesyow** palace

123

¹pan² [pan] *m* when

²pan [pan] *hg* what

pana² [pana] *hg* what

panda ['panda] *g* **+s** panda

pandra ['pandra] *rh* what

pann ['pan:] *g* **+ow** cloth, woven fabric

pannell ['pan:el] *g* **+ow** panel (of people)

paper ['pa·per] *g* **+yow** paper

paper-nowodhow [ˌpa·pernɔ'wɔ·ðɔw] *g*
  paperyow-n. newspaper

papynjay [ˌpapɪn'dʒaɪ] *g* **+s** parrot

¹par ['pa:r] *g* **+ow** equal, sort, kind; **tus a'n par na**
  such people

²par [par] *av* as, just as

para ['pa·ra] *g* **parys** team, gang, squad, flock

paradhis [pa·ra·ðɪs] *b* paradise

pareusi [pa·rœ·zi] *v* prepare, make ready

Paris ['pa·rɪs] *le* Paris

park ['park] *g* **+ow** field, park

park-kerri [ˌpark'ker:i] *g* **parkow-k.** car-park

parkya ['parkja] *v* park

paros ['pa·rɔs] *g* **+yow** party wall

parow ['pa·rɔw] *hg* even (of numbers)

parsell ['parsel] *g* **+s** band of people, cast of a play

parth ['parθ] *b* **+ow** behalf, act of a play, zone

parti ['parti] *g* **+ow** political party, side in a conflict

parys ['pa·rɪs] *hg* ready, prepared

¹pas ['pa:z] *g* **+ow** cough

²pas ['pa:s] *g* **+ys** pace, step

pasa ['pa·sa] *v* cough

Pask ['pa:sk] *g* **+ow** Easter

past ['pa:st] *g* **+ow** paste

pasta ['pa·sta] *g* pasta

124

past-dyns [past'dɪns] *g* **pastow-dyns** tooth-paste

pasti ['pasti] *g* **+ow** pasty

patatys [pa'taːtɪs] *hk* **+enn** potatoes

patron ['patrɔn] *g* **+yow** pattern, example, model

paw ['paw] *b* **+yow, diwbaw** *hd* paw, claw of crab, fluke of anchor, hand (pejoratively)

pawgenn ['pawɡen] *g* **+ow** moccasin, slipper

payn ['paɪn] *g* **+ys** pain, torment, torture

paynt ['paɪnt] *g* **+ow** paint

payntya ['paɪntja] *v* paint (a surface)

paynya ['paɪnja] *v* torture, inflict pain

pe ['peː] *v* pay, pay for, settle accounts with

peber ['peːber] *g* **-oryon** baker (male)

pebores [pe'bɔːres] *b* **+ow** baker (female)

Peder ['peːder] *hp* Peter

peder ['peːder] *niv* four (f.)

pedrek ['pedrek] *hg* square: *g* **-ogow** square

pedrenn ['pedren] *b* **+ow, diwbedrenn** *hd* buttock, hind-quarter

pedrevan [pe'dreːvan] *b* **-es** lizard

pedrevanas [ˌpedre'vaːnas] *v* creep on all fours

pedri ['pedri] *v* rot, decay, fester, corrupt

pegh ['peːx] *g* **+ow** sin

pegha ['peːxa] *v* sin

pel ['peːl] *b* **+yow** ball, sphere

peldroes ['peldrʏs] *b* football

pell ['peːl] *hg* far, distant, remote

pellder ['pelder] *g* **+yow** distance

pellenn ['pelen] *b* **+ow** ball, dumpling, lump, bullet

pellennik [pe'lenɪk] *b* **-igow** pill, sleeping pill

pellgewsel [pel'ɡewzel] *v* telephone

pellgowser [pel'ɡɔwzer] *g* **+yow** telephone

pellhe [pel'heː] *v* send far away, expel, banish

pellskrifenn [pel'skri·fen] *b* **+ow** fax (message)

pellvotonek [pelvɔ'tɔ·nek] *b* **-egi** remote control

pellwolok [pel'wɔ·lɔk] *b* **pellwologow** television

Penkost ['penkɔst] *g* **+ow** Whitsuntide, Pentecost

penn ['pen:] *g* **+ow** head, end, summit

penn-bloedh [pen'blo:ð] *g* **pennow-bloedh** birthday, anniversary; **penn-bloedh lowen!** happy birthday!

penn-droppya [ˌpen'drɔp:ja] *v* nod

penneglos [pen'eglɔs] *b* **+yow** cathedral

pennfenten [pen'fenten] *b* **-tynyow** head-spring, source of stream

penn-gwynn [ˌpen'gwin:] *g* **pennow-gwynn** penguin

pennhembrenkyas [ˌpenhem'brenkjas] *g* **pennhembrynkysi** general of army

penn-medhow [ˌpen'meðɔw] *g* **pennow-medhow** drunkard

pennobereth [penɔ'be·reθ] *b* **+ow** masterpiece

pennrewler [pen'reʊler] *g* **-oryon** director

penn-rudh [ˌpen'ry:ð] *hg* red-haired

Pennsans [ˌpen'sans] *le* Penzance

pennserneth [pen'serneθ] *b* architecture (art of)

pennseviges [penze'vi·ges] *b* **+ow** princess

pennsevik [pen'ze·vɪk] *g* **-igyon**; **-igyow** prince

pennseythun [pen'seɪθyn] *b* **+yow** weekend

pennsita [pen'si·ta] *b* **-sitys** capital city

pennskol ['penskɔl] *b* **+yow** university, institution of higher education

Penntorr [ˌpen'tɔr:] *le* Torpoint

pennwari [pen'wa·ri] *g* **+ow** final (game)

pennwisk ['penwisk] *g* **+ow** head-dress, headgear

¹per ['pe:r] *g* **+yow** crock, large jar

²per ['pe:r] *hk* **+enn** pears

perfydh ['perfɪð] *hg* perfect, entire

perghenn ['perxen] *g* **+ow** owner, proprietor

perghennek [per'fienːek] *g* **-ogyon** owner

perl ['perl] *g* **+ys** pearl

persil ['persɪl] *hk* **+enn** parsley

person ['persɔn] *g* **+s** person

personel [per'sɔːnel] *hg* personal

perthi ['perθi] *v* endure, tolerate; **perthi kov a**
remember; **perthi own** be afraid

perthyans ['perθjans] *g* **+ow** endurance, patience,
toleration, experience

pervedh ['perveð] *g* **+ow** interior, inside

pervedhel [per've·ðel] *hg* interior

peryll ['pe·rɪl] *g* **+ow** danger, peril, risk, hazard

peryllus [pe'rɪl:ys] *hg* dangerous, risky

¹pes ['pe:z] ; **pes da** in a good mood; **drog pes** in
a bad mood

²pes ['pe:z] *av* how many

peswar ['pezwar] *niv* four (m.)

peswardhek [pez'warðek] *niv* fourteen

peswarlamm [pez'warlam] *g* **+ow** gallop

peswarlemmel [,pezwar'lemːel] *v* gallop

peswar-ugens [,pezwar'y·gens] *niv* eighty

peswora [pez'wɔ·ra] *niv* fourth

pesya ['pe·zja] *v* last, continue

pesyans ['pe·zjans] *g* **+ow** continuation

peub ['pœ:b] *rh* all

peul ['pœ:l] *g* **+yow** pole

peulge ['pœlge] *g* **+ow** railing

peulweyth ['pœlweɪθ] *g* scaffolding

peuns ['pœns] *g* **+ow** pound (money or weight)

p'eur⁵ ['pœ:r] *av* when

peuri ['pœ·ri] *v* graze, feed

piano [pɪ'a·nɔ] *g* **+s** piano

pib ['pi:b] *b* **+ow** pipe; **an Bib** the Underground;
   pibow sagh bagpipes

pibell ['pi·bel] *b* **+ow** pipe

pibenn ['pi·ben] *b* **+ow** tube

pies ['pi·es] *hk* **+enn** magpies

piknik ['piknik] *g* **+ow** picnic

pilenn ['pi·len]; **+ow, pil** *hk* fringe

pin ['pi:n] *hk* **+enn** pine-trees

pinaval [pin'a·val] *g* **+ow** pineapple

pisas ['pi·zas] *g* urine

pith ['pi:θ] *hg* greedy, avaricious, stingy, mean

piw ['piw] *rh* who

piwas ['piʊas] *g* **+ow** reward, prize

piwpynag [piʊpɪ'na:g] *rh* whoever

planet ['pla·net] *g* **+ow** planet

plank ['plank] *g* **plenkys** plank, board

plansa ['planza] *v* plant

plas ['pla:s] *g* **plasow** country seat

plasenn ['pla·zen] *b* **+ow** record (sound-recording)

plastek ['pla·stek] *hg* plastic: *g* **-ogow** plastic

plaster ['pla·ster] *g* **+yow** plaster

plastra ['plastra] *v* plaster

plat ['pla:t] *g* **+yow**; **+ys** plate

platt ['plat] *hg* flat

plattya ['plat:ja] *v* cower

ple⁵ ['ple:] *av* where

pleg ['ple:g] *g* **+ow** fold, bend

plegya ['ple·gja] *v* fold; **mar pleg** please

plen ['ple:n] *hg* plain: *g* **+ys** plain; **plen an gwari**
   open-air theatre

plesour ['ple·sur] *g* **+s** pleasure

plesya ['ple·zja] *v* please

plisk ['pli:sk] *hk* **+enn** husks

plit ['pli:t] *g* **+ys** plight, predicament, condition

plommer ['plɔmːer] *g* **-oryon** plumber

plos ['plɔːz] *hg* dirty, filthy, foul; **plos y daves** foul-mouthed

plosegi [plɔ'zeːgi] *v* get dirty

ploumenn ['pluːmen] *b* **+ow** plum

Pluto ['plyːtɔ] *le* Pluto

pluv ['plyːv] *hk* **+enn** plumage, feathers

pluvek ['plyːvek] *b* **pluvogow** cushion, pillow

pluvenn ['plyːven] *b* **+ow, pluv** *hk* pen, feather, quill; **pluvenn blomm** pencil

pluw ['plyw] *b* **+ow** parish

po [pɔ] *m* or

pobas ['pɔ·bas] *v* bake

pobel ['pɔ·bel] *b* **poblow** people, folk

poblans ['pɔblans] *g* **+ow** population

poblek ['pɔblek] *hg* public; **an poblek** the public

poblogethek [pɔblɔ'geːθek] *hg* republican: *g* **-ogyon** republican

poder ['pɔ·der] *g* rot

podik ['pɔ·dɪk] *g* **-igow** jug

podredhek [pɔ'dreːðek] *hg* corrupt, festering

podrek ['pɔdrek] *hg* corrupt, rotten: *g* **podrogyon** depraved person

poell ['pɤlːː] *g* **+ow** intelligence, reason

poellek ['pɤlːek] *hg* intelligent

poenvos ['pɤnvɔs] *g* **+ow** trouble, misery

poenya ['pɔ·nja] *v* run

poes ['pɔːz] *hg* heavy, sultry: *g* **+ow** weight, pressure

poesa ['pɔ·sa] *v* lean, weigh

poesedhek [pɤ'zeːðek] *hg* positive

129

poesek ['po·sek] *hg* important, weighty

poeslev ['po·slev] *g* **+ow** accent, stress, emphasis

poeth ['po:θ] *hg* scorching, hot

poken [pɔ'ke:n] *m* or else, otherwise

poket ['pɔ·ket] *g* **+ow** pocket

pokya ['pɔ·kja] *v* poke, thrust

polisi ['pɔlisi] *g* **+s** policy

politeger [,pɔlɪ'te·ger] *g* **-oryon** politician

politegieth [pɔl,ɪte'gi·eθ] *b* politics

politek [pɔ'li·tek] *hg* political

poll ['pɔl:] *g* **+ow** pool, pond; **poll neuvya** swimming pool

polonek [pɔ'lɔ·nek] *hg* Polish

Polonek [pɔ'lɔ·nek] *g* Polish language

Poloni [pɔ'lɔ·ni] *le* Poland

pols ['pɔls] *g* **+yow** moment, instant, short time, short distance

polter ['pɔlter] *g* **+yow** powder, dust

pompell ['pɔmpel] *b* **+ow** pump

pompya ['pɔmpja] *v* pump

pompyon ['pɔmpjɔn] *g* **+s** pumpkin, gourd

pons ['pɔns] *g* **+yow** bridge

popett ['pɔ·pet] *g* **+ow** puppet

popti ['pɔpti] *g* **+ow** bakery, baker's shop

por ['pɔ:r] *hk* **+enn** leeks

poran [pɔ'a:n] *av* quite, exactly, rightly

porres [pɔr're:z] *av* absolutely

¹**porth** ['pɔrθ] *g* **+ow** gateway, entrance, porch

²**porth** ['pɔrθ] *g* **+ow** cove, harbour, port

Porthia [pɔr'θi·a] *le* St Ives

portmantell [pɔrt'mantel] *g* **+ow** portmanteau

Portyngal ['pɔrtɪngal] *le* Portugal

portyngalek [,pɔrtɪn'ga·lek] *hg* Portuguese

Portyngalek [ˌpɔrtɪnˈɡaˑlek] *g* Portuguese language

¹post [ˈpɔːst] *g* **+ow** post, pole, pillar

²post [ˈpɔːst] *g* post, mail

pott [ˈpɔt] *g* **+ow** pot

pow [ˈpɔw] *g* **+yow** country, province, countryside;
Pow Sows England; **Pow Frynk** France; **Pow
Belg** Belgium; **Pow Grek** Greece

powes [ˈpɔʊes] *g* **+ow** rest, truce, interval, pause: *v*
pause, take a rest

pows [ˈpɔʊz] *b* **+yow** frock, dress; **pows nos** night-
dress

prag [ˈpraːɡ] *av* why, wherefore, what for, how come

praktisya [prakˈtiˑsja] *v* practise

pras [ˈpraːz] *g* **+ow** meadow, common pasture

pratt [ˈprat] *g* **+ys** trick, prank; **gul pratt** play a trick

Predennek [preˈdenˑek] *hg* British

preder [ˈpreˑder] *g* **+ow** thought, worry, anxiety

prederi [preˈdeˑri] *v* consider, think, ponder, worry

prederus [preˈdeˑrys] *hg* careful

prena [ˈpreˑna] *v* buy, purchase, pay for; **ty a'n pren**
you'll pay for it, you'll call it

prenas [ˈpreˑnas] *g* **+ow** purchase, shopping

prenn [ˈprenː] *g* **+yer** timber, wood, sawn log

prenna [ˈprenːa] *v* bar, bolt, lock

prest [ˈpreːst] *av* continually, always, constantly

previ [ˈpreˑvi] *v* prove, test, taste, try

pri [ˈpriː] *g* **+ow** clay; **pri gwynn** china-clay

pria [ˈpriˑa] *v* daub

pries [ˈpriˑes] *g* **priosow** spouse

prileghenn [prileˑxen] *b* **+ow** tile

pris [ˈpriːs] *g* **+yow** price, value, reputation

prison [ˈpriˑzon] *g* **+yow** prison, jail

privedh [ˈpriˑveð] *hg* private

privedhyow [pri'veˑðjɔw] *lp* toilet, lavatory

priweyth ['priˑweɪθ] *g* pottery (craft)

priweythor ['priweɪθɔr] *g* **+yon** potter

priweythva [pri'weɪtva] *b* **+ow** clay-works, pottery (factory)

profya ['proˑfja] *v* proffer, suggest, propose, offer

profyans ['proˑfjans] *g* **+ow** offer

pronter ['prɔnter] *g* **+yon** priest, parson, clergyman, vicar

Protestant ['prɔtestant] *g* **-ans** Protestant: *hg* Protestant

prov ['prɔːv] *g* **+ow** proof, test, trial

prow ['prɔw] *g* gain, profit, benefit, advantage

prydydh ['prɪˑdɪð] *g* **+yon** poet

prynt ['prɪnt] *g* **+ow** print

pryntya ['prɪntja] *v* print

prys ['priːz] *g* **prysyow** time, meal-time; **prys gwari** playtime; **yn gwella prys** fortunately; **yn gwettha prys** unfortunately

prysweyth ['prɪˑzweɪθ] *b* **+yow** moment, occasion, epoch, instant of time

pryv ['prɪːv] *g* **+es**; **+yon** worm, creeping creature

pub [pyb] *hg* each, every

pub-dydhyek [pəb'dɪðjek] *hg* daily

puber ['pyˑber] *g* **+yow** pepper

pubonan [pyb'ɔˑnan] *rh* everyone, everybody

pup-prys [pəp'priːz] *av* always

pup-tra [pəp'traː] *g* everything

pur² ['pyːr] *hg* pure, absolute: *av* very; **pur dha** very good

pursywya [pyr'sɪʊja] *v* pursue

pusketti [pys'ketːi] *g* **+ow** aquarium

pusorn ['pyˑsɔrn] *g* **+ow** bundle, bale, burden

puth [ˈpyːθ] *g* **+ow** well

py [pɪ] *rh* which, what; **py par** what kind of

pyffyer [ˈpɪfːjer] *g* **-s** dolphin

pyg [ˈpɪːg] *g* **+ow** pitch, tar

pygans [pɪˈgans] *g* wherewithal, requisites, necessities, means

pygemmys [pɪˈgemːɪs] *av* how much

pymp [ˈpɪmp] *niv* five

pympes [ˈpɪmpes] *niv* fifth

pymthek [ˈpɪmθek] *niv* fifteen

pynchya [ˈpɪntʃja] *v* pinch

pyneyl [pɪˈneɪl] *rh* which (of two)

pynn [ˈpɪnː] *g* **+ow** pin, dowel, peg

pynsel [ˈpɪnsel] *g* **+s** artist's paint-brush

pys [ˈpɪːz] *hk* **+enn** peas

pysadow [pɪˈzaˈdɔw] *g* prayer, supplication, entreaty

pysi [ˈpɪˈzi] *v* pray, entreat, beg **my a'th pys** I pray thee

pysk [ˈpɪːsk] *g* **puskes** fish; **pysk hag askloes** fish and chips

pyskador [pɪsˈkaˈdɔr] *g* **+yon** fisherman

pyskess [pɪsˈkesːa] *v* fish

pystiga [pɪsˈtiˈga] *v* harm, hurt, injure

pystik [ˈpɪˈstɪk] *g* **pystigow** harm, hurt, injury

pystri [ˈpɪˈstri] *g* magic

pystrier [pɪsˈtriˈer] *g* **-oryon** sorcerer, magician, wizard

pyth [ˈpɪːθ] *rh* what

pyth [ˈpɪːθ] *g* **+ow** thing, property; **pythow** riches

pytt [ˈpɪt] *g* **+ow** pit

R

rach ['raːtʃ] *g* caution, care, attention
radyo ['raˑdjɔ] *g* **+yow** radio
rag [rag] *rg* for, in order to: *m* for
ragarghas [rag'arxas] *g* **+ow** reservation
ragdres ['ragdres] *g* **+ow** project
ragerghys [rag'erxɪs] *hg* reserved, booked
raglev ['raglev] *g* **+ow** vote
ragleva [rag'leˑva] *v* vote
ragsettyans [rak'setːjans] *g* **+ow** prescription
ragskeus ['rakskœs] *g* **+ow** pretext
rakan ['raˑkan] *g* **+ow** garden rake
rakhemma [rak'hemːa] *m* wherefore
rakhenna [rak'henːa] *m* therefore
rann ['ran] *b* **+ow** part, share, portion, division
ranna ['ranːa] *v* share, divide, distribute, part
ranndir ['ran,diˑr] *g* **+yow** region, district
rannji ['ran,dʒiˑ] *g* **+ow** flat, apartment
rannles ['ranles] *g* **+ow** commission (money)
rannriv ['ran,riˑv] *g* **+ow** fraction (maths.)
rannvro ['ran,vrɔˑ] *b* **+yow** province
rastell ['raˑstel] *b* **restell** hayrake, grill, rack, grid
rastella [ras'telːa] *v* grill
rath ['raːθ] *g* **+es** rat
ratha ['raˑθa] *v* scrape, rasp
rathell ['raˑθel] *b* **+ow** rasp
ravna ['ravna] *v* ravage, violate, rape
ravnans ['ravnans] *g* rape
¹re ['reː] *rh* some, persons, things, some people, one;
an re goth the old people
²re² *av* too; **re vras** too big
³re² *rg* by (in oaths); **re Varia!** by Mary!

134

reden ['reˑden]; **+enn** bracken, ferns
redik ['reˑdɪk] *hk* **redigenn** radishes
redya ['reˑdja] *v* read
reken ['reˑken] *g* **reknow** bill, invoice
rekna ['rekna] *v* reckon, count, calculate
reknell ['reknel] *b* **+ow** calculator
rekord ['reˑkɔrd] *g* **+ys** record, witness, testimony
rekordya [re'kɔrdja] *v* record, witness
remm ['remː] *g* rheumatism
remova [re'mɔˑva] *v* displace
renk ['renk] *g* **+ow** rank
renka ['renka] *v* rank in order
renkas ['renkas] *g* **+ow** social class
renki ['renki] *v* snore, snort, gurgle, croak
rent ['rent] *g* **+ow** rent
reowta [re'ɔuta] *g* dignity, respect
repoblek [re'pɔblek] *b* **-ogow** republic
¹res ['reːz] *g* need, necessity; **res yw dhymm mos**
 I must go; **mars yw res** if necessary
²res ['reːz] *g* **+ow** race, course, flow
³res ['reːz] *b* **+yow** row (line of objects)
resayt [re'saɪt] *g* **+yow** recipe
resegydh [re'zeˑgɪð] *g* **+yon** runner
resek ['reˑsek] *v* run (of liquids and people), race
reser ['reˑzer] *g* **-oryon** runner, racer
resna ['rezna] *v* reason
reson ['reˑzɔn] *g* **+s** reason
restra ['restra] *v* arrange, tidy, organize, lay the table
restrans ['restrans] *g* **+ow** organization (abst.),
 arrangement
restrenn ['restren] *b* **+ow** file, dossier
reswisk ['reˑzwɪsk] *g* tracksuit
resyas ['reˑzjas] *g* **+ow** rhythm

reudh ['rœ:ð] *g* distress, upset

reudhi ['rœ·ði] *v* upset, distress

reun ['rœ:n] *g* **+yon** seal (mammal)

reverthi [re'verθi] *b* **+ow** spring tide

1rew ['rew] *g* **+yow** row (line of objects)

2rew ['rew] *g* **+yow** frost, ice; **rew du** black ice

rewell ['re·wel] *b* **+ow** freezer

rewi ['re·wi] *v* freeze

rewl ['reʊl] *b* **+ow** rule, order, regulation; **rewl voes** diet (as in "go on a diet")

rewlell ['reʊlel] *b* **+ow** ruler (tool)

rewler ['reʊler] *g* **-oryon** ruler (head of state)

rewlya ['reʊlja] *v* rule (trans.)

Rewynys [reʊ'ɪ·nɪs] *le* Iceland

rewynysek [reʊɪ'nɪ·zek] *hg* Icelandic

rewynysek [reʊɪ'nɪ·zek] *g* Icelandic language

Rewynyser [reʊɪ'nɪ·zer] *g* Icelander

reydh ['reɪð] *b* **+ow** sex, gender

reydhel ['reɪðel] *hg* sexual

reyn ['reɪn] *g* **+ys** reign

reynya ['reɪnja] *v* reign

reyth ['reɪθ] *hg* right, regular: *g* **+yow** right

ri ['ri:] *v* give, grant, render, present

ribin ['ri·bin] *g* **+ow** streak

ris ['ri:s] *hk* **+enn** rice

riv ['ri:v] *g* **+ow** number

ro ['rɔ:] *g* **rohow** gift, present

roas ['rɔ·as] *g* **+ow** talent

robot ['rɔ·bɔt] *g* **+ow** robot

roemm ['rɤm:] *g* rum

roes ['rɔ:z] *b* **+ow** net

roesweyth ['rɔ·zweɪθ] *g* **+yow** network

roeth ['rɔ:θ] *g* **+ow** shape

roev ['roːv] *b* **+ow** oar
rol ['rɔːl] *b* **+yow** list, inventory
rolbrenn ['rɔlbren] *g* **+yer** wooden roller
rolven ['rɔlven] *g* **rolveyn** stone roller
rol-voes [ˌrɔˑlˈvoːz] *b* **rolyow-boes** menu (of food)
rolya ['rɔˑlja] *v* roll
Rom ['rɔːm] *le* Rome
Roman ['rɔˑman] *g* **+s**; **+yon** Roman
romanek [rɔˈmaˑnek] *hg* Roman, Romance
Romani [rɔˈmaˑni] *le* Romania
romans ['rɔˑmans] *g* **+ow** novel
rombenn ['rɔmben] *b* **+ow** lozenge (shape)
rond ['rɔnd] *hg* round
ronk ['rɔnk] *g* **+ow** snore
¹ros ['rɔːz] *b* **+ow** wheel
²ros ['rɔːz] *g* **+yow** hill-spur, promontory
³ros ['rɔːz] *hk* **+enn** roses
rostya ['rɔˑstja] *v* roast
rosva ['rɔzva] *b* **+ow** promenade, avenue
rosya ['rɔˑzja] *v* ramble, hike
rosyas ['rɔˑzjas] *g* **+ow** stroll
rout ['ruːt] *g* **+ys** rabble
router ['ruˑter] *g* **+s** director, controller, producer
routyans ['ruˑtjans] *g* direction (e.g. of a film)
roweth ['rɔʊeθ] *g* importance
rudh ['ryːð] *hg* red
rudhek ['ryˑðek] *g* **-ogyon** robin
rudhloes [ˌryˑðˈloːz] *hg* russet
rudhvelyn [ryðˈveˑlɪn] *hg* orange (colour)
rumanek [ryˈmaˑnek] *hg* Rumanian
Rumanek [ryˈmaˑnek] *g* Rumanian language
rusk ['ryːsk] *b* **+enn** bark of a tree, rind, peel
russek ['rysːek] *hg* Russian

137

Russek ['rysːek] *g* Russian language
Russi ['rysːi] *le* Russia
rutya ['ryˑtja] *v* rub, apply friction
rutyer ['ryˑtjer] *g* **+yow** eraser
ruvanes [ryˈvaˑnes] *b* **+ow** queen
ryb [rɪb] *rg* beside, by, close to, next to
rych ['rɪːtʃ] *hg* rich
rychys ['rɪˑtʃɪs] *g* wealth, riches
rydh ['rɪːð] *hg* free
rydhhe [rɪðˈheː] *v* set free
rydhses ['rɪðzes] *g* freedom, liberty
ryllik ['rɪlːɪk] *b* groove
Rysrudh [rɪzˈryːð] *le* Redruth

S

¹'s [s] *rh* her, it
²'s [s] *rh* them
sad ['saːd] *hg* serious, steadfast, solemn
Sadorn ['saˑdɔrn] *g* Saturn, Saturday
sagh ['saːx] *g* **seghyer** bag **sagh koska** sleeping-bag
salad ['saˑlad] *g* **+ys** salad
salow ['saˑlɔw] *hg* safe, well, healthy
sand ['sand] *g* **+ow** course of meal, dish
sans ['sans] *hg* holy, sacred: *g* **syns** saint (male)
sanses ['sanzes] *b* **+ow** saint (female)
sarf ['sarf] *b* **serf** snake, serpent
Sarsyn ['sarsɪn] *g* **+s** Moor
Satnas ['satnas] Satan
sav ['saːv] *g* stand, stance, erect posture

savla-kyttrin [ˌsavlakɪtˈriːn] *g* **savleow-kyttrin**
bus-stop

saw [ˈsaw] *hg* safe: *m* except, unless

sawer [ˈsawer] *g* **+yow** savour, flavour, taste

sawya [ˈsaʊja] *v* save from danger, rescue, preserve,
heal

sawyas [ˈsaʊjas] *g* **-ysi** rescuer

sebon [ˈseˈbɔn] *g* **+ow** soap

sedhbrenn [ˈseðbren] *g* **+yer** diving board

sedhi [ˈseˈði] *v* sink, dip, dive, submerge, set (of Sun)

segi [ˈseˈgi] *v* soak

¹sel [ˈseːl] *b* **+yow** base, foundation

²sel [ˈseːl] *b* **+yow** seal (for document)

selder [ˈselder] *g* **+yow** cellar, basement

selsigenn [selˈsiˈgen] *b* **+ow**, **selsik** *hk* sausage

selya [ˈseˈlja] *v* seal

semlans [ˈsemlans] *g* **+ow** appearance

sempel [ˈsempel] *hg* simple, ordinary

Sen Ostell [senˈɔˈstel] *le* St Austell

senedh [ˈseˈneð] *g* **+ow** senate, parliament, synod

seni [ˈseˈni] *v* sound (of an instrument), play an
instrument, ring a bell

ser [ˈseːr] *g* **+i**; **ser men** mason

Serb [ˈserb] *g* **+yon** Serb

serbek [ˈserbek] *hg* Serbian

Serbek [ˈserbek] *hg* Serbian language

Serbi [ˈserbi] *le* Serbia

serghek [ˈserxek] *hg* dependent

serghi [ˈserxi] *v* cling

serjont [ˈserdʒɔnt] *g* **serjons** sergeant

serri [ˈserːi] *v* annoy, vex, provoke

serrys [ˈserːɪs] *hg* angry, cross

sertan [ˈsertan], certain, sure *av* certainly, surely

serth ['serθ] *hg* steep

servis ['servɪs] *g* **+yow** service (including in church)

servya ['servja] *v* serve

servyades [serv'jaˑdes] *b* **+ow** servant (female), waitress

servyas ['servjas] *g* **-ysi** servant (male), waiter

servyour ['servjur] *g* **+s** tray

seson ['seˑsɔn] *g* **+yow**; **+s** season, period of time

¹seth ['seˑθ] *b* **+ow** arrow

²seth ['seˑθ] *g* **+ow** large jar

sether ['seˑθer] *g* gannet; **An Sether** Sagittarius

settya ['setˑja] *v* set, place, appoint

seudhel ['sœˑðel] *g* **+yow, dewseudhel** *hd* heel

seul² ['sœːl] *rh* whoever

seulabrys [sœlaˑbrɪːz] *av* formerly, already, in the past

sevel ['seˑvel] *v* stand, rise, get up; **sevel orth** stand against, resist

sevi ['seˑvi] *hk* **+enn** strawberries

sevur ['seˑvyr] *hg* severe, serious, grave

sewena [se'weˑna] *b* success, prosperity, welfare

seweni [se'weˑni] *v* succeed, prosper, thrive

seytek ['seɪtek] *niv* seventeen

seyth ['seɪθ] *niv* seven

seythun ['seɪθyn] *b* **+yow** week

seythunyek [seɪˈθyˑnjek] *hg* weekly

shafta ['ʃafta] *g* **-ys** mine-shaft

sham ['ʃaːm] *g* **+ys** shame, disgrace

shamya ['ʃaˑmja] *v* shame

shapya ['ʃaˑpja] *v* fashion

sherewa [ʃe'reʊa] *g* **sherewys** rogue

sherewynsi [ˌʃere'wɪnzi] *g* wickedness

shora ['ʃɔˑra] *g* **+ys** fit, seizure, convulsion

shyndya ['ʃɪndja] *v* injure, hurt, ruin, harm

sider ['siˑder] *g* cider

sidhel ['siðel] *g* **sidhlow** filter, strainer

sidhla ['siðla] *v* filter, sift

sigarik [siˈgaˑrɪk] *g* **-igow** cigarette

sim ['siːm] *g* **+yon** monkey

siment ['siˑment] *g* cement

sin ['siːn] *g* **+ys**; **+yow** sign, symptom

sina ['siˑna] *v* sign, signal

sinans ['siˑnans] *g* **+ow** signature

sinema ['siˑnema] *g* **+ow** cinema

sita ['siˑta] *b* **sitys** city

skala ['skaˑla] *g* **+ys** dish, bowl, saucer

skampi ['skampi] *k* scampi

skansenn ['skanzen] *b* **+ow**, **skans** *hk* fish-scale

skant ['skant] *hg* scarce: *av* scarcely, hardly

skaphwyth ['skaphwɪθ] *g* **+ow** draught of wind

skath ['skaːθ] *b* **+ow** boat

skath-roevya [ˌskaˑθˈroˑvja] *b* **skathow-roevya** rowing-boat

skath-woelya [ˌskaˑθˈwoˑlja] *b* **skathow-goelya** sailing-boat

skav ['skaːv] *hg* light, nimble, swift

skavell ['skaˑvel] *b* **+ow** stool

skavell-groenek [ˌskaˑvelˈgroˑnek] *b* **skavellow-kroenek** toadstool, mushroom

skethenn ['skeˑθen] *b* **+ow** strip, tatter

skeul ['skœːl] *b* **+yow** ladder

skeulya ['skœˑlja] *v* scale

skeus ['skœːz] *g* **+ow** shadow

skeusenn ['skœˑzen] *b* **+ow** photograph

skevens ['skeˑvens] *lp* lungs

ski ['skiː] *g* **+ow**, **dewski** *hd* ski

141

skia ['skiˑa] *v* ski

skians ['skiˑans] *g* **+ow** knowledge, sense; **mes a'y skians** out of his wits

skiansek [skɪˈanzek] *hg* intellectual, knowledgeable

skiber ['skiˑber] *b* **+yow** barn

skiens ['skiˑens] *g* **+ow** science

skila ['skiˑla] *b* **skilys** reason

skit ['skiːt] *g* **+ys** diarrhoea

skityans ['skiˑtjans] *g* **+ow** injection

skochfordh ['skɔtʃfɔrð] *b* **+ow** short-cut, alley, passage

skoedh ['skoːð] *b* **+ow, diwskoedh** *hd* shoulder

skoedhya ['skoˑðja] *v* support

skoedhyans ['skoˑðjans] *g* **+ow** support (abst.)

skoedhyer ['skoˑðjer] *g* **-oryon** supporter

skoellva ['skɤlva] *b* **+ow** rubbish-tip, dump

skoellya ['skɤlːja] *v* waste, squander, spill; **skoellya a-les** disperse

skoellyek ['skɤlːjek] *hg* extravagant: *g* **-ogyon** waster

skoes ['skoːz] *g* **+ow** shield

skol ['skɔːl] *b* **+yow** school; **skol veythrin** nursery school; **skol varghogeth** riding school

skoler ['skoˑler] *g* **-oryon** scholar (male)

skolheygel [skɔlˈheɪgel] *hg* scholarly

skolores [skɔlˈɔˑres] *b* **+ow** scholar (female)

skon ['skɔːn] *av* quickly, soon, at once

skonya ['skoˑnja] *v* refuse, reject, shun

skorrenn ['skɔrːen] *b* **+ow** branch, bough, seam of ore

skovarn ['skoˑvarn] *b* **skovornow, diwskovarn** *hd* ear, handle of jar

skovarnek [skoˑˈvarnek] *g* **-ogyon** hare

skovva ['skɔvːa] *b* **+ow** shelter, refuge

skown ['skɔʊn] *b* **+yow** bench

skrif ['skriːf] *g* **+ow** writing, article, script

skrifa ['skriˑfa] *v* write

skrifedh ['skriˑfeð] *b* **+ow** writing, inscription, writ

skrifenn ['skriˑfen] *b* **+ow** document

skrifennyades [ˌskrifen'jaˑdes] *b* **+ow** secretary (female)

skrifennyas [skrɪ'fenːjas] *g* **-ysi** secretary (male)

skrifer ['skriˑfer] *g* **-oryon** writer

skrij ['skriːdʒ] *g* **+ow** scream

skrija ['skriˑdʒa] *v* screech, scream, shriek

skryp ['skrɪːp] *g* **+ys** wallet

skuba ['skyˑba] *v* sweep, brush

skubell ['skyˑbel] *b* **+ow** broom (implement)

skubell-sugna [ˌskybel'sygna] *b* **skubellow-sugna** vacuum-cleaner

skubyllenn [sky'bɪlːen] *b* **+ow** small brush, mop; **skubyllenn baynt** paint-brush; **skubyllenn dhyns** tooth-brush

skudell ['skyˑdel] *b* **+ow** dish, bowl

skwadron ['skwadrɔn] *g* **+s** squadron

skwardya ['skwardja] *v* tear, rip, rend, lacerate

skwattya ['skwatːja] *v* crush, hit, squash

skwith ['skwiːθ] *hg* tired, weary

skwitha ['skwiˑθa] *v* tire

skwithhe [skwiˑθ'heː] *v* exhaust

skwith-marow [ˌskwiθ'marɔʊ] *hg* exhausted

skwithter ['skwiˑθter] *g* fatigue, tiredness, weariness

skwithus ['skwiˑθys] *hg* tiring, boring

skwych ['skwɪːtʃ] *g* **+ys** jerk, twitch, spasm

skwychell ['skwɪˑtʃel] *b* **+ow** switch (electric)

skwychya ['skwɪˑtʃja] *v* switch; **skwychya yn fyw** switch on; **skwychya yn farow** switch off

skyll ['skɪlː] *hk* **+enn** sprouts

Slav ['slaːv] *g* **Slevyon** Slav

Slavek ['slaˑvek] *hg* Slav

sleygh ['sleɪx] *hg* clever, skilful

sleyghneth ['sleɪxneθ] *b* skill, dexterity, cleverness

Slovaki [slɔˈvaˑki] *le* Slovakia

Sloveni [slɔˈveˑni] *le* Slovenia

slynk ['slɪŋk] *g* **+ow** slide, skid

slynkya ['slɪŋkja] *v* slide, slip, skid

snell ['snelː] *hg* quick, speedy

snod ['snoːd] *g* **+ow** tape

soedh ['soːð] *b* **+ow** office, job, occupation

soedhek ['soˑðek] *g* **-dhogyon** officer, official

soedhogel [sʏˈðɔˑgel] *hg* official

soedhva ['sʏðva] *b* **+ow** office, work-place, place of employment; **soedhva dornyaseth** tourist office

sokor ['sɔˑkɔr] *g* succour, aid

solempnita [ˌsɔˈlempnita] *g* **-nitys** solemnity, ceremony

solempnya [sɔˈlempnja] *v* celebrate

soler ['sɔˑler] *g* **+yow** loft, attic, upper floor

sommenn ['sɔmːen] *b* **+ow** sum, total

son ['sɔːn] *g* **+yow** sound (noise)

sonskrifa [sɔnˈskriˑfa] *v* record

soper ['sɔˑper] *g* **+yow** supper

sordyans ['sɔrdjans] *g* **+ow** rising

sorr ['sɔrː] *g* anger

¹sort ['sɔrt] *g* **+ow** sort, kind

²sort ['sɔrt] *g* **+es** hedgehog

sos ['sɔːs] *g* friend(s)

Soth ['sɔːθ] *g* South

soubenn ['suˑben] *b* **+ow** soup, broth

souder ['suˑder] *g* **-oryon** soldier

sowdhan ['souðan] *g* surprise

sowdhanas [sou'ðaːnas] *v* surprise

soweth [sɔ'weːθ] *esk* alas: *av* unfortunately

sows ['souz] *g* **+ow** sauce

Sows ['souz] *g* **+on** Englishman, Saxon

Sowses ['souzes] *b* **+ow** Englishwoman

sowsnek ['souznek] *hg* English

Sowsnek ['souznek] *g* English language

spal ['spaːl] *g* **+yow** fine, penalty

spas ['spaːs] *g* **+ow** space (not astron.)

Spayn ['spain] *le* Spain

spaynek ['spainek] *hg* Spanish

Spaynek ['spainek] *g* Spanish language

Spayner ['spainer] *g* **-oryon** Spaniard

spedhas ['speˑðas] *hk* **+enn** brambles, briars

spena ['speˑna] *v* spend, use up

spiser ['spiˑser] *g* **-oryon** grocer

spisti ['spiˑsti] *g* **+ow** grocer's shop

splann ['splanː] *hg* splendid

splanna ['splanːa] *v* shine

splannder ['splander] *g* **+yow** brightness, brilliance

spong ['spɔŋ] *g* **+ow** sponge

sport ['spɔrt] *g* **+ow** sport, game; **sportow dowr** water sports

sportva ['spɔrtva] *b* **+ow** stadium

sportyas ['spɔrtjas] *g* **-ysi** professional sportsman

spyrys ['spiˑris] *g* **+yon** spirit, fairy; **An Spyrys Sans** The Holy Spirit

spys ['spiːz] *g* period (of time), interval; **a verr spys** soon

stag ['staːg] *hg* fixed

staga ['staˑga] *v* tether, fix, attach

stagell ['staˑgel] *b* **+ow** attachment (physical,

including e-mail)

stamp ['stamp] *g* **+ys; +ow** stamp

stanch ['stantʃ] *hg* impervious

stat ['staːt] *g* **+ow** state (political), estate

sten ['steːn] *g* tin (metal)

stenor ['steˑnɔr] *g* **+yon** tinner

sterenn ['steˑren] *b* **+ow, ster** *hk* star; **sterenn lostek** comet

stervarner [ster'varner] *g* **-oryon** astronaut

stevell ['steˑvel] *b* **+ow** room

stevell-dhybri [ˌsteˑvel'ðɪbri] *b* **stevellow-dybri** dining-room

stevell-omwolghi [ˌsteˑveləm'wɔlxi] *b* **stevellow-omwolghi** bathroom

stevnik ['stevnɪk] *b* **-igow** palate, roof of mouth

stif ['stiːf] *b* **+ow** squirt

stifa ['stiˑfa] *v* squirt, spray

stoff ['stɔf] *g* **+ys** material, stuff, substance

stoffyans ['stɔfːjans] *g* **+ow** stuffing

stoppya ['stɔpːja] *v* stop (trans.), block

strech ['streːtʃ] *g* **+ys** delay

stredh ['streːð] *b* **+ow** stream, brook

strekys ['streˑkɪs] *b* **strokosow** stroke, blow

stret ['streːt] *b* **+ow** street

strik ['striːk] *hg* active, nimble

striw ['striw] *g* **+yow** sneeze

striwi ['striwi] *v* sneeze

stroeth ['stroːθ] *hg* tight, strict, stringent

strus ['stryːz] *g* **+yow** ostrich

studh ['styːð] *g* **+yow** state, condition, predicament

studhva ['styθfa] *b* **+ow** study (room)

studhya ['styˑðja] *v* study

studhyans ['styˑðjans] *g* **+ow** study (piece of work)

146

studhyer ['sty·ðjer] *g* **studhyoryon** student
stumm ['stymː] *g* **+ow** bend, turning
stumma ['stymːa] *v* turn, bend
styr ['stıːr] *g* **+yow** meaning, sense
styrya ['stı·rja] *v* mean, explain, define
stywya ['stıʊja] *v* stew
sugal ['sy·gal] *hk* **+enn** rye
sugen ['sy·gen] *g* **+yow** juice, sap, syrup, essence
sugna ['sygna] *v* suck
sugra ['sygra] *g* sugar
Sul ['syːl] *g* **+yow** Sunday
sur ['syːr] *hg* sure: *av* surely
surheans [syr'he·ans] *g* **+ow** insurance, assurance
swedek ['swe·dek] *hg* Swedish
Swedek ['swe·dek] *g* Swedish language
Sweden ['swe·den] *le* Sweden
sybwydh ['sı·bwıð] *hk* **+enn** fir-trees, evergreen
   trees
syg ['sıːg] *b* **+ow** attachment (physical), bond, link
sygera [sı'ge·ra] *v* ooze, dawdle, leak slowly
sygh ['sıːx] *hg* dry
sygha ['sı·xa] *v* dry, wipe
syghes ['sı·xes] *g* thirst; **yma syghes dhymm**
   I am thirsty
sylli ['sıl·i] *b* **+es** eel
synsell ['sınzel] *b* **+ow** clip (e.g. paper-clip)
synsi ['sınzi] *v* hold
syrk ['sırk] *g* **+ow** circus (show)
syrr ['sırː] *g* **+ys** sir
system ['sı·stem] *g* **+ow** system
syth ['sıːθ] *hg* direct, upright
sywya ['sıʊja] *v* follow; **a syw** following
sywyans ['sıʊjans] *g* **+ow** result, consequence

T

tabour ['ta·bur] *g* **+yow** drum, tabor

tag ['ta:g] *g* **+ow** choking, strangulation, traffic jam

taga ['ta·ga] *v* choke, stifle, strangle, constrict, clog

takel ['takel] *g* **taklow** thing

taksi ['taksi] *g* **+ow** taxi

takya ['ta·kja] *v* clap hands

tal ['ta:l] *b* **+yow** brow, forehead, temple (of head)

talas ['ta·las] *g* **+ow** payment

talgell ['talgel] *b* **+ow** pantry

talik ['ta·lɪk] *g* **-igow** garret, attic

talvesa [tal've·za] *v* value, prize, be worth

talvosek [tal'vɔ·zek] *hg* valuable

talvosogeth [ˌtalvɔzɔ·geθ] *b* **+ow** value, worth

tamm ['tam:] *g* **temmyn** piece, bit, fragment; **tamm ha tamm** gradually, bit by bit

tan ['ta:n] *g* **+yow** fire; **gans tan** on fire

tanbellenn [tan'bel:en] *b* **+ow** bomb, shell

tanbellenna [ˌtanbe'len:a] *v* bomb, bombard

tanbrenn ['tanbren] *g* **-yer** match, lucifer

tangasor [tan'gazɔr] *g* **+yon** fireman

tanow ['tanɔw] *hg* thin, rare, scarce

tanses ['tanzes] *g* **+yow** bonfire, blaze

tanta ['tanta] *v* woo, court

tapp ['tap] *g* **+ow** tap (e.g. of bath)

taran ['ta·ran] *b* thunder

tardh ['tarð] *g* **+ow** bang, explosion, burst, eruption

tardha ['tarða] *v* explode, burst, break (of day), erupt

tardra ['tardra] *v* bore (a hole), drill

tarosvann [ta'rɔzvan] *g* **+ow** ghost, spectre, phantom

tarosvannus [ˌtarɔz'van:ys] *hg* ghostly

tarow ['tarɔw] *g* **terewi** bull

tartenn ['tarten] *b* **+ow** tart (food)

tas ['taːz] *g* **+ow** father

tas-besydh [ˌtaːz'beˑzɪð] *g* **tasow-vesydh** godfather

tasek ['taˑzek] *g* **tasogyon** patron saint

tas-gwynn [ˌtaːz'gwɪːn] *g* **tasow-wynn** grandfather

tasik ['taˑzɪk] *g* **-igyon** dad

tava ['taˑva] *v* touch, stroke

tavern ['taˑvern] *g* **+yow** tavern, inn

tavernor [ta'vernɔr] *g* **+yon** licensee (of inn)

taves ['taˑves] *g* **tavosow** tongue, language

tavosa [ta'vɔˑza] *v* scold, tell off

taw ['taw] *g* silence, quiet; **taw taves!** silence!, be quiet!

tawesek [ta'weˑzek] *hg* silent, taciturn

te ['teː] *g* **+ow** tea

tebel ['teˑbel] *hg* evil, wicked

tebeldhyghtya [ˌtebel'ðɪxtja] *v* abuse, ill-treat

tebott ['teˑbɔt] *g* **+ow** teapot

teg ['teːg] *hg* fine, beautiful, pretty

tegenn ['teˑgen] *b* **+ow** trinket, jewel

teghes ['teˑxes] *v* flee

teghyas ['teˑxjas] *g* **-ysi** fugitive, refugee

teknegydh [tek'neˑgɪð] *g* **+yon** technician

teknek ['teknek] *g* **-ogow** technique

teknogel [tek'nɔˑgel] *hg* technical

tekst ['tekst] *g* **+ow** text

tekter ['tekter] *g* beauty, finery

telli ['telːi] *v* bore holes, drill holes

telynn ['teˑlɪn] *b* **+ow** harp

telynnyer [te'lɪnːjer] *g* **-oryon** harpist

tempel ['tempel] *g* **templow** temple (building)

tempra ['tempra] *v* temper

tempredh ['tempreð] *g* **+ow** temperature

149

tempredhell [tem'preˑðel] *b* **+ow** thermometer

tenewen [te'newen] *g* **tenwennow** side, flank

tenn ['ten:] *g* **+ow** pull, drag, tug, draught (drink), shot

tenna ['ten:a] *v* pull, drag, attract, shoot

tennis ['ten:is] *g* tennis

terghi ['terxi] *v* wreathe, coil

terlenki [ter'lenki] *v* gulp

terlentri [ter'lentri] *v* glisten

termyn ['termin] *g* **+yow** time, period of time; **an termyn eus passys** the past; **an termyn a dheu** the future

ternos ['ternɔs] *av* next day; **ternos vyttin** tomorrow morning

terras ['terːas] *g* **+ow** terrace

terri ['terːi] *v* break, pick (e.g. flowers)

terroes ['terːʏs] *g* **+ow** havoc, destruction, disaster

terrys ['terːis] *hg* broken

terthenn ['terθen] *b* **+ow** fever, influenza, flu

tervans ['tervans] *g* **+ow** tumult, turmoil

tes ['teːz] *g* heat, warmth

tesa ['teːza] *v* heat, warm in the sunshine

tesenn ['teˑzen] *b* **+ow** cake; **tesenn gales** biscuit

testskrif ['teˑstskrif] *g* **+ow** certificate, testimonial

teth ['teːθ] *b* **+i**; **+ow** teat

teudhi ['tœˑði] *v* melt, smelt, thaw, fuse

teurek ['tœˑrek] *hk* **teurogenn** bugs

tevesiges [ˌteveˈziˑges] *b* **+ow** adult (female)

tevesik [teˈveˑzik] *hg* adult: *g* **-igyon** adult (male)

tevi ['teˑvi] *v* grow

tew ['tew] *hg* thick, fat

tewal ['teʊal] *hg* dark

tewedh ['teweð] *g* **+ow** storm

150

tewel ['tewel] *v* be silent, cease speaking

tewes ['tewes] *hk* **+enn** sand

tewhe [teʊ'heː] *v* thicken, fatten

tewl ['teʊl] *hg* dark

tewlder ['teʊlder] *g* darkness

tewlel ['teʊlel] *v* throw, cast, toss, fling

tewlhe [teʊl'heː] *v* darken, obscure

tewlwolow [tʊwl'wɔ·lɔw] *g* dusk, twilight

tewlyjyon [teʊl'ɪˈdʒjɔn] *g* obscurity

tewolgow [te'wɔlgɔw] *g* darkness

tewynn ['te·wɪn] *g* **+ow** dune

Tewynn Pleustri [ˌtewɪn'plœ·stri] *le* Newquay

teyl ['teɪl] *g* manure

teylu ['teɪly] *g* **+yow** family, household

teyr³ ['teɪr] *niv* three (fem.)

teyrgweyth ['teɪrgweɪθ] *av* thrice

teyrros ['teɪrːɔs] *b* **+ow** tricycle

ti ['tiː] *v* swear

tiek ['ti·ek] *g* **tiogyon** farmer (male)

tigenn ['ti·gen] *b* **+ow** hand-bag

tiger ['ti·ger] *g* **tigri** tiger

tin ['tiːn] *b* **+yow** arse, rump, backside

tioges [ti'ɔ·ges] *b* **+ow** farmer (female), countrywoman

tir ['tiːr] *g* **+yow** land, ground, territory; **tir meur** mainland

tira ['ti·ra] *v* land, come ashore

tirwel ['ti·rwel] *b* **+yow** landscape

titel ['ti·tel] *g* **titlow** legal title

to ['tɔː] *g* **tohow** roof

toella ['tɤlːa] *v* deceive, cheat, fool

toellwisk ['tɤlwɪsk] *g* **+ow** disguise

toellwiska [tɤl'wi·ska] *v* disguise

151

toemm ['tʏm:] *hg* warm, ardent

toemma ['tʏm:a] *v* warm

toemmder ['tʏmder] *g* warmth

toemmheans-kres [tʏm,heˈansˈkreːz] *g* central heating

¹toes ['toːz] *g* dough

²toes ['toːz] *g* **+ow** tuft, tassel, bunch

toeth ['toːθ] *g* speed, haste, hurry; **toeth men** quickly

toethya ['toˈθja] *v* speed

tokyn ['tɔˈkɪn] *g* tokynyow ticket, symptom, token

tokynva [tɔˈkɪnva] *b* **+ow** ticket-office, booking office

¹toll ['tɔl:] *g* **tell** hole

²toll ['tɔl:] *b* **+ow** tax, duty

tollgorn ['tɔlgɔrn] *g* tollgern flute

tollwas ['tɔllwas] *g* -wesyon customs officer

tommenn ['tɔm:en] *b* **+ow** earth-bank, embankment

ton ['tɔːn] *g* **+yow** tune, melody, tone; **ton kerdh** march (tune)

¹tonn ['tɔn:] *g* **+ow** turf

²tonn ['tɔn:] *b* **+ow** wave, billow

tonnas ['tɔn:as] *g* **+ow** ton, tonne

tonnek ['tɔn:ek] *hg* flock

tonteth ['tɔnteθ] *b* impudence, cheek, impertinence

torgh ['tɔrx] *g* **+es** boar

torn ['tɔrn] *g* **+ow** turn, deed, tour

tornyas ['tɔrnjas] *g* -ysi tourist

tornyaseth [tɔrnˈjaˈzeθ] *b* tourism

¹torr ['tɔr:] *b* **+ow** belly, abdomen

²torr ['tɔr:] *b* **+ow** tor

torrva ['tɔrva] *b* breach, rupture; **torrva dhemmedhyans** divorce

152

torth ['tɔrθ] *b* **+ow** loaf; **torth hir** baguette

toul ['tu:l] *g* **+ow** tool, implement

tour ['tu:r] *g* **+yow** tower, steeple

tournay ['turnaɪ] *g* **+s** tournament

towell ['tɔʊel] *g* **+ow** towel

towl ['tɔʊl] *g* **+ow** throw, plan, design

towlenn ['tɔʊlen] *b* **+ow** programme, schedule

tra ['traː] *b* **+ow** thing, article, object, affair

trammhyns ['tramhɪns] *g* **+ow** tramway

travalya [tra'vaˑlja] *v* walk far, travel, trudge

travyth ['traˑvɪθ] *b* nothing, anything (in neg. phrases)

trayson ['traɪsɔn] *g* treason, treachery

trayta ['traɪta] *v* betray

traytour ['traɪtur] *g* **+s** traitor

tre ['treː] *b* **trevow** farmstead, village, town, home; **yn tre** at home

tredan ['treˑdan] *g* electricity

tredanek [tre'daˑnek] *hg* electric

tredaner [tre'daˑner] *g* **-oryon** electrician

tregh ['treːx] *g* **+ow** section, slice, tranch

treghi ['treˑxi] *v* cut, carve

tremen ['treˑmen] *g* corridor

tremena [trɛˈmeˑna] *v* pass, die

tremengummyas [ˌtremenˈgymːjas] *g* **+ow** passport

tremenyas [treˈmeˑnjas] *g* **-ysi** traveller

tremmynn ['tremːɪn] *g* **+ow** face, look, aspect

tren ['treːn] *g* **+ow** railway train; **tren toeth bras (T.T.B.)** high speed train

trenk ['trenk] *hg* acid, sharp (of taste or smell), sour

trenyans ['treˑnjans] *g* training

tresa ['treˑsa] *v* draw (as in art)

tresas ['treˑsas] *g* **+ow** drawing

153

tresor ['trɛˑzɔr] *g* **+yow** treasure
tressa ['trɛsːa] third; **Tressa Bys** Third World
treth ['trɛːθ] *g* **+ow** beach, strand, sea-shore
treth ['trɛːθ] *g* **+yow** ferry, passage over water
treusi ['trœˑzi] *v* cross, pass over, traverse
treusperthi [trœsˈpɛrθi] *v* transfer
treusporth ['trœsporθ] *g* **+ow** transfer, transport
treusva ['trœˑsfa] *b* **+ow** crossing
treusweladow [ˌtrœzweˈlaˑdɔw] *hg* transparent
trevas ['trɛˑvas] *b* **+ow** harvest, crop
treveglos [treˈveglɔs] *b* **+yow** churchtown, village
trevesiga [ˌtreveˈziˑga] *v* settle (on new land)
trevesigeth [ˌtreveˈziˑgeθ] *b* **+ow** colony, settlement
¹treveth ['treˑveθ] *b* **+ow** farm
²treveth ['treˑveθ] *b* **+yow** occasion (time)
trew ['trew] *g* saliva
treweythyow [treˈweɪθjɔw] *av* sometimes, occasionally, now and then
treylouba [treɪˈluˑba] *v* stir
treylya ['treɪlja] *v* turn, convert, translate
treylyans ['treɪljans] *g* **+ow** translation
treynwas ['treɪnwas] *g* **-wesyon** straggler
tri³ ['triː] *niv* three (m.)
trial ['triˑal] *g* **+s** trial (legal)
trig ['triːg] *g* low tide
triga ['triˑga] *v* dwell, live (at a place), reside, stay, remain
trigva ['trɪgva] *b* **+ow** address (place), abode, dwelling-place
trihorn ['triˑhɔrn] *g* **trihern** triangle
trist ['triːst] *hg* sad, mournful
tri-ugens [triˈyˑgens] *niv* sixty, threescore; **deg ha tri-ugens** seventy

tro ['trɔ:] *b* **+yow** turn

trobla ['trɔbla] *v* trouble, vex, bother

troe'lergh ['trolerx] *g* **+ow** footpath

troen ['trɔ:n] *g* **+yow** nose, snout, point of land, trunk of animal

troengornvil [trɤn'gɔrnvil] *g* **+es** rhinoceros

troenhwytha [trɤn'hwɪ·θa] *v* snuffle

troes ['trɔ:z] *g* **treys, dewdroes** *hd* foot (Anat.)

troesell ['trɔ·zel] *b* **+ow** pedal

troesella [trɤ'zel:a] *v* pedal

troespons ['trɔ·spɔns] *g* **+ow** footbridge

trog ['trɔ:g] *g* **+ow** case, box, trunk, suitcase

trogenter [trɔ'genter] *b* **-gentrow** screw

trogentra [trɔ'gentra] *v* screw

trogentrell [trɔ'gentrel] *b* **+ow** screw-driver

trogh ['trɔ:x] *hg* cut, cracked: *g* **+ow** cut, incision

trog-tenna [ˌtrɔ·k'ten:a] *g* **trogow-tenna** drawer (furniture)

troha ['trɔ·ha] *rg* towards

tromm ['trɔm:] *hg* sudden, brusque; **yn tromm** suddenly

tronkys ['trɔnkɪs] *g* ablutions; **gul tronkys** take a bath

tros ['trɔ:z] *g* **+ow** noise, clamour

trosek ['trɔ·zek] *hg* noisy

troyll ['trɔɪl:] *g* **+yow** spin, ceilidh, fest-noz

tru ['try:] *esk* alas

truan ['try·an] *hg* wretched

truedh ['try·eð] *g* pity, compassion, pathos, sad state of affairs; **kemmeres truedh a** have pity on

Truru ['try·ry] *le* Truro

truth ['try:θ] *g* **+ow** trout

trydhek ['trɪ·ðek] thirteen

trygh ['trɪːx] *hg* superior, victorious, triumphant: *g* **+ow** victory, triumph

tryghi ['trɪˈfiː] *v* conquer, triumph

trymis ['trɪˈmis] *g* **+yow** school term, quarter (of a year), three months

trynn ['trɪnː] *b* **+ow** trouble

tu ['tyː] *g* **+yow** direction, side; **tu ha** towards; **bos heb tu** abstain in a vote; **tu a-rag** forward part

tuedh ['tyˈeð] *g* **+ow** trend, tendency

Turk ['tyrk] *g* **+ys**; **+yon** Turk

turkek ['tyrkek] *hg* Turkish

Turkek ['tyrkek] *g* Turkish language

Turki ['tyrki] *le* Turkey

tus ['tyːz] *lp* people, persons, men

tus-dha [ˌtyˈzˈðaː] *lp* in-laws

ty² ['tiː] *rh* you (sg.), thou

tybi ['tɪˈbi] *v* imagine, think, hold an opinion

tybyans ['tɪˈbjans] *g* **+ow** opinion, thought, idea

tykki-Duw [ˌtɪkiˈdyw] *b* **tykkies-Duw** butterfly

tylda ['tɪlda] *g* **tyldow** tent

tyli ['tɪˈli] *v* owe, recompense

tyller ['tɪlˈer] *g* **+yow** place, spot, location

tynn ['tɪnː] *hg* tight, intense, sharp, cruel, taut

tynnhe [tɪnˈheː] *v* tighten

tynnow ['tɪnːɔw] *lp* tights

tyskenn ['tɪˈsken] *b* **+ow** sheaf, bunch

U

ufern ['y·fern] *g* **+yow, dewufern** *hd* ankle

ugens ['y·gens] *niv* twenty

ughel ['y·fiel] *hg* high, lofty, loud (of sound)

ughelder [y'fielder] *g* **+yow** height, altitude, elevation, stature

ugheldir [y'fieldir] *g* **+yow** high ground

ughelgompesenn [ˌyfielgɔm'p·ezen] *b* **+ow** plateau

ughgapten [yfi'gapten] *g* **+yon** major (rank)

ughverk ['yfiferk] *g* **+ow** accent (in writing); **ughverk to** circumflex; **ughverk tylda** tilde

Ukrayn ['ykraın] *le* Ukraine

ukraynek [y'kraınek] *hg* Ukrainian

Ukraynek [y'kraınek] *g* Ukrainian language

unn ['yn:] *hg* one, only, sole: a certain

unnek ['yn:ek] *niv* eleven

unnik ['yn:ık] *hg* single, unique

unnlagasek [ˌynla'ga·zek] *hg* one-eyed

unnses ['ynzes] *g* **+ow** unity, unit

unnweyth ['ynweıθ] *av* once

unnwisk ['ynwısk] *g* uniform

unnwoes ['ynwɤs] *hg* akin, related by blood

unyans [y'njans] *g* **+ow** union, alliance; **Unyans Europek** European Union

unys ['y·nıs] *hg* united, unified

Uranus ['y·ranys] *le* Uranus

urdh ['yrð] *b* **+yow** order (organization)

¹us ['y:z] *g* **+yow** use, habit

²us ['y:z] *g* **+ow** yell

usa ['y·za] *v* yell, bawl

usadow [y'za·dɔw] *g* usage, custom; **herwydh usadow** as usual

uskis ['yˑskɪs] *hg* quick, nimble, fast; **yn uskis** quickly

uskisell [ɪsˈkiˑzel] *b* **+ow** accelerator

uskishe [ɪskɪsˈheˑ] *v* accelerate

usya ['yˑzja] *v* use; **dell yw usys** usually

V

vanshya ['vanʃja] *v* disappear

venimya [veˈniˑmja] *v* poison

visour ['viˑzur] *g* **+s** mask

votya ['vɔˑtja] *v* vote

votyans ['vɔˑtjans] *g* **+ow** poll

¹vy ['vɪ], ['vɪː] *rh* me (enclitic)

²vy ['vɪː] *rh* me (obj.)

vyaj ['vɪˑadʒ] *g* **+yow** journey, expedition, voyage, trip

vyajyer [vɪˈaˑdʒjer] *g* **-oryon** passenger

vyth ['vɪːθ] *hg* any (in neg. expressions), at all; **gorthyp vyth** no answer

vytholl ['vɪˑθɔl] *av* at all

W

¹war² [war] *rg* on, upon; **war euryow** now and then

²war ['waːr] *hg* aware, wary; **bydh war!** look out!

war-barth [warˈbarθ] *av* together

war-dhelergh [warðeˈlerx] *av* backwards

war-eun [warˈœːn] *av* directly

war-lergh [war'lerx] *rg* after
warlyna [war'lɪ·na] *av* last year
war-rag [war'ra:g] *av* forward(s)
west ['we:st] *hg* west: *g* west
wor'tiwedh [wɔr'tiʋeð] *av* in the end, finally
wosa ['wɔ·za] *rg* after
wostiwedh [wɔs'tiʋeð] *av* at last

Y

¹y⁵ [ɪ] *rh* his, its
²y² [ɪ] *pv* (verbal particle)
ya ['ɪ·a] *esk* yes
yagh ['ja:x] *hg* healthy, well
yaghhe [jaɦ'he:] *v* cure, heal
yaghhes [jaɦ'he:z] *hg* cured
yaghus ['ja·xys] *hg* healthful, health-giving
yalgh ['jalx] *b* **+ow** purse
yar ['ja:r] *b* **yer** hen
ydhnik ['ɪðnɪk] *g* **-igow** chick
Yedhow ['je·ðɔw] *g* **Yedhewon** Jew
yedhowek [je'ðɔʋek] *hg* Jewish
Yedhowek [je'ðɔʋek] *g* Yiddish language
yeghes ['je·xes] *g* health; **yeghes da!** good health!
yerik ['je·rɪk] *b* **-igow** chicken
yes ['je:z] *v* absolve (of sins), shrive
yet ['je:t] *b* **yetys** gate
yeth ['je:θ] *b* **+ow** language
yethador [je'θa·dɔr] *g* **+yow** grammar book
yewgenn ['jeʋgen] *g* **+ow** ferret, stoat, marten, polecat

159

yeyn ['jeɪn] *hg* cold

yeynder ['jeɪnder] *g* cold, chill

yeynell ['jeɪnel] *b* **+ow** refrigerator

ylyn ['ɪˑlɪn] *hg* limpid

y'm [ɪm] *in* in my

¹yn [ɪn] *rg* in

²yn⁵ [ɪn] *pv* -ly (adverbial suffix), e.g. **yn ta** well

y'n [ɪn] *rg* in the

yn-bann [ɪn'banː] *av* upward(s), up

yn-dann² [ɪn'danː] *rg* under, beneath

yndella [ɪn'delːa] *av* like that, thus, similarly

yndellma [ɪn'delma] *av* like this, in this way

yndellna [ɪn'delna] *av* in that way

ynk ['ɪnk] *g* **+ow** ink

ynkleudhva [ɪn'klœðva] *b* **+ow** cemetery, graveyard

ynkleudhyans [ɪn'klœˑðjans] *g* **+ow** burial, interment

ynkleudhyas [ɪn'klœˑðjas] *v* bury

yn-mes [ɪn'meːz] *av* out, outside

ynn ['ɪnn] *hg* narrow, slender

yn-nans [ɪn'nans] *av* downward(s)

ynni ['ɪnːi] *g* **+ow** urge, pressure

ynnia [ɪ'niˑa] *v* urge, incite, force, exhort

ynniadow [ˌɪni'aˑdow] *g* urgency: *hg* urgent

yn-rag [ɪn'raːg] *av* forward, onward

yntanys [ɪn'taˑnɪs] *hg* excited

yntra ['ɪntra] *rg* between

ynwedh [ɪn'weːð] *av* also, likewise, as well

ynys ['ɪˑnɪs] *b* **+ow** island, isolated place; **Ynysow Karibek** Antilles

ynysek [ɪ'nɪˑzek] *b* **-egi** archipelago

yogort ['jɔˑgort] *g* **+ow** yoghurt

yorgh ['jɔrx] *b* **yergh** roedeer

yos [ˈjɔːz] *g* gruel; **yos kergh** porridge

Yow [ˈjɔw] *g* Jupiter, Thursday

Yowann [ˈjɔwan] John

yowynk [ˈjɔwɪnk] *hg* young

yowynkneth [jɔˈwɪnkneθ] *b* youth (abst.)

ys [ˈiːz] *hk* **+enn** corn

yskynna [ɪsˈkɪnːa] *v* ascend, climb, go up

yskynnans [ɪsˈkɪnːans] *g* **+ow** ascent, ascendancy

Ysrael [ˌɪzraˈel] *le* Israel

Ysraelyas [ˌɪzraˈeljas] *g* **-ysi** Israeli

yssynsi [ɪsˈsɪnzi] *v* contain

ystynn [ˈɪˈstɪn] *v* extend, stretch

ystynnans [ɪsˈtɪnːans] *g* **+ow** extension

yth [ɪθ] *pv* (verbal particle)

y'th[5] [ɪθ] *rg* in thy

ytho [ɪˈθɔː] *m* then, so

yurl [ˈjyrl] *g* **+ys** count (noble)

ywin [ˈɪˈwɪn] *hk* **+enn** yew

Z

zebra [ˈzebra] *g* **+s** zebra

SOWSNEK-KERNEWEK

ENGLISH-CORNISH

An taves Sowsnek

An taves Sowsnek a veu dres dhe Vreten Veur
y'n pympes kansblydhen. Ev o moy haval orth
Almaynek es dell yw lemmyn, ha haval lowr
orth an yeth kewsys yn Norgagh hag yn
Danmark. Pan dheuth tus alena rag trevesiga
rannow a Bow Sows, an Sowsnek koth a veu
sempelhes, rag may halla an Sowson keskewsel
gansa.

Pan goedhas an pow yn-dann rewl an
Normanes, y teuth meur a eryow Frynkek
a-berth y'n taves. An Sowsnek a gollas
lostelvennow gramasek ha reydh yn henwyn.
Y'n pymthegves kansblydhen, son an
bogalennow a janjyas (henwys *Great Vowel
Shift*), mes an lytherennans o ogas an keth. Yn
kettermyn, y tegemmeras lies ger diworth Latin
ha Greka.

Sowsnek a veu degys dhe bub rann an
Emperoureth Predennek. Y'n ugensves

kansblydhen, y teuth ha bos yeth keswlasek.
Yma neb 400 milvil a dus a gews Sowsnek avel
yeth-vamm, ha martesen an niver dien a
gowsoryon yw moy es 1000 milvil.

Gis-leveryans an Sowsnek

Avel gerlyvrigow erell y'n kevres, yth yw
diskwedhys gis-leveryans a eryow Sowsnek.
Gwrys yw yn Lytherennek Fonetek Keswlasek
(IPA), ha kemmerys yw diworth *English
Pronouncing Dictionary* (Everyman), gans
Jones ha Gimson (1991), mes [a] re beu gorrys
yn le [æ], hag [ɔ] yn le [ɒ]. An gis yw *Received
Pronunciation* (RP), hag yw tamm dihaval
diworth gis-leveryans an pennskrifer. An
arwoedhyow yw kepar dell syw (an ensamplow
yw re Jones ha Gimson):

Bogalennow

[iː]	b**ea**n	[ɪ]	p**i**t
[ɑː]	b**ar**n	[e]	p**e**t
[ɔː]	b**or**n	[a]	p**a**t
[uː]	b**oo**n	[ʌ]	p**u**tt
[ɜː]	b**ur**n	[ɔ]	p**o**t
		[ə]	**a**nother

Diwvogalennow

[eɪ]	b**ay**	[əʊ]	n**o**
[aɪ]	b**uy**	[aʊ]	n**ow**
[ɔɪ]	b**oy**	[ɪə]	p**eer**
		[eə]	p**air**
		[ʊə]	p**oor**

Kessonennow

[p]	**p**in	[b]	**b**in
[t]	**t**in	[d]	**d**in
[k]	**c**ome	[g]	**g**um
[tʃ]	**ch**ain	[dʒ]	**J**ane
[f]	**f**ine	[v]	**v**ine
[θ]	**th**ink	[ð]	**th**is
[s]	**s**eal	[z]	**z**eal
[ʃ]	**sh**eep	[ʒ]	mea**s**ure
[h]	**h**ow	[ŋ]	su**ng**
[m]	su**m**	[n]	**S**un
[l]	**l**ight	[r]	**r**ight
[w]	**w**et	[j]	**y**et

Ynwedh, liw an gessonenn [r] yw diskwedhys dre an arwoedh [ʳ]. ['] a dhiskwedh bos kynsa poeslev war an syllabenn a syw, ha [ˌ] a dhiskwedh bos warnedhi nessa poeslev.

Berrheansow gramasek y'n gevrenn ma

a	adjective	hanow-gwann
adv	adverb	asverb
art	article	erthyglenn
coll	collective noun	hanow kuntellek
conj	conjunction	mellenn
f	feminine	benow
interj	interjection	eskarm
m	masculine	gorow
n	noun	hanow
num	number	niver
pl	plural	liesplek
prep	preposition	rag-ger
pron	pronoun	rakhanow
ptl	verbal particle	perthyglenn
sg.	singular	unnplek
v	verb	verb

A

a [ˈeɪ, ə] *art (not usually translated)*

abandon [əˈbandən] *v* gasa

abandonment [əˈbandənmənt] *n* forsakyans *m* +ow

abbey [ˈabi] *n* abatti *m* +ow

abbot [ˈabət] *n* abas *m* +ow

able [ˈeɪbl] *adj* abel; **be able** galloes

abort [əˈbɔːt] *v* erthylya

about [əˈbaʊt] *prep* a-dro dhe, yn kever; **about you** y'th kever

above [əˈbʌv] *prep* a-ugh, dres; **above all** dres oll: *adv* a-vann

abscess [ˈabses] *n* gorenn *f* +ow

absent [ˈabsənt] *adj* estrigys

absolutely [ˈabsəluːtli] *adv* porres

accelerate [akˈseləreɪt] *v* uskishe

accelerator [akˈseləreɪtər] *n* uskisell *f* +ow

accent [ˈaksent] *n (speech)* poeslev *m* +ow; *(diacritic)* ughverk *m* +ow

accept [əkˈsept] *v* degemmeres

accident [ˈaksɪdənt] *n* droglamm *m* +ow

accompany [əˈkʌmpəni] *v* keveylya

according [əˈkɔːdɪŋ] **according to** herwydh *prep*

accordion [əˈkɔːdjən] *n* karjel *m* +yow

account [əˈkaʊnt] *n (financial)* akont *m* +ow; **take account of** gul vri a

accumulate [əˈkjuːmjuleɪt] *v* kreuni

accusation [ˌakjuːˈzeɪʃən] *n* kabel *m*, kuhudhans *m* +ow

accuse [əˈkjuːz] *v* kuhudha

acid [ˈasɪd] *adj* trenk

acquaintance [əˈkweɪntəns] *n (knowledge)* aswonnvos *m; (person)* kothman *m* +s

across [əˈkrɔs] *prep* a-dreus: *adv* a-dreus

act [ˈakt] *v* gwari

action [ˈakʃən] *n* gweythres *m* +ow

activate [ˈaktɪveɪt] *v* bywhe

active [ˈaktɪv] *adj* bywek

activity [akˈtɪvɪti] *n* bywder *m* +yow

actor [ˈaktər] *n* gwarier *m* -oryon

adapt [əˈdapt] *v* aswiwa

address [əˈdres] *n (place)* trigva *f* +ow; *(talk)* areth *f* +yow

administration [ədˌmɪnɪˈstreɪʃən] *n* menystrans *m* +ow

admiral [ˈadmərəl] *n* amiral *m* -elyon

admit [ədˈmɪt] *v* amyttya, degemmeres a-berth

adolescence [adəˈlesəns] *n* lanketh *f*

adult [ˈadʌlt] *n (female)* tevesiges *f* +ow; *(male)* tevesik *m* -igyon

advance [ədˈvɑːns] *v* avonsya

advantage [ədˈvɑːntɪdʒ] *n* les *m*, prow *m*

advantageous [ˌadvənˈteɪdʒəs] *adj* lesus

adventure [ədˈventʃər] *n* aneth *m* +ow

adverb [ˈadvɜːb] *n* asverb *m* +ow

advertising [ˈadvətaɪzɪŋ] *n* argemmynnans *m*

advice [ədˈvaɪs] *n* avis *m* +yow, kusul *f* +yow

advise [ədˈvaɪz] *v* kusulya, avisya

aeroplane [ˈeərəpleɪn] *n* jynn-ebron *m* jynnow-ebron

affair [əˈfeər] *n* negys *m* +yow

Africa [ˈafrɪkə] *place* Afrika

African [ˈafrɪkan] *adj* afrikanek: *n* Afrikan *m* +s

after [ˈɑːftər] *prep* wosa, war-lergh

afternoon [ɑ:ftə'nu:n] *n* dohajydh *m* +yow, androw *m* +yow

afternoon-time [ɑ:ftə'nu:n'taim] *n* androweyth *f* +yow

afterwards ['ɑ:ftəwədz] *adv* a-wosa

again [ə'ɡein] *adv* arta

against [ə'ɡenst] *prep* erbynn

age ['eidʒ] *n* oes *m* +ow

agitate ['adʒiteit] *v* amovya

agitation [ˌadʒi'teiʃən] *n* amovyans *m* +ow

ago [ə'ɡəʊ] *adv* nans yw; **a week ago** nans yw seythun; **long ago** nans yw pell

agree [ə'ɡri:] *v* akordya

agreement [ə'ɡri:mənt] *n* akord *m*; *(contract)* kevambos *m* +ow

agriculture ['aɡrikʌltʃəʳ] *n* ammeth *f*

aground [ə'ɡraʊnd] **run aground** kammdira

aid ['eid] *n* gweres *m*

aim ['eim] *n* amkan *m* +ow

air ['eəʳ] *n* ayr *m*: *v* ayra

aircraft ['eəkrɑ:ft] *n* jynn-ebron *m* jynnow-ebron

airport ['eəpɔ:t] *n* ayrborth *m* +ow

aisle ['ail] *n* kasel *f* +yow

akin [ə'kin] *adj* unnwoes

alarm [ə'lɑ:m] *n* **alarm clock** difunell *f*

alas [ə'las] *int* soweth, tru

Albania [al'beiniə] *place* Albani

album *n* albom *m* +ow

alcohol ['alkəhɒl] *n* las *m* +ow

alder-tree [ˌɔ:ldər'tri:] *n* gwernenn *f* +ow, gwern *coll*

alien ['eiljən] *n* estren *m* +yon: *adj* estren

alive [ə'laiv] *adj* byw, yn fyw

all ['ɔ:l] *pron* peub; **at all** vytholl: *adj* oll

alley ['alɪ] *n* skochfordh *f* +ow

allow [ə'laʊ] *v* gasa; **be allowed to** kavoes kummyas dhe

ally ['alaɪ] *n* keffrysyas *m* -ysi

almighty [ɔl'maɪtɪ] *adj* ollgalloesek

almond ['almənd] *n* alamand *m* +ow +ys

almost ['ɔːlməʊst] *adv* nammna, ogas; **I almost fell** nammna goedhis

alms ['ɑːmz] *pl* alusen *f* +ow

alphabet ['alfəbet] *n* lytherennek *f* -egi

already [ɔːl'redɪ] *adv* seulabrys

Alsace [el'zas] *place* Elzas

also ['ɔːlsəʊ] *adv* ynwedh, keffrys

although [ɔːl'ðəʊ] *conj* kyn; *(before vowels and [h-])* kynth

always ['ɔːlweɪz] *adv* bykken, pup-prys, prest

amass [ə'mas] *v* gronna

amateur ['amətɜːʳ] *n* bodhesik *m* -igyon

ambassador [am'basədəʳ] *n* kannas *f* +ow

ambulance ['ambjʊləns] *n* karr-klavji *m* kerri-klavji

America [ə'merɪkə] *place* Amerika; **North America** Amerika Kledh; **South America** Amerika Dyghow; **Latin America** Amerika Latin

American [ə'merɪkən] *adj* amerikanek

among [ə'mʌŋ] *prep* yn mysk

amount [ə'maʊnt] *n* myns *m* +ow

amuse [ə'mjuːz] *v* didhana

amusement [ə'mjuːzmənt] *n* didhan *m* -enyow

amusing [ə'mjuːzɪŋ] *adj* didhan

anchor ['aŋkəʳ] *n* ankor *m* +yow: *v* ankorya

and [and] *conj (before consonants)* ha; *(before vowels)* hag

angel ['eɪndʒəl] *n* el *m* +edh

172

anger ['aŋgər] n sorr m

angle ['aŋgl] n elin m +yow

angry ['aŋgri] adj serrys; **become angry** omserri

anguish ['aŋgwɪʃ] n angoes m

animal ['anɪml] n enyval m +es, mil m +es

ankle ['aŋkl] n ufern m +yow, dewufern dual

anniversary [ˌanɪˈvɜːsəri] n penn-bloedh m pennow-bloedh

annoy [əˈnɔɪ] v serri, annia

annual ['anjuəl] adj blydhenyek

another [əˈnʌðər] adj arall

answer ['ɑːnsər] n gorthyp m gorthybow: v gorthybi

Antarctica [antˈɑrktɪkə] place Antartika

Antilles [anˈtɪliːz] place Ynysow Karibek

anxiety [aŋˈzaɪəti] n fienas m +ow

any ['eni] adj neb; (in neg. expressions) vyth; **any other** nahen; **any more** namoy

anybody ['enɪˌbɔdi] pron nebonan; (with implied neg.) denvyth m

anyone ['enɪwʌn] pron nebonan; (with implied neg.) denvyth m

anything ['enɪθɪŋ] pron neppyth m; (in neg. phrases) travyth f

apparently [əˈparəntli] adv dell hevel

appear [əˈpɪər] v omdhiskwedhes

appearance [əˈpɪərəns] n semlans m +ow

appetite ['apɪtaɪt] n (for food) ewl boes m

apple ['apl] n aval m +ow

approach [əˈprəʊtʃ] v dos nes dhe, neshe

approximately [əˈprɒksɪmətli] adv a-dro dhe

April ['eɪprəl] n mis-Ebrel m misyow-E.

apron ['eɪprən] n apron m +yow

aquarium [əˈkweəriəm] n pusketti m +ow

Aquarius [əˈkweərɪəs] *name* An Dowrer

Arab [ˈarəb] *n* Arab *m* Arebyon

Arabia [əˈreɪbɪə] *place* Arabi

Arabic [ˈarəbɪk] *adj* arabek; **Arabic language** Arabek *m*

arch [ˈɑːtʃ] *n* gwarak *f* -egow

archipelago [ˌɑːkɪˈpelɪgəʊ] *n* ynysek *f* -egi

architecture [ˈɑːkɪtektʃəʳ] *n (art of)* pennserneth *f*

archive *n* kovskrifenn *f* +ow

Arctic [ˈɑːktɪk] *place* Arktik

arduous [ˈɑːdjʊəs] *adj* kales

area [ˈeərɪə] *n* arenebedh *m* +ow

Argentina [ˌɑːdʒəntiːnə] *place* Arghantina

argument [ˈɑːgjʊmənt] *n* dadhel *f* dadhlow, argyans *m* +ow

arithmetic [əˈrɪθmetɪk] *n* niveronieth *f* +ow

arm [ˈɑːm] *n (limb)* bregh *f* +ow, diwvregh *dual*; *(weapon)* arv *f* +ow: *v* arva

armchair [ˌɑːmˈtʃeəʳ] *n* kador-vregh *f* kadoryow-bregh

arm-pit [ˈɑːmpɪt] *n* kasel *f* +yow, diwgasel *dual*

army [ˈɑːmi] *n* lu *m* +yow

around [əˈraʊnd] *prep* yn kyrghynn: *adv* a-dro

arrange [əˈreɪndʒ] *v* restra, ordena

arrangement [əˈreɪndʒmənt] *n* restrans *m* +ow

arrive [əˈraɪv] *v* devos

arrow [ˈarəʊ] *n* seth *f* +ow

art [ˈɑːt] *n* art *m* +ow +ys

artisan [ˌɑːtɪˈzan] *n* krefter *m* -oryon

artist [ˈɑːtɪst] *n* artydh *m* +yon; *(painter)* lymner *m* lymnoryon

as [az] *conj* dell; **as if** kepar dell; *(comparison)* **as ... as** maga ... avel, mar ... avel; **as white as crystal**

maga hwynn avel an gwrys; **as heavy as stone** mar boes avel men; **as many as** kemmys; **as much as** kemmys; **as soon as** kettell; **as well** maga ta; **as usual** dell yw usys

ascendant [əˈsendənt] *n* yskynnans *m* +ow

ashamed [əˈʃeɪmd] *adj* methek

ashes [ˈaʃɪz] *plur* lusu *coll* +enn

ash-tree [ˌaʃˈtriː] *n* onnenn *f* +ow, onn *coll*

Asia [ˈeɪʃə] *place* Asi

Asiatic [ˌeɪʃiˈatɪk] *adj* Asiek

ask [ˈɑːsk] *v* govynn

aspect [ˈaspekt] *n* tremmynn *m* +ow

ass [ˈas] *n* asen *m* +es

assailant [əˈseɪlənt] *n* omsettyer *m* -yoryon

assemble [əˈsembl] *v (intrans.)* omguntell; *(trans.)* keskorra

assembly [əˈsembli] *n* kuntelles *m* +ow

assent [əˈsent] *n* assentyans *m* +ow

association [əˌsəʊsiˈeɪʃən] *n* kowethyans *m* +ow

assurance [əˈʃʊərəns] *n* surheans *m* +ow

astride [əˈstraɪd] *adv* yn howlek

astronaut [ˈastrənɔːt] *n* stervarner *m* -oryon

asylum [əˈsaɪləm] *n* herbereth *f*; **place of asylum** meneghi *m*; **give asylum** ri herbereth

at [at] *prep* orth, dhe; **at all** vyth

athletics [aθˈletɪks] *plur* athletieth *f*

atmosphere [ˈatməˌsfɪəʳ] *n* ayrgylgh *m* +yow

attached [əˈtatʃt] *adj* stag

attachment [əˈtatʃmənt] *n (physical, including e-mail)* stagell *f* +ow

attack [əˈtak] *n* omsettyans *m* +ow: *v* settya war

attempt [əˈtempt] *v* assaya

attention [əˈtenʃən] *n* rach *m*

attic ['atɪk] *n* soler *m* +yow

August ['ɔːɡəst] *n* mis-Est *m* misyow-Est

aunt ['ɑːnt] *n* modrep *f* modrebedh

Australia [ɔ'streɪliə] *place* Ostrali

Australian [ɔ'streɪliən] *adj* Ostralek

Austria [ɔ'striə] *place* Ostri

Austrian [ɔ'striən] *adj* ostrek

author ['ɔːθər] *n* awtour *m* +s

autumn ['ɔːtəm] *n* kynyav *m* +ow

avenue ['avənjuː] *n* rosva *f* +ow

average ['avərɪdʒ] *n* kresek *m* kresogow: *adj* kresek *m* kresogow

awake [ə'weɪk] *adj* difun

away [ə'weɪ] *adj* a-ves: *adv* dhe-ves

axe ['aks] *n* boel *f* +yow

B

baby ['beɪbi] *n* baban *m* +es

back ['bak] *n* keyn *m* +ow

backside [bak'saɪd] *n (rump)* tin *f* +yow

backwards ['bakwədz] *adv* war-dhelergh

bacon ['beɪkən] *n* meghin *m* +yow

bad ['bad] *adj* drog

badger ['badʒər] *n* brogh *m* +es

bag ['baɡ] *n* sagh *m* seghyer

bagpipes ['baɡpaɪps] *plur* pibow-sagh

bail ['beɪl] *n* mewgh *m* +yow

baguette [ba'ɡet] *n* torth hir *m* torthow hir

bake ['beɪk] *v* pobas

baker ['beɪkər] *n* peber *m* -oryon, pebores *f* +ow

bakery ['beɪkəri] *n* popti *m* +ow

balance ['baləns] *n* mantol *f* +yow: *v* mantola

balcony ['balkəni] *n* balegva *f* +ow

bald ['bɔːld] *adj* blogh, moel

bale ['beɪl] *n* pusorn *m* +ow

ball ['bɔːl] *n* pel *f* +yow; pellenn *f* +ow

banana [bə'nɑːnə] *n* banana *m* +s

band ['band] *n (group of people)* parsell *m* +s; *(musical)* band *m* +ys

bandage ['bandɪdʒ] *n* lystenn *f* +ow: *v* lystenna

bank ['baŋk] *n (for money)* arghantti *m* +ow; *(of river)* glann *f* +ow; *(topographical)* bankenn *f* +ow

banker ['baŋkər] *n* arghanser *m* -oryon

banquet ['baŋkwɪt] *n* gwledh *f* +ow

baptise [bap'taɪz] *v* besydhya

baptism ['baptɪzm] *n* besydh *m* +yow

bar [bɑːr] *v* prenna

bard ['bɑːd] *n (female)* bardhes *f* +ow; *(male)* bardh *m* berdh

bare ['beər] *adj* lomm

barefoot ['beəfʊt] *adj* diarghen, dieskis

bark ['bɑːk] *n (of a dog)* harth *m* +ow; *(of a tree)* rusk *f* +enn: *v* hartha

barn ['bɑːn] *n* skiber *f* +yow

barrel ['barəl] *n* balyer *m* +yow +s

barrier ['barɪər] *n* lett *m* +ow +ys

basin ['beɪsn] *n* **large basin** bason *m* +yow +ys; **small basin** bolla *m* bollow bollys

basket ['bɑːskɪt] *n* kanstell *f* +ow

Basque ['bask] *adj* euskadek; **Basque language** Euskadek *m*; **Basque Country** Euskadi

bath ['bɑːθ] *n* **take a bath** gul tronkys

bathe ['beɪð] *v* badhya

177

bathroom ['bɑ:θrʊm] *n* golghva *f* +ow, stevell-omwolghi *f* stevellow-omwolghi

battery ['batəri] *n (elec.)* batri *m* +ow

battle ['batl] *n* batel *f* +yow, kas *f* +ow

bawl ['bɔ:l] *v* uja

bay ['beɪ] *n (coastal indentation)* kammas *f* +ow, baya *m* +ys

be ['bi:] *v* bos, bones

beach ['bi:tʃ] *n* treth *m* +ow

beak ['bi:k] *n* gelvin *m* +es

beam ['bi:m] *n (radiation)* dewynn *m* +ow; *(structural)* keber *f* kebrow

bean ['bi:n] *n* favenn *f* +ow, fav *coll*

beard ['bɪəd] *n* barv *f* +ow

bearded ['bɪədɪd] *adj* barvek

beast ['bi:st] *n* best *m* +es

beat ['bi:t] *v* gweskel

beautiful ['bju:təfʊl] *adj* teg

beauty ['bju:ti] *n* tekter *m*

because [bɪ'kɒz] *conj* drefenn

become [bɪ'kʌm] *v* dos ha bos

bed ['bed] *n* gweli *m* +ow; **bed and breakfast** gweli ha hansel

bedroom ['bedrʊm] *n* chambour *m* +yow

beef ['bi:f] *n* bewin *m*

beer ['bɪər] *n* korev *m* +ow

beetle ['bi:tl] *n* hwil *m* +es

before [bɪ'fɔ:r] *prep* a-dherag, a-rag; *(in time)* kyns

begin [bɪ'gɪn] *v* dalleth

beginner [bɪ'gɪnər] *n* dallether *m* -oryon

beginning [bɪ'gɪnɪŋ] *n* derow *m* +yow

behalf [bɪ'hɑ:f] *n* parth *f* +ow

behave [bɪ'heɪv] *v* fara

behaviour [bɪ'heɪvjəʳ] *n* fara *m*

behind [bɪ'haɪnd] *prep* a-dryv: *adv* a-dhelergh, a-dryv

belfry ['belfri] *n* kleghti *m* +ow

Belgium ['beldʒəm] *place* Pow Belg

believe [bɪ'liːv] *v* krysi

bell ['bel] *n* klogh *m* klegh; **door-bell** klogh daras *m* klegh daras

beloved [bɪ'lʌved] *adj* karadow, meurgerys

below [bɪ'ləʊ] *adv* a-woeles

belt ['belt] *n* grogys *m* +yow

bench ['bentʃ] *n* bynk *f* +yow

bend ['bend] *n* stumm *m* +ow: *v* stumma, plegya

bent ['bent] *adj* kamm

bequeath [bɪ'kwiːð] *v* kemmynna

besides [bɪ'saɪdz] *prep* dres

best ['best] *adj* gwella

bet ['bet] *n* kenwoestel *m* kenwoestlow: *v* kenwoestla

betray [bɪ'treɪ] *v* traysya

better ['betəʳ] *adj* gwell; **get better** omwellhe

between [bɪ'twiːn] *prep* yntra

beyond [bɪ'jɔnd] *prep* dres

bib ['bɪb] *n* bronnlenn *f* +ow

bicycle ['baɪsɪkl] *n* diwros *f* +ow

big ['bɪg] *adj* bras

bilingual [baɪ'lɪŋgwəl] *adj* diwyethek

bill ['bɪl] *n (financial)* reken *m* reknow

billion ['bɪljən] *n* bilvil

bind ['baɪnd] *v* kelmi

binoculars [bɪ'nɔkjʊləz] *pl* diwlagatell *f* +ow

biological [ˌbaɪəʊ'lɔdʒɪkl] *adj* bywoniethel

birch-tree [ˌbətʃ'triː] *n* besowenn *f* +ow, besow *coll*

bird ['bɜːd] *n* edhen *f* ydhyn

birth ['bɜːθ] *n* dineythyans *m* +ow, genesigeth *f* +ow;

give birth dineythi

birthday ['bɜːθdeɪ] *n* penn-bloedh *m* pennow-bloedh

biscuit ['bɪskɪt] *n* tesenn gales *f* tesennow kales

bishop ['bɪʃəp] *n* epskop *m* epskobow

bit ['bɪt] *n* tamm *m* temmyn, darn *m* +ow

bite ['baɪt] *n* brath *m* +ow: *v* dynsel, bratha

bitter ['bɪtər] *adj* hwerow

black ['blak] *adj* du

blackbird ['blakbɜːd] *n* molgh-dhu *f* molghi-du

blacksmith ['blaksmɪθ] *n* gov *m* +yon

blade ['bleɪd] *n* lown *m* +yow

blame ['bleɪm] *n* blam *m* +ys, kabel *m*: *v* blamya, kabla

blanket ['blaŋkɪt] *n* pallenn *f* +ow

blast ['blɑːst] *v (of wind)* hwytha

bleed ['bliːd] *v* goesa

bless ['bles] *v* benniga

blessing ['blesɪŋ] *n* bennath *f* +ow

blind ['blaɪnd] *adj* dall: *v* dallhe, dalla

blink ['blɪŋk] *v* dewwynkya

blister ['blɪstər] *n* bothell *f* +ow, gusigenn *f* +ow

block ['blɔk] *v* lettya

blood ['blʌd] *n* goes *m*

blow ['bləʊ] *n* boemmenn *f* +ow, hwaff *m* +ys: *v (wind)* hwytha

blue ['bluː] *adj* glas

boar ['bɔːr] *n* torgh *m* +es

board ['bɔːd] *n (group of people)* kesva *f* +ow; *(timber)* astell *f* estyll, plank *m* plenkys +ow; **diving board** sedhbrenn *m* +yer

boat ['bəʊt] *n* skath *f* +ow; **fishing boat** kok *m* kokow

Bodmin ['bɒdmɪn] *place* Bosvenegh

body ['bɔdi] *n* korf *m* +ow

bog ['bɔg] *n* keunegenn *f* +ow

boil ['bɔɪl] *v* bryjyon

boiler ['bɔɪləʳ] *n* *(for domestic heating)* forn-doemma *f* fornow-toemma

bold ['bəʊld] *adj* hardh, bold

bomb ['bɔm] *n* tanbellenn *f* +ow: *v* tanbellenna

bombard ['bɔmbard] *n* *(musical instrument)* bombard *f* +ow

bond ['bɔnd] *n* *(link)* syg *f* +ow

bone ['bəʊn] *n* askorn *m* eskern

bonfire ['bɔnfaɪəʳ] *n* tanses *m* +yow

bonnet ['bɔnɪt] *n* kogh *m* +ow

book ['bʊk] *n* lyver *m* lyvrow

bookshop ['bʊkʃɔp] *n* lyverji *m* +ow

boot ['buːt] *n* *(footwear)* botasenn *f* +ow

border ['bɔːdəʳ] *n* or *f* +yon, amal *m* emlow

bore ['bɔːʳ] *v* tardra; **bore holes** telli

born ['bɔːn] *adj* genys

borrow ['bɔrəʊ] *v* chevisya

Bosnia-Herzegovina ['bɔznɪəˌheərtsəgəˈviːnə] *place* Bosni

boss ['bɔs] *n* *(employer)* arvethor *m* +yon

both ['bəʊθ] *adj (f.)* an dhiw, an eyl ha'y ben; **both of you** agas diw; *(m.)* an dhew, an eyl ha'y gila; **both of you** agas dew

bother ['bɔðəʳ] *v* ankombra, trobla

bottle ['bɔtl] *n* botell *m* +ow

bottom ['bɔtəm] *n* goeles *m* +ow

bout ['baʊt] *n* fytt *m* +ys +ow

bow ['bəʊ] *n* *(arc)* gwarak *f* -egow

bow ['baʊ] *v* omblegya

bowels ['baʊəlz] *n* kolodhyon *coll* +enn

bowl ['bəʊl] *n* bolla *m* bollow bollys

box ['bɒks] *n (container)* kist *f* +yow; *(tree)* boks *m* byksyn

boy ['bɔɪ] *n* maw *m*

bra ['brɑː] *n* diwvronner *m* +yow

bracelet ['breɪslɪt] *n* breghellik *m* -igow

braggart ['bragət] *n* braggyer *m* +s

bragging ['bragɪŋ] *n* braggyans *m*

brake ['breɪk] *n (curb)* fronn *f* +ow

brambles ['bramblz] *plur* spedhas *coll* +enn

branch ['brɑːntʃ] *n* skorr *m* +ow, skorrenn *f* +ow

Brazil [brəˈzɪl] *place* Brazil

brave ['breɪv] *adj* kolonnek

bread ['bred] *n* bara *m*

break ['breɪk] *v* terri; *(waves, day)* tardha

breakfast ['brekfəst] *n* hansel *m* +yow

breast ['brest] *n* bronn *f* +ow, diwvronn *dual*

breath ['breθ] *n* anall *f*, *(one breath)* hwyth *m* +ow

breathe ['briːð] *v* anella

breeze ['briːz] *n* awel glor *f* awelyow klor

Breton ['bretən] *n (man)* Breton *m* +yon; *(woman)* Bretones *f* +ow; **Breton speaker** Bretoneger *m* -oryon: *adj* bretonek *m*; **Breton language** Bretonek *m*

brick ['brɪk] *n* brykk *m* +ow

bridge ['brɪdʒ] *n* pons *m* +yow

brigade [brɪˈɡeɪd] *n* brigadenn *f* +ow

brightness ['braɪtnɪs] *n* splannder *m* +yow, golewder *m* +yow

bring ['brɪŋ] *v* dri, kyrghes

Britain ['brɪtn] *place* Breten; **Great Britain** Breten Veur

British ['brɪtɪʃ] *adj* Predennek

182

Briton ['brɪtn] *n* Brython *m* +yon

Brittany ['brɪtəni] *place* Breten Vyghan

broad ['brɔːd] *adj* ledan, efan

broken ['brəʊkən] *adj* terrys, bryw

brooch ['brəʊtʃ] *n* brocha *m* brochys

brook ['brʊk] *n* gover *m* +ow, stredh *f* +ow

broom ['bruːm] *n* (implement) skubell *f* +ow; (plant in general) banadhel *coll* banadhlenn

brother ['brʌðər] *n* broder *m* breder

brother-in-law [ˌbrʌðərɪn'lɑː] *n* broder dre lagha *m* breder dre lagha

brown ['braʊn] *adj* **light brown** gell; **dark brown** gorm

brush ['brʌʃ] *n* skubyllenn *f* +ow; **pastry brush** skubyllenn-bast *f* skubyllennow past: *v* skuba

brusque ['bruːsk] *adj* tromm

bubble ['bʌbl] *n* hwythenn *f* +ow

buck ['bʌk] *n* (male goat) bogh *m* +es

bucket ['bʌkɪt] *n* kelorn *m* kelern

bud ['bʌd] *n* egin *m* +yow

buff ['bʌf] *n* (colour) liw bual *m*

bug ['bʌg] *n* teurogenn *f* +ow, teurek *coll*

build ['bɪld] *v* (trans.) drehevel

building ['bɪldɪŋ] *n* drehevyans *m* +ow

bulb ['bʌlb] *n* (for lamp) bollenn *f* +ow

Bulgaria [bʌl'geəriə] *place* Bulgari

Bulgarian [bʌl'geəriən] *adj* bulgarek; **Bulgarian language** Bulgarek *m*

bull ['bʊl] *n* tarow *m* terewi

bullet ['bʊlɪt] *n* pellenn *f* +ow

bump ['bʌmp] *n* bonk *m* +ys

bunch ['bʌntʃ] *n* gronn *m* +ow, tyskenn *f* +ow

burden ['bɜːdn] *n* begh *m* +yow, pusorn *m* +ow

burgess ['bɜːdʒes] *n* burjes *m* burjysi

burn ['bɜːn] *v* leski, dewi

burrow ['bʌrəʊ] *n* dordoll *m* dordell

burst ['bɜːst] *v* tardha

bury ['beri] *v* ynkleudhyas

bus ['bʌs] *n* kyttrin *m* +yow; **bus stop** savla-kyttrin *m* savleow-k.

business ['bɪznɪs] *n* negys *m* +yow

but ['bʌt] *conj* mes

butcher ['bʊtʃər] *n* kiger *m* -oryon; **pork butcher** kiger mogh *m* kigoryon vogh

butchery ['bʊtʃəri] *n (trade)* kigereth *f*

butter ['bʌtər] *n* amanynn *m* +ow: *v* amanynna

butterfly ['bʌtəflaɪ] *n* tykki-Duw *f* tykkies-Duw

buttock ['bʌtək] *n* pedrenn *f* +ow, diwbedrenn *dual*

button ['bʌtn] *n* boton *m* +yow: *v* botona

buy ['baɪ] *v* prena

by [baɪ] *prep* gans, ryb, er; **by Christmas** erbynn Nadelik; **two by two** dew ha dew

C

cabin ['kabɪn] *n* krowji *m* +ow

cage ['keɪdʒ] *n* kowell *m* +ow

cake ['keɪk] *n* tesenn *f* +ow

calculate ['kalkjʊleɪt] *v* kalkya, rekna

calculation [ˌkalkjʊ'leɪʃən] *n (an individual)* kalkyans *m* +ow; *(as a science)* kalkonieth *f*

calculator ['kalkjʊleɪtər] *n (instrument)* reknell *f* +ow

calendar ['kalɪndər] *n (book)* lyver-dydhyow *m* lyvrow-dydhyow

calf ['kɑːf] *n (animal)* leugh *m* +i; *(of leg)* bil an arr *m* bilyow an arr

call ['kɔːl] *n* galow *m* +yow: *v* gelwel

calm ['kɑːm] *n* kalmynsi *m: adj* hebask: *v* hebaskhe; **calm down** omdhiserri

Camborne ['kambɔːn] *place* Kammbronn

camel ['kaməl] *n* kowrvargh *m* -vergh

camera ['kamrə] *n* kamera *m* +s

camp ['kamp] *n* kamp *m* +ow +ys: *v* kampya

camp-site ['kampsaɪt] *n* kampva *f* +ow

Canada ['kanədə] *place* Kanada

Canadian [kə'neɪdiən] *adj* Kanadek

cancel ['kansəl] *v* dilea

cancer ['kansəʳ] *n* kanker *m* kankres

candidate ['kandɪdeɪt] *n* ombrofyer *m* -oryon

candle ['kandl] *n* kantol *f* +yow

cannon ['kanən] *n* kanon *m* +yow

canteen [kan'tiːn] *n* bywdern *m* +ow

cap ['kap] *n* kappa *m* kappow

capable ['keɪpəbl] *adj* abel

capital ['kapɪtl] *n (city)* pennsita *f* -sitys

Capricorn ['kaprɪkɔːn] *name* An Aver

captain ['kaptɪn] *n* kapten *m* +yon

car ['kɑːʳ] *n* karr *m* kerri

caravan ['karavan] *n* karavan *m* +s

card ['kɑːd] *n* kartenn *f* +ow

cardigan ['kɑːdɪgən] *n* kardigan *m* +s

care ['keəʳ] *n (keeping)* gwith *m* +yow; *(responsibility)* charj *m* +ys; *(worry)* govison *m*; *(solicitude)* rach *m*; **care home** chi gwith

carefree ['keəfriː] *adj* digeudh

careful ['keəfʌl] *adj* prederus

caress [kə'res] *v* chershya

185

car-park ['kɑːˈpɑːk] *n* park-kerri *m* parkow-k.

carpet ['kɑːpɪt] *n* leurlenn *f* +ow

carriage ['karɪdʒ] *n (vehicle)* kocha *m* kochow kochys

carry ['kari] *v* degi, doen

carve ['kɑːv] *v* kervya

case ['keɪs] *n* kas *m* +ys; *(box)* trog *m* +ow

cash ['kaʃ] *n* mona *coll*

casket ['kɑːskɪt] *n* kofrynn *m* +ow

cast ['kɑːst] *v* deghesi, tewlel

castle ['kɑːsl] *n* kastell *m* kastylli kestell

cat ['kat] *n* kath *f* kathes

Catalan ['katəlan] *adj* katalunek; **Catalan language** Katalunek *m*

Catalonia ['katələʊnjə] *place* Kataluni

catch ['katʃ] *v* kachya

category ['katəgəri] *n* klass *m* +ow

cathedral [kəˈθiːdrəl] *n* penneglos *f* +yow

Catholic ['kaθəlɪk] *adj* katholik

cattle ['katl] chatel *coll* +enn; **horned cattle** gwarthek *coll*

cauldron ['kɔːldrən] *n* chek *m* +ys

cauliflower ['kɔlɪˌflaʊə] *n* kowlvleujenn *f* +ow

cause ['kɔːz] *n* acheson *m* +yow +ys, kaws *m* +ys

cease ['siːs] *v* hedhi

ceilidh ['keɪli] *n* troylh *m* +yow

ceiling ['siːlɪŋ] *n* nen *m* +yow

celebrate ['selɪbreɪt] *v* solempnya

cellar ['selər] *n* dorgell *f* +ow, selder *m* +yow

Celt ['kelt] *n* Kelt *m* +yon

Celtic ['keltɪk] *adj* keltek; **Celtic language** Keltek *m*

cement [sɪˈment] *n* siment *m* +ys

cemetery ['semɪtri] *n* korflann *f* +ow

centralize ['sentrəleiz] *v* kresenni

centre ['sentər] *n* (*building*) kresenn *f* +ow, kresva *f* +ow; (*in sport*) kreswas *m* -wesyon; (*middle*) kres *m* +yow: *v* kresenni

century ['sentʃʊri] *n* kansblydhen *f* kansblydhynyow

cereal ['sıərıəl] *n* greunvoes *m* +ow

ceremony ['serıməni] *n* solempnita *m* -nytys

certain ['sɜːtn] *adj* kowgans, sertan

certainly ['sɜːtnli] *adv* devri, heb wow

certainty ['sɜːtnti] *n* kowganseth *f* +ow

certificate [sə'tıfıkət] *n* testskrif *m* +ow

chain ['tʃeın] *n* kadon *f* +yow

chair ['tʃeər] *n* kador *f* +yow

chalk ['tʃɔːk] *n* krey *m* +ow

champion ['tʃampjən] *n* kampyer *m* -oryon

chance ['tʃɑːns] *n* chons *m* +yow; **by chance** dre happ

change ['tʃeındʒ] *n* (*money*) mona *coll*; **small change** mona munys: *v* chanjya

channel ['tʃanl] *n* kanel *f* kanolyow; **the English Channel** An Chanel

chapel ['tʃapl] *n* chapel *m* +yow

chapter ['tʃaptər] *n* chaptra *m* chapters

character ['karəktər] *n* gnas *f* +ow

charge ['tʃɑːdʒ] *n* (*responsibility*) charj *m* +ys: *v* (*e.g. a battery*) karga

chatter ['tʃatər] *n* klapp *m*: *v* klappya

chauffeur ['ʃəʊfɜːr] *n* lewyas *m* -ysi

cheap ['tʃiːp] *adj* iselgostek

cheat ['tʃiːt] *n* hyger *m* -oryon: *v* hyga, toella

check ['tʃek] *v* chekkya

cheek ['tʃiːk] *n* (*Anat.*) bogh *f* +ow, diwvogh *dual*; (*rudeness*) tonteth *f*

187

cheese ['tʃiːz] *n* keus *m* +yow
chemical ['kemɪkl] *adj* kymyk: *n* kymygenn *f* +ow
chemist ['kemɪst] *n* feryl *m* +yow
chemistry ['kemɪstri] *n* kymygieth *f*
cheque ['tʃek] *n* chekkenn *f* +ow
chess ['tʃes] *n* goedhboell *m*
chest ['tʃest] *n (container)* argh *f* +ow
chestnut ['tʃestnʌt] *n* kestenenn *f* +ow, kesten *coll*
chew ['tʃuː] *v* knias
chick ['tʃɪk] *n* ydhnik *m* -igow
chicken ['tʃɪkɪn] *n* yerik *f* -igow
child ['tʃaɪld] *n* flogh *m* fleghes
childhood ['tʃaɪldhʊd] *n* flogholeth *f*
chimney ['tʃɪmni] *n* chymbla *m* chymblys
chin ['tʃɪn] *n* elgeth *f* +yow
China ['tʃaɪnə] *place* China
Chinese [ˌtʃaɪˈniːz] *adj* chinek; **Chinese language**
  Chinek *m*
chocolate ['tʃɔkələt] *n* choklet *coll* +enn
choice ['tʃɔɪs] *n* dewis *m* +yow
choke ['tʃəʊk] *v* moga, taga
choose ['tʃuːz] *v* dewis
chough ['tʃʌf] *n* palores *f* +ow
Christ ['kraɪst] *name* Krist
Christendom ['krɪʃndəm] *n* Kristonoleth *f*
Christian ['krɪstʃən] *n (male)* Kristyon *m* Kristonyon:
  adj Kristyon *m* Kristonyon
Christianity [ˌkrɪstiˈanɪti] *n* Kristonedh *m*
Christmas ['krɪsməs] *n* Nadelik *m* -igow; **Merry
  Christmas!** Nadelik Lowen!
church ['tʃɜːtʃ] *n* eglos *f* +yow
churchtown ['tʃɜːtʃtaʊn] *n* treveglos *f* +yow
churchyard ['tʃɜːtʃjɑːd] *n* korflann *f* +ow

cider ['saɪdər] *n* sider *m*

circle ['sɜːkl] *n* kylgh *m* +yow

circumference [sə'kʌmfərəns] *n* krennhys *m* +ow

circumflex ['sɜːkəmfleks] *n (diacritic)* ughverk to *m* -verkow to

circus ['sɜːkəs] *n (show)* syrk *m* +ow

city ['sɪti] *n* sita *f* sitys; **city hall** hel an sita

clap ['klap] *v* **clap hands** takya

class ['klɑːs] *n* klass *m* +ow; **social class** renkas *m* +ow

classical ['klasɪkl] *adj* klassek

classification [ˌklasɪfɪ'keɪʃən] *n* klassans *m* +ow

claw ['klɔː] *n* ewin *m* +es; *(of crab)* paw *f* +yow, diwbaw *dual*

clay ['kleɪ] *n* pri *m* +ow

clean ['kliːn] *adj* glan: *v* glanhe

clear ['klɪər] *adj* kler: *v* klerhe

clergy ['klɜːdʒi] *n* klerji *coll*

clever ['klevər] *adj* konnyk

click ['klɪk] *v* klykkya

cliff ['klɪf] *n* als *f* +yow, kleger *m* +ow

climate ['klaɪmɪt] *n* hin *f* +yow

climb ['klaɪm] *v* krambla, yskynna

cling ['klɪŋ] *v* serghi, glena

clinic ['klɪnɪk] *n* medhegva *f* +ow

clip ['klɪp] *n* **paper-clip** synsell paper

cloakroom ['kləʊkrʊm] *n* gwiskva *f* +ow

clock ['klɒk] *n* klokk *m* +ow

clog ['klɒg] *n* eskis prenn *m* -yow prenn

close ['kləʊz] *v* degea

closed ['kləʊzd] *adj* deges, klos

cloth ['klɒθ] *n (individual)* kweth *f* +ow; *(material)* pann *m* +ow

clothes [ˈkləʊðz] *n* dillas *coll* +enn

clothing [ˈkləʊðɪŋ] *n* dillas *coll* +enn

cloudy [ˈklaʊdi] *adj* kommolek

clover [ˈkləʊvə] *n* mellyon *coll* +enn

coach [ˈkəʊtʃ] *n (vehicle)* kocha *m* kochow

coal [ˈkəʊl] *n (in bulk)* glow *coll* +enn

coast [ˈkəʊst] *n* arvor *m* +yow

coat [ˈkəʊt] *n* kota *m* kotow; *(of paint)* gwiskas *m* +ow

coating *n* gwiskas *m* +ow

cock [ˈkɒk] *n (male bird)* kulyek *m* -ogyon

cockerel [ˈkɒkərəl] *n* kulyek *m* -ogyon

code *n* kodenn *f* +ow

coffee [ˈkɒfi] *n* koffi *m* +ow

coffin [ˈkɒfɪn] *n* geler *f* +yow

cohabit [kəʊˈhabɪt] *v* kesvywa

coin [ˈkɔɪn] *n* bath *m* +ow

col [ˈkɒl] *n* bolgh *m* +ow

cold [ˈkəʊld] *adj* yeyn

collaborate [kəˈlabəreɪt] *v* kesoberi

collar [ˈkɒlər] *n* kolorenn *f* +ow

collect [kəˈlekt] *v (intrans.)* omguntell; *(trans.)* kuntell

collection [kəˈlekʃən] *n* kuntell *m* +ow

collective [kəˈlektɪv] *adj* kuntellek

college [ˈkɒlɪdʒ] *n* kollji *m* +ow

colony [ˈkɒləni] *n* trevesigeth *f* +ow

colour [ˈkʌlər] *n* liw *m* liwyow: *v* liwa

colt [ˈkɒlt] *n* ebel *m* ebeli

column [ˈkɒləm] *n* koloven *f* +yow

comb [ˈkəʊm] *n* krib *f* +ow: *v* kribas

come [ˈkʌm] *v* dos, dones; **come back** dehweles; **come in!** deus a-ji!

comet [ˈkɒmɪt] *n* sterenn lostek *f* sterennow lostek

comfort ['kʌmfət] *n (ease)* cs *m; (spiritual)* konfort *m* +s: *v* konfortya

comfortable ['kʌmfətəbl] *adj* attes

command [kə'mɑːnd] *n* gorhemmynn *m* +ow: *v* gorhemmynna

commission [kə'mɪʃən] *n (group of persons)* desedhek *m* desedhogow; *(money)* rannles *m* +ow

commodities [kə'mɔdɪtiz] *plur* gwara *coll* gwarenn

common ['kɔmən] *adj* kemmyn

compact ['kɔmpakt] *adj* kewask

companion [kəm'panjən] *n (female)* kowethes *f* +ow; *(male)* koweth *m* +a

company ['kʌmpəni] *n* kowethyans *m* +ow

compare [kəm'peəʳ] *v* keheveli

compel [kəm'pel] *v* kompella

compensate ['kɔmpənseɪt] *v* astiveri

compensation [kɔmpən'seɪʃən] *n* astiveryans *m* +ow

competent ['kɔmpɪtənt] *adj* abel

competition [ˌkɔmpɪ'tɪʃən] *n* kesstrif *m* +ow

competitor [kəm'petɪtəʳ] *n* kesstrivor *m* +yon

complain [kəm'pleɪn] *v* krodhvolas

complaint [kəm'pleɪnt] *n* krodhvol *m* +yow; *(medical)* grevons *m* +ys

complete [kəm'pliːt] *adj* kowal: *v* kowlwul

completely [kəm'pliːtli] *adv* yn tien, glan

complexion [kəm'plekʃən] *n* fisment *m* fismens

complicated ['kɔmplɪkeɪtɪd] *adj* komplek

computer [kəm'pjuːtəʳ] *n* jynn-amontya *m* jynnow-amontya; amontyell *f* +ow; **computer science** amontieth *f* +ow; **computer scientist** amontydh *m* +yon

computing [kəm'pjuːtɪŋ] *n* amontieth *f*

comrade ['kɔmreɪd] *n* kothman *m* +s, mata *m* matys

conceal [kən'siːl] *v* keles, kudha
conceive [kən'siːv] *v* konsevya
concerning [kən'sɜːnɪŋ] *prep* a-dro dhe, yn kever
conclusion [kən'kluːʒən] *n* gordhiwedh *m* +ow
concrete ['kɔŋkriːt] *n* kentevynn *m* +ow
condemn [kən'dem] *v* dampnya
condition [kən'dɪʃən] *n* studh *m* +yow
confess [kən'fes] *v* avowa; *(of sins)* yes
confidence ['kɔnfɪdəns] *n* fydhyans *m*, kyfyans *m*
conjunction [kən'dʒʌŋkʃən] *n* kevrenn *f* +ow
connect [kə'nekt] *v* junya
consent [kən'sent] *n* bodh *m* +ow
consider [kən'sɪdər] *v* prederi
consolation [ˌkɔnsə'leɪʃən] *n* konfort *m* +s
console ['kɔnsəʊl] *v* konfortya
constabulary [kən'stabjʊləri] *n* kreslu *m* +yow
consumer [kən'sjuːmər] *n* devnydhyer *m* -yoryon
contact ['kɔntakt] *n* kestav *m* +ow: *v* kestava
contain [kən'teɪn] *v* yssynsi
contaminate [kən'tamɪneɪt] *v* mostya
contemporary [kən'tempərəri] *adj* kevoes
contempt [kən'tempt] *n* bismer *m*
continent ['kɔntɪnənt] *n* brastir *m* +yow
continuation [kənˌtɪnjʊ'eɪʃən] *n* pesyans *m* +ow
continue [kən'tɪnjuː] *v* pesya
contract ['kɔntrakt] *n* ambos *m* +ow
contrary ['kɔntrəri] *adj* gorth, konter
control [kən'trəʊl] *n* maystri *m*
conversation [ˌkɔnvə'seɪʃən] *n* keskows *m* +ow
converse [kən'vɜːs] *v (speech)* keskewsel
cook ['kʊk] *n* keginer *m* -oryon; *(female)* koges *f* +ow;
    (male) kog *m* +ow: *v* kegina
cooked ['kʊkt] *adj* keginys

192

cooker ['kʊkə^r] *n* kogforn *f* +ow
cookery ['kʊkəri] *n* keginieth *f*
co-operate [kəʊ'ɒpəreɪt] *v* kesoberi
copper ['kɒpə^r] *n* kober *m*
copy ['kɒpi] *n* dasskrif *m* +ow: *v* dasskrifa
cord ['kɔːd] *n* kordenn *f* kerdyn
cork ['kɔːk] *n* *(stopper)* korkynn *m* +ow
corkscrew ['kɔːkskruː] *n* alhwedh-korkynn *m* alhwedhow-korkynn
cormorant ['kɔːmərənt] *n* morvran *f* -vrini
corner ['kɔːnə^r] *n* korn *m* kernow, kornell *f* +ow
Cornish ['kɔːnɪʃ] *n* *(language)* Kernewek *m*: *adj* kernewek
Cornishman ['kɔːnɪʃmən] *n* Kernow *m* +yon
Cornishwoman ['kɔːnɪʃwʊmən] *n* Kernewes *f* +ow
Cornwall ['kɔːnwəl] *place* Kernow
corporal ['kɔːpərəl] *n* korporal *m* +s
corpse ['kɔːps] *n* korf marow *m* +ow
correct [kə'rekt] *adj* ewn: *v* ewnhe
corridor ['kɒridə^r] *n* tremen *m* +yow
corrupt [kə'rʌpt] *adj* podrek
Corsica ['kɔːsɪkə] *place* Korsika
Corsican ['kɔːsɪkən] *adj* korsek; **Corsican language** Korsek *m*
cost ['kɒst] *n* kost *m* +ow: *v* kostya
costly ['kɒstli] *adj* ker, kostek
cotton ['kɒtən] *n* koton *m* -enyow
cough ['kɒf] *n* pas *m* +ow: *v* pasa
council ['kaʊnsl] *n* konsel *m* +yow
count ['kaʊnt] *n* *(census)* niveryans *m* +ow; *(noble)* yurl *m* +ys: *v* nivera
country ['kʌntri] *n* bro *f* +yow, pow *m* +yow, gwlas *f* +ow; **in the country** y'n pow

couple ['kʌpl] *n* kopel *m* koplow; *(people)* dewdhen *m*: *v* kopla

courage ['kʌrɪdʒ] *n* kolonnekter *m*

course ['kɔːs] *(route)* *n* res *m* +ow

cousin ['kʌzn] *n (female)* keniterow *f* keniterwi; *(male)* kenderow *m* kenderwi

cover ['kʌvəʳ] *n* gorher *m* +yow: *v* gorheri

cow ['kaʊ] *n* bugh *f* +es

coward ['kaʊəd] *n* ownek *m* ownogyon

cower ['kaʊəʳ] *v* plattya

cowshed ['kaʊʃed] *n* bowji *m* +ow

crab ['krab] *n* kanker *m* kankres

crack ['krak] *n* krakk *m* +ys: *v* krakkya

cracked ['krakt] *adj* trogh, felsys

cradle ['kreɪdl] *n* kowell lesk *m* kowellow lesk

cramp ['kramp] *n* godramm *m* +ow

crane ['kreɪn] *n* garan *f* +es

crawl ['krɔːl] *v* kramya

cream ['kriːm] *n* dyenn *m* +ow

create [kriːˈeɪt] *v* gwruthyl

creep ['kriːp] *v* kramya

crew ['kruː] *n* mayni *m* +ow

crime ['kraɪm] *n* drogober *m* +ow, galweyth *m* +yow

criminal ['krɪmɪnl] *n* drogoberer *m* -oryon, gal *m* +yon: *adj* galweythel

crisis ['kraɪsɪs] *n* barras *m* +ow

criticize ['krɪtɪsaɪz] *v* arvreusi

Croat ['krəʊat] *n* Kroat *m* +yon

Croatia [krəʊˈeɪʃə] *place* Kroati

Croatian [krəʊˈeɪʃən] *adj* kroatek; **Croatian language** Kroatek *m*

crocodile ['krɒkədaɪl] *n* krokodil *m* +es

crooked ['krʊkɪd] *adj* kamm

crop [ˈkrɔp] *n* trevas *f* +ow

cross [ˈkrɔs] *n* krows *f* +yow: *adj* serrys: *v* treusi

crossing [ˈkrɔsɪŋ] *n* treusva *f* +ow

crossroads [ˈkrɔsrəʊdz] *n* krowsfordh *f* +ow

crow [ˈkrəʊ] *n* bran *f* brini

crowd [ˈkraʊd] *n* bush *m* +ys

crown [ˈkraʊn] *n* kurun *f* +yow: *v* kuruna

cruel [ˈkrʊəl] *adj* fell, tynn

cruise [ˈkruːz] *n* krowsvyaj *m* +yow

crumb [ˈkrʌm] *n (of loaf)* hwigenn *f*

crush [ˈkrʌʃ] *v* skwattya, brywi

crutch [ˈkrʌtʃ] *n* kroch *m* +ow +ys; **pair of crutches** dewgroch *dual*

cry [ˈkraɪ] *n* kri *m* +ow: *v* kria

cube [ˈkjuːb] *n* kub *m* +ow

cultivate [ˈkʌltɪveɪt] *v (crops)* gonis

cultural [ˈkʌltʃərəl] *adj* gonisogethel

culture [ˈkʌltʃər] *n* gonisogeth *f* +ow, megyans *m* +ow

cup [ˈkʌp] *n* hanaf *m* +ow

cupboard [ˈkʌbəd] *n* amari *m* +ow +s

cure [ˈkjʊər] *v* yaghhe

cured [ˈkjʊəd] *adj* yaghhes

curly [ˈkɜːli] *adj* krullys

current [ˈkʌrənt] *n (flow)* fros *m* +ow

curtain [ˈkɜːtn] *n* kroglenn *f* +ow

curved [ˈkɜːvd] *adj* kromm

cushion [ˈkʊʃən] *n* pluvek *f* pluvogow

custody [ˈkʌstədi] *n* gwith *m*

custom [ˈkʌstəm] *n* gis *m* +yow, usadow *m* +yow

customs [ˈkʌstəmz] *n* **customs officer** tollwas *m* -wesyon

cut [ˈkʌt] *n* **short cut** skochfordh *f* +ow *v* treghi

cylinder ['sɪlɪndər] *n* hirgrennenn *f* +ow
Cypriot ['sɪprɪət] *n* Kobrynyser *m* -oryon
Cyprus ['saɪprəs] *place* Kobrynys
Czech ['tʃek] *adj* chekk; **Czech language** Chekk
   m; **Czech Republic** Repoblek Chekk

D

dad ['dad] *n* tasik *m* -igyon
daffodil ['dafədɪl] *n* lili Gorawys *f* lilis Korawys
daily ['deɪlɪ] *adj* pub-dydhyek
dairy ['deərɪ] *n* le'ti *m* +ow
daisy ['deɪzɪ] *n* kaja *f* kajow
dam ['dam] *n* arge *m* +ow
damage ['damɪdʒ] *n* kisyans *m* +ow: *v* kisya
damaged ['damɪdʒd] *adj* kisys
damn ['dam] *v* dampnya
damned ['damd] *adj* dampnys
damp ['damp] *adj* gwlygh
dance ['dɑːns] *n* dons *m* +yow: *v* donsya
danger ['deɪndʒər] *n* peryll *m* +ow
dangerous ['deɪndʒərəs] *adj* deantell, peryllus
Danish ['deɪnɪʃ] *adj* danek; **Danish language**
   Danek *m*
dare ['deər] *v* bedha, lavasos; **I dare say** bedhav y di
daring ['deərɪŋ] *adj* bedhek, bold
dark ['dɑːk] *adj* tewal, tewl
darken ['dɑːkn] *v* tewlhe
darkness ['dɑːknɪs] *n* tewlder *m*, tewolgow *m*
darling ['dɑːlɪŋ] *n* keresik *m* -igyon: *adj* hwegoll
date ['deɪt] *n* (*specific day*) dydhyas *m* +ow

date [ˈdeɪt] *n (fruit)* datesenn *f* +ow, dates *coll*

datum [ˈdeɪtəm] *n* datum *m* data

daub [ˈdɔːb] *v* pria, mostya

daughter [ˈdɔːtər] *n* myrgh *f* myrghes

daughter-in-law [ˈdɔːtərɪnlɔː] *n* gohydh *f* +ow

dawn [ˈdɔːn] *n* bora *m* +ow

day [ˈdeɪ] *n* dydh *m* +yow; **duration of a day** dydhweyth *f* +yow; **next day** ternos *adv*

daylight [ˈdeɪlaɪt] *n* golow dydh

dead [ˈded] *adj* marow

deaf [ˈdef] *adj* bodhar

deafen [ˈdefn] *v* bodharhe

deafening [ˈdefnɪŋ] *adj* bodharel

dealer [ˈdiːlər] *n* marchont *m* -ons

dear [ˈdɪər] *adj* ker

death [ˈdeθ] *n* mernans *m* +ow; *(personified)* ankow *m*

debate [dɪˈbeɪt] *n* dadhelva *f* +ow: *v* dadhla

debt [ˈdet] *n* kendon *f* +ow

deceive [dɪˈsiːv] *v* toella

December [dɪˈsembər] *n* mis-Kevardhu *m* misyow-K.

decent [ˈdiːsnt] *adj* onest

decide [dɪˈsaɪd] *v* ervira

decision [dɪˈsɪʒn] *n* ervirans *m* +ow

deck [ˈdek] *n (of ship)* flour *m* +yow

deck-chair [ˈdektʃeər] *n* kador-dreth *f* kadoryow-treth

declare [dɪˈkleə] *v* disklerya

decline [dɪˈklaɪn] *v* nagha

decoder [dɪˈkəʊdər] *n* digodennell *f* +ow

decor [ˈdeɪkɔːr] *n* afinans *m* +ow

decorate [ˈdekəreɪt] *v* afina

decoration [ˌdekəˈreɪʃən] *n* afinans *m* +ow

deep ['diːp] *adj* down
deer ['dɪər] *n* karow *m* kerwys
defeat [dɪ'fiːt] *v* fetha: *n* fethans *m* +ow
defeated [dɪ'fiːtɪd] *adj* fethys
defect ['diːfekt] *n* defowt *m* +ow, gwall *m* +ow
defend [dɪ'fend] *v* defendya
defender [dɪ'fendər] *n* difennyas *m* -ysi
deferred [dɪ'fɜːd] *adj* delatys
deform [dɪ'fɔːm] *v* difurvya
degree [dɪ'griː] *n* gradh *m* +ow
delay [dɪ'leɪ] *n* ardak *m* -dagow: *v* delatya
delegate ['delɪgɪt] *n* kannas *f* +ow
delicate ['delɪkət] *adj* bleudh
delight [dɪ'laɪt] *n* delit *m* +ys
deliver [dɪ'lɪvər] *v* delivra
delivery [dɪ'lɪvəri] *n* livreson *m*
democrat ['deməkrat] *n* gweriniethor *m* +yon
demonstration [ˌdemən'streɪʃən] *n* *(show)* diskwedhyans *m* +ow
Denmark ['denmɑːk] *place* Danmark
denounce [dɪ'nəʊns] *v* kuhudha
dense ['dens] *adj (physically)* does
deny [dɪ'naɪ] *v* nagha
departure [dɪ'pɑːtʃər] *n* dibarth *f* +ow
depend ['dɪpend] *v*; **depend on** kregi war
descend [dɪ'send] *v* diyskynna
descent [dɪ'sent] *n* diyskynn *m* +ow
desert *n* difeyth *m* +yow
desiccated [ˌdesɪ'ketɪd] *adj* desyghys
desire [dɪ'zaɪər] *n* hwans *m* +ow: *v* desirya, hwansa
desk ['desk] *n* desk *m* +ys
dessert [dɪ'zɜːt] *n* melyssand *m* +ys
destroy [dɪ'strɔɪ] *v* distrui

destruction [dɪ'strʌkʃən] *n* distruyans *m*, terroes *m* +ow

detach [dɪ'tatʃ] *v* digelmi, distaga

detached [dɪ'tatʃt] *adj* distag

detail ['diːteɪl] *n* **details** manylyon

detergent [dɪ'tɜːdʒənt] *n* lin sebon *m* linyow s.

deteriorate [dɪ'tɪərɪəreɪt] *v* gwethhe

detest [dɪ'test] *v* kasa

detestable [dɪ'testəbl] *adj* kasadow

develop [dɪ'veləp] *v* displegya

devil ['devl] *n* dyowl *m* dywolow; **the devil** an jowl

Devon ['devn] *place* Dewnens

dew ['djuː] *n* gluth *m* +ow

diamond ['daɪəmənd] *n* adamant *m* +ow +ys

diarrhoea [ˌdaɪə'riːə] *n* skit *m* +ys

dice ['daɪs] *n* dis *m* +yow

dictionary ['dɪkʃənrɪ] *n* gerlyver *m* -lyvrow

diet ['daɪət] *n (as in "go on a diet")* rewl voes *f* rewlow boes

difference ['dɪfərəns] *n* dihevelepter *m* +yow, dyffrans *m* +ow

different ['dɪfrənt] *adj* dihaval

differentiate [ˌdɪfə'renʃɪeɪt] *v (maths.)* dyffransegi

difficult ['dɪfɪkəlt] *adj* kales

difficulty ['dɪfɪkəltɪ] *n* kaletter *m* +yow

dig ['dɪg] *v* palas; **dig a trench** kleudhya

dimension [dɪ'menʃən] *n* myns *m* +ow

dining-room ['daɪnɪŋrʊm] *n* stevell-dhybri *f* stevellow-dybri

dinner ['dɪnər] *n* kinyow *m* kinyewow; **late dinner** koen *f* +yow; **eat late dinner** koena *v*

dinosaur ['daɪnəsɔːr] *n* arghpedrevan *m* +es

direct [dɪ'rekt] *adj* syth: *v* brennya

direction [dɪ'rekʃən] *n (geog.)* tu *m* +yow; *(e.g. of a film)* routyans *m*

directly [dɪ'rektli] *adv* hware

director [dɪ'rektər] *n* lewydh *m* +yon

dirt ['dɜːt] *n* mostedhes *m*

dirty ['dɜːti] *adj* plos; **get dirty** plosegi: *v* mostya

disappear [ˌdɪsəpɪər] *v* vanshya

disappointed [ˌdɪsə'pɔɪntɪd] *adj* diswaytys

disaster [dɪ'zɑːstər] *n* terroes *m* terroesedhow

disconnect [ˌdɪskə'nektɪd] *v* disjunya

discover [dɪs'kʌvər] *v* diskudha

discuss [dɪs'kʌs] *v* dadhla

disdain [dɪs'deɪn] *n* fi: *v* fia

disease [dɪ'ziːz] *n* dises *m* +ys

disembark [ˌdɪsɪm'bɑːk] *v* dilestra

disentangle [ˌdɪsɪ'taŋgl] *v* digelmi

disguise [dɪs'gaɪz] *n* toellwisk *m* +ow: *v* toellwiska

disgust [dɪs'gʌst] *n* divlas *m* +ow

disgusting [dɪs'gʌstɪŋ] *adj* divlas

dish ['dɪʃ] *n (container)* skala *m* +ys; *(food)* sand *m* +ow

disobey [ˌdɪsə'beɪ] *v* disobaya

disorder [dɪs'ɔːdə] *n* deray *m* +s, disordyr *m*

dispatch [dɪs'patʃ] *v* dannvon

displace [dɪs'pleɪs] *v* removya, dilea

display [dɪ'spleɪ] *n* displetyans *m* +ow: *v* displetya

displease [dɪs'pliːz] *v* displesya

dissociate [dɪ'səʊʃieɪt] *v* digelmi

distance ['dɪstəns] *n* pellder *m* +yow

distinct [dɪ'stɪŋkt] *adj* diblans

distinguish [dɪ'stɪŋgwɪʃ] *v* dissernya

distracted [dɪs'traktɪd] *adj* distennys

distress [dɪ'stres] *n* reudh *m*: *v* reudhi

200

distribute [dɪs'trɪbjuːt] *v* lesranna

disturb [dɪs'tɜːb] *v* ankresya

disturbing [dɪs'tɜːbɪŋ] *adj* ankresus

ditch ['dɪtʃ] *n* kleudh *m* +yow, kleys *m* +yow

dive ['daɪv] *v* sedhi

diverse [daɪ'vɜːs] *adj* divers

divide [dɪ'vaɪd] *v* ranna

divorce [dɪ'vɔːs] *n* torrva dhemmedhyans *f* torrvaow demmedhyans

do ['duː] *v* gul, oberi

doctor ['dɒktəʳ] *n* medhek *m* medhogyon; *(title)* doktour *m* +s

document ['dɒkjument] *n* skrifenn *f* +ow

doe ['dəʊ] *n (female deer)* ewik *f* +ow

dog ['dɒg] *n* ki *m* keun

doll ['dɒl] *n* dolli *f* +ow

dolphin ['dɒlfɪn] *n* pyffyer *m* +s

domestic [də'mestɪk] *adj (of animal)* dov: servyas *m* -ysi

domesticate [də'mestɪkeɪt] *v* dovhe

domino ['dɒmɪnəʊ] *n* domino *m* +yow

donkey ['dɒŋki] *n* asen *m* -es

door ['dɔːʳ] *n* daras *m* +ow

dope ['dəʊp] *v* dopi

doping ['dəʊpɪŋ] *n* dopyans *m*

dormitory ['dɔːmətri] *n* hunva *f* +ow

dossier ['dɒsieɪ] *n* restrenn *f* +ow

double ['dʌbl] *adj* dewblek

doubt ['daʊt] *n* dout *m* +ys, mar *m*; **without doubt** heb mar: *v* doutya

dough ['dəʊ] *n* toes *m*

dove ['dʌv] *n* kolomm *f* kelemmi

downhearted [ˌdaʊn'hɑːtɪd] *adj* digolonnek

downland ['daʊnlənd] *n* goen *f* +yow

dozen ['dʌzn] *n* dewdhek *m* -egow

drag ['drag] *v* draylya

drain ['dreɪn] *v* sygera, bera

draught ['drɑːft] *n (wind)* skaphwyth *m* +ow

draw ['drɔː] *v (as in art)* delinya, tresa; *(drag)* tenna

drawer ['drɔːər] *n (furniture)* trog-tenna *m* trogow-tenna

drawing ['drɔːɪŋ] *n* delinyans *m* +ow, tresas *m* +ow

dream ['driːm] *n* hunros *m* +ow: *v* hunrosa

dreamer ['driːmər] *n* hunrosyer *m* -yoryon

dress ['dres] *n (garment)* pows *f* +yow; *(clothing)* gwisk *m*, dillas *coll* +enn: *v* gwiska

drink ['drɪŋk] *n* diwes *m* diwosow: *v* eva

drinker ['drɪŋkər] *n* evyas *m* -ysi

drip ['drɪp] *v* devera

drive ['draɪv] *v* lewya; **drive away** fesya: *n* rosva *f* +ow

driver ['draɪvər] *n* lewyer *m* -yoryon

drizzle ['drɪzl] *n* niwllaw *m*: *v* gul niwllaw

drop ['drɒp] *n* banna *m* bannaghow, lomm *m* +ow: *v* gasa dhe goedha, droppya

drown ['draʊn] *v* beudhi

druid ['druːɪd] *n* drewydh *m* +yon

drum ['drʌm] *n* tabour *m* +yow

drunk ['drʌŋk] *adj* medhow

drunkard ['drʌŋkəd] *n* penn-medhow *m* pennow-vedhow

dry ['draɪ] *adj* sygh: *v* sygha

duck ['dʌk] *n* hos *m* heyji

duke ['djuːk] *n* duk *m* +ys

dumb ['dʌm] *adj* avlavar

dune ['djuːn] *n* tewynn *m* +ow

202

during [ˈdjʊərɪŋ] *prep* dres
dusk [ˈdʌsk] *n* mo *m* +yow, tewlwolow *m*
dust [ˈdʌst] *n* doust *m*
dustbin [ˈdʌstbɪn] *n* atalgist *f* +yow
duty [ˈdjuːti] *n* dever *m* +ow; *(tax)* toll *f* +ow
duvet [ˈduːveɪ] *n* kolghes *f* +ow
dwarf [ˈdwɔːf] *n* korr *m* +yon
dynamism [daɪnəˈmɪzm] *n* dynamekter *m*

E

each [ˈiːtʃ] kettep, pub
eagerness [ˈiːgənes] *n* mall *m*
eagle [ˈiːgl] *n* er *m* +yon
ear [ˈɪər] *n* skovarn *f* skovornow, diwskovarn *dual*
early [ˈɜːli] *adv* a-brys, a-varr
earn [ˈɜːn] *v* dendil
ease [ˈiːz] *n* es *m*; **at ease** attes
Easter [ˈiːstər] *n* Pask *m* +ow
easy [ˈiːzi] *adj* es; **make easy** esya
eat [ˈiːt] *v* dybri; **eat lunch** livya
eater [ˈiːtər] *n* dybrer *m* -oryon
eccentric [ekˈsentrɪk] *adj (off-centre)* eskresek;
  (strange) koynt
echo [ˈekəʊ] *n* dasson *m* +yow: *v* dasseni
ecologist [ɪˈkɒlədʒɪst] *n* ekologydh *m* +yon
economics [ˌiːkəˈnɒmɪks] *plur* erbysieth *f*
economy [ɪˈkɒnəmi] *n (system)* erbysiedh *m* +ow
edge [ˈedʒ] *n* amal *m* emlow
education [ˌedʒʊˈkeɪʃən] *n* adhyskans *m* +ow
effect [ɪˈfekt] *n* effeyth *m* +yow

effective [ɪ'fektɪv] *adj* effeythus

egg ['eg] *n* oy *m* +ow

eight ['eɪt] *num* eth

eighteen [ˌeɪ'tiːn] *num* etek

eighty ['eɪti] *num* peswar-ugens

elbow ['elbəʊ] *n* elin *m* +yow, dewelin *dual*

election [ɪ'lekʃən] *n* etholans *m* +ow

electric [ɪ'lektrɪk] *adj* tredanek

electrician [ˌɪlek'trɪʃən] *n* tredaner *m* -oryon

electricity [ˌɪlek'trɪsəti] *n* tredan *m*

elephant ['elɪfənt] *n* olifans *m* +es

eleven [ɪ'levn] *num* unnek

elf ['elf] *n* korrigan *m* +es

eliminate [ɪ'lɪmɪneɪt] *v (exclude)* eskeas

eliminatory [ɪˌlɪmɪ'neɪtəri] *adj* eskeansek

elm-tree ['elmˌtriː] *n* elowenn *f* +ow, elow *coll*

else ['els] *adv* ken; **did you see anybody else?** a welsys denvyth ken?; **nothing else** travyth ken; **or else** poken

e-mail ['iːmeɪl] *n* e-bost *m* +yow

embankment [ɪm'baŋkmənt] *n* bour *m* +yow

embroider [ɪm'brɔɪdər] *v* brosya

embroidery [ɪm'brɔɪdəri] *n* brosweyth *m*

emergency [ɪ'mɜːdʒənsi] *n* goredhomm *m* +ow

emperor ['empərər] *n* emperour *m* +s

empire ['empaɪər] *n* empereureth *f* +ow

employee [ˌemplɔɪ'iː] *n* arvethesik *m* -igyon

employer [ɪm'plɔɪər] *n* arvethor *m* +yon

empty ['empti] *adj* gwag; *v* gwakhe

enclosure [ɪn'kləʊzjʊər] *n* kew *f* +yow

encourage [ɪn'kʌrɪdʒ] *v* kennertha

end ['end] *n* diwedh *m* +ow, fin *f* +yow, penn *m* +ow

endure [ɪn'djʊər] *v* perthi

enemy ['enəmi] *n* envi *m*, eskar *m* eskerens

energy ['enədʒi] *n* nerth *m* +ow

engine ['endʒin] *n* jynn *m* +ow +ys

engineer [ˌendʒɪ'nɪəʳ] *n* jynnweythor *m* +yon

England ['ɪŋglənd] *place* Pow Sows

English ['ɪŋglɪʃ] *adj* sowsnek; **English language** Sowsnek; **English Channel** An Chanel *place*

Englishman ['ɪŋglɪʃmən] *n* Sows *m* +on

Englishwoman ['ɪŋglɪʃwumən] *n* Sowses *f* +ow

enjoy [ɪn'dʒɔɪ] *v* **enjoy oneself** omlowenhe; **I enjoy** da yw genev

enlarge [ɪn'lɑːdʒ] *v* brashe

enough [ɪ'nʌf] *adj* lowr

ensign ['ensaɪn] *n (rank)* isleftenant *m* -ans

entertain [ˌentə'teɪn] *v* didhana

entirely [ɪn'taɪəʳli] *adv* yn tien

envelope ['envələʊp] *n* maylyer *m* +s

environment [ɪn'vaɪərənmənt] *n* kyrghynnedh *m* +ow

envoy ['envɔɪ] *n* kannas *f* +ow

envy ['envi] *n* avi *m* +ow

epoch ['iːpɔk] *n (instant of time)* prysweyth *f* +yow; *(period of time)* oesweyth *f* +yow

equal ['iːkwəl] *n* par *m* +ow: *adj* kehaval

equally ['iːkwəli] *adv* yn kehaval

equator [ɪ'kweɪtəʳ] *n* kehysedh *m* +ow

equip [ɪ'kwɪp] *v* darbari

equipment [ɪ'kwɪpmənt] *n* daffar *m*

era ['iərə] *n* oesweyth *f* +yow

eraser [ɪ'reɪzəʳ] *n* rutyer *m* +yow

error ['erəʳ] *n* kammweyth *m* +yow

escape [ɪ'skeɪp] *n* diank *m* +ow: *v* diank *m* +ow

escort [es'kɔːt] *v* hembronk

especially [ɪ'speʃli] *adv* yn arbennik, dres oll

essence ['esns] *n* sugen *m* +yow

establish [ɪ'stablɪʃ] *v* fondya

Estonia [es'təʊniə] *place* Estoni

Estonian [es'təʊniən] *adj* estonek

estuary ['estjuari] *n* heyl *m* +yow

Eurasia [jʊə'reɪʃə] *place* Eurasi

euro ['jʊərəʊ] *n (currency)* euro *m* +yow

Europe ['jʊərəp] *place* Europa

European [ˌjʊərə'piːən] *adj* europek

even ['iːvn] *adj* leven; *(of numbers)* parow

evening ['iːvnɪŋ] *n* gorthugher *m* +ow; **in the evening** gorthugherweyth *adv*; **this evening** haneth *adv*

event [ɪ'vent] *n* darvos *m* +ow

ever ['evər] *adv (in the past)* bythkweth; *(in the future)* byth, bykken; **Cornwall for ever!** Kernow bys vykken!

every ['evri] *adj* kettep, pub

everybody ['evriˌbɒdi] *pron* pubonan, pub huni

everyone ['evrɪwʌn] *pron* pubonan, pub huni

everything ['evrɪθɪŋ] *n* pup-tra *m*

everywhere ['evrɪweər] *adv* pub le

evidence ['evɪdəns] *n* dustuni *m* dustuniow

evil ['iːvl] *n* drog *m* +ow: *adj* tebel

exact [ɪg'zakt] *adj* kewar

exactly [ɪg'zaktli] *adv* poran

examination [ɪgˌzamɪ'neɪʃən] *n* apposyans *m* +ow

examine [ɪg'zamɪn] *v* hwithra; *(of knowledge)* apposya

example [ɪg'zɑːmpl] *n* ensampel *m* -plow -plys; **for example** rag ensampel

excellent ['eksəlnt] *adj* koeth

except [ɪkˈsept] *conj* marnas, saw

exchange [ɪksˈtʃeɪndʒ] *n* keschanj *m* +yow: *v* keschanjya

excited [ɪkˈsaɪtɪd] *adj* yntanys

exclude [ɪksˈkluːd] *v* eskeas

excuse [ɪkˈskjuːz] *n* digeredh *m* +ow: *v* digeredhi; **excuse me!** gav dhymm!

exercise [ˈeksəsaɪz] *n (piece of work)* oberenn *f* +ow

exhaust [ɪgˈzɔːst] *v* skwithhe

exhausted [ɪgˈzɔːstɪd] *adj* skwith-marow

exhibition [ˌeksɪˈbɪʃən] *n* diskwedhyans *m* +ow

exit [ˈeksɪt] *n* mesporth *m* +ow

expect [ɪkˈspekt] *v* gwaytyas

expedition [ˌekspɪˈdɪʃən] *n* eskerdh *m* +ow

expel [ɪkˈspel] *v* estewlel

expense [ɪkˈspens] *n* kost *m* +ow

expensive [ɪkˈspensɪv] *adj* ker, kostek

experience [ɪkˈspɪərɪəns] *n (something experienced)* perthyans *m* +ow

explain [ɪkˈspleɪn] *v* displegya

explode [ɪkˈspləʊd] *v* tardha

explosion [ɪkˈspləʊʒn] *n* tardh *m* +ow

export [ˈekspɔːt] *n* esporth *m* +ow: *v* esperthi

extend [ɪksˈtend] *v* ystynn

extension [ɪksˈtenʃən] *n* ystynnans *m* +ow

extensive [ɪksˈtensɪv] *adj* efan

extinguisher [ɪkˈstɪŋgwɪʃər] *n* difeudhell *f* +ow

extraordinary [ɪkˈstrɔːdnri] *adj* koynt, gorusadow

extravagant [ɪksˈtravəgənt] *adj* skoellyek

extremely [ɪkˈstriːmli] *adv* fest

eye [ˈaɪ] *n* lagas *m* +ow, dewlagas *dual*

eyelid [ˈaɪlɪd] *n* kroghen an lagas *f* kreghyn an lagas

F

fable ['feɪbl] *n* henhwedhel *m* +ow

face ['feɪs] *n* bejeth *f* +ow, fas *m* fasow; **face to face** orth ganow

facilitate [fa'sɪlɪteɪt] *v* esya

facing ['feɪsɪŋ] *prep* a-dal

fact ['fakt] *n* gwirenn *f* +ow

factor ['faktər] *n (maths.)* faktor *m* +yow

factory ['faktri] *n* gweythva *f* +ow

fail ['feɪl] *v* fyllel

failure ['feɪljʊər] *n* fall *m*

faint ['feɪnt] *n* klamder *m* +yow: *v* klamdera

fair ['feər] *adj (just)* ewn; *(beautiful)* teg

fairy ['feəri] *n* spyrys *m* +yon

faith ['feɪθ] *n* fydh *f* +yow

faithful ['feɪθfʊl] *adj* lel

falcon ['falkən] *n* falghun *m* +es

fall ['fɔːl] *n* koedh *m* +ow: *v* koedha

Falmouth ['falməθ] *place* Aberfala

false ['fɔːls] *adj* fals

fame ['feɪm] *n* ger-da *m* geryow-da

family ['faməli] *n* teylu *m* +yow

famous ['feɪməs] *adj* gerys-da

fantasy ['fantəsi] *n* fantasi *m* +s

far ['faː] *adj* pell

farce ['faːs] *n (theatre)* fars *m* +ys

farewell [ˌfeə'wel] *int* farwell

farm ['faːm] *n* bargen-tir *m* bargenyow-tir

farmer ['faːmər] *n* tiek *m* tiogow tiogyon

fart ['faːt] *n* bramm *m* bremmyn: *v* bramma

fashion ['faʃən] *n* gis *m* +yow: *v* shapya

fashionable ['faʃənəbl] *adj* herwydh an gis

fast [ˈfɑːst] *adj (fixed)* fast; *(speedy)* uskis

fasten [ˈfɑːsn] *v* fastya

fat [ˈfat] *n* blonek *m* -egow: *adj* tew

father [ˈfɑːðər] *n* tas *m* +ow

father-in-law [ˈfɑːðərɪnlɔː] *n* hwegron *m* +yon

fault [ˈfɔːlt] *n* fowt *m* +ys +ow; *(geological)* dorfols *m* +ow

favourable [ˈfeɪvərəbl] *adj* faveradow

fax [ˈfaks] *n (message)* pellskrifenn *f* +ow

fear [ˈfɪər] *n* own *m*

feather [ˈfeðər] *n* pluvenn *f* +ow, pluv *coll*

February [ˈfebruəri] *n* mis-Hwevrer *m* misyow-H.

feed [ˈfiːd] *v* maga, boesa

feel [ˈfiːl] *v* klewes

feeling [ˈfiːlɪŋ] *n* omglewans *m* +ow

fellow [ˈfeləʊ] *n* gwas *m* gwesyon

felt [ˈfelt] *n (material)* leuvbann *m* +ow

female [ˈfiːmeɪl] *adj* benow

feminine [ˈfemɪnɪn] *adj* benel, gwregel

fence [ˈfens] *n* kloes *f* +yow

ferry [ˈferi] *n* kowbal *m* +yow

fertilizer [ˈfɜːtɪlaɪzər] *n* godeyl *m* +yow

festival [ˈfestəvl] *n* goel *m* +yow

fetch [ˈfetʃ] *v* kyrghes

fever [ˈfiːvər] *n* terthenn *f* +ow

few [ˈfjuː] *n* nebes *m*

fiction [ˈfɪkʃən] *n* fugieth *f*

field [ˈfiːld] *n (large)* gwel *m* +yow; *(enclosed)* park *m* +ow

fifteen [ˌfɪfˈtiːn] *num* pymthek

fifth [ˈfɪfθ] *num* pympes

fifty [ˈfɪfti] *num* hanter-kans

fight [ˈfaɪt] *n* kas *f* +ow, kevammok *m* -ogow

209

fighter [ˈfaɪtər] *n* kasor *m* -oryon

figure [ˈfɪɡər] *n* (*shape*) figur *m* +ys

figurine [fɪɡəˈriːn] *n* figurenn *f* +ow

file [faɪl] *n* (*document*) restrenn *f* +ow

fill [ˈfɪl] *v* lenwel; **fill with** lenwel a

film [ˈfɪlm] *n* (*cinema, T.V., video*) fylm *m* +ow: *v* (*shoot a film*) fylmya

filter [ˈfɪltər] *n* sidhel *m* sidhlow: *v* sidhla

fin [ˈfɪn] *n* (*of fish*) askell *f* eskelli

final [ˈfeɪnəl] *n* (*game*) pennwari *m* +ow: *adj* finel

find [ˈfaɪnd] *v* kavoes; **find again** daskavoes

fine [ˈfaɪn] *n* (*penalty*) spal *m* +yow: *adj* teg; **fine arts** artow fin

finger [ˈfɪŋɡər] *n* bys *m* bysies; **ring finger** bys bysow

finger-nail *n* ewin *m* +es

finish [ˈfɪnɪʃ] *v* gorfenna

finished [ˈfɪnɪʃt] *adj* gorfennys

Finland [ˈfɪnlənd] *place* Fynndir

Finn [ˈfɪn] *n* Fynn *m* +yon

Finnish [ˈfɪnɪʃ] *adj* fynnek; **Finnish language** Fynnek *m*

fire [ˈfaɪər] *n* tan *m* +yow

fireman [ˈfaɪəmən] *n* tangasor *m* +yon

fireplace [ˈfaɪəpleɪs] *n* oeles *f* +ow

firm [ˈfɜːm] *adj* (*fixed*) fast, fyrv

first [ˈfɜːst] *num* kynsa: *adj* kynsa

fish [ˈfɪʃ] *n* pysk *m* puskes: *v* pyskessa

fisherman [ˈfɪʃəmən] *n* pyskador *m* +yon

fishing-rod [ˈfɪʃɪŋrəd] *n* gwelenn-byskessa *f* gwelynni-pyskessa

fist [ˈfɪst] *n* dorn *f* +ow, diwdhorn *dual*

fit [ˈfɪt] *n* (*illness*) shora *m* +ys: *adj* gwiw: *v* desedha

five ['faɪv] *num* pymp

fix ['fɪx] *v (attach)* staga

flame ['flaɪm] *n* flamm *m* +ow

flannel ['flanel] *n* gwlanenn *f* +ow

flat ['flat] *n* rannji *m* +ow: *adj* gwastas

flatter ['flatər] *v* flattra

flay ['flaɪ] *v* kroghena

flea ['fliː] *n* hwannenn *f* +ow

flee ['fliː] *v* teghes

Fleming ['flemɪŋ] *n* Flemen *m* +yon

flesh ['fleʃ] *n* kig *m* +yow

flexible ['fleksəbl] *adj* gwedhyn

flock ['flɔk] *n* tonnek *m* -egow

flood ['flʌd] *n* liv *m* +ow: *v* liva

floor ['flɔːr] *n* leur *m* +yow

flour ['flauər] *n* bleus *m* +yow

flow ['fləu] *v* bera, frosa

flower ['flauə] *n* bleujenn *f* +ow, bleujyow *coll*

fluent ['fluːənt] *adj* freth

flute ['fluːt] *n* tollgorn *m* tollgern

fly ['flaɪ] *n* kelyonenn *f* +ow, kelyon *coll*: *v* nija

foam ['fəum] *n* ewyn *coll* +enn

focus ['fəukəs] *n* fog *f* +ow: *v* fogella

fog ['fɔg] *n* niwl *m* +ow

foggy ['fɔgi] *adj* niwlek

fold ['fəuld] *n (bend)* pleg *m* +ow: *v* plegya

folk ['fəuk] *n* gwerin *f*

follow ['fɔləu] *v* sywya, holya

following ['fɔləuɪŋ] *adj* a syw

food ['fuːd] *n* boes *m* +ow

fool ['fuːl] *n* foll *m* fellyon

foolish ['fuːlɪʃ] *adj* foll

foot ['fʊt] *n (Anat.)* troes *m* treys, dewdroes *dual*

football ['futbɔːl] *n* peldroes *f*

footbridge ['futbrɪdʒ] *n* troespons *m* +ow

footpath ['futpɑːθ] *n* troe'lergh *m* +ow

for [fɔː] *prep* rag: *conj* rag

forbid [fəˈbɪd] *v* difenn; **forbid someone to do something** difenn orth nebonan a wul neppyth; **God forbid** Duw difenn

force ['fɔːs] *v* nerth *m* +yow

forearm ['fɔrɑːm] *n* arvregh *f* +ow

forecast ['fɔːkɑːst] *n* dargan *f* +ow: *v* dargana

forehead ['fɔrɪd] *n* tal *f* +yow

foreign ['fɔrən] *adj* estrenyek

foreigner ['fɔrɪnər] *n (male)* estren *m* +yon; *(female)* estrenes *f* +ow

forest ['fɔrɪst] *n* koeswik *f* -igow

forget [fəˈget] *v* ankevi

forgive [fəˈgɪv] *v* gava

forgiveness [fəˈgɪvnɪs] *n* gevyans *m* +ow

fork ['fɔːk] *n (tool)* forgh *f* fergh; *(Y-shape)* gowl *f* +ow

form ['fɔːm] *n* furv *f* +ow: *v* furvya

formation [fɔːˈmeɪʃən] *n* furvyans *m* +ow

former ['fɔːmər] *adj* kyns

fortunately ['fɔːtʃənətli] *adv* y'n gwella prys

forty ['fɔːti] *num* dew-ugens

forward ['fɔːwəd] *adj* a-rag; **forward part** tu a-rag *m* +yow a-rag: *adv* war-rag

foul ['faul] *adj* plos

found ['faund] *v* fondya

founder ['faundər] *n* fondyer *m* -oryon

fountain ['fauntɪn] *n* fenten *f* fentynyow

four ['fɔːr] *num (m.)* peswar; *(f.)* peder; **go on all fours** pedrevanas

fourteen [ˌfɔːˈtiːn] *num* peswardhek
fourth [ˈfɔːθ] *num* peswora
Fowey [ˈfɔɪ] *place* Fowydh
fox [ˈfɔks] *n* lowarn *m* lewern
fraction [ˈfrakʃən] *n* darnas *m* +ow; *(math.)* rannriv *m* +ow
fragile [ˈfradʒaɪl] *adj* hedorr
fragment [ˈfragmənt] *n* darn *m* +ow
frame [ˈfreɪm] *n* fram *m* +yow: *v* framya
France [ˈfrɑːns] *place* Pow Frynk
freckle [ˈfrekl] *n* brithenn *f* +ow
free [ˈfriː] *adj* rydh: *v (set free)* rydhhe
freedom [ˈfriːdəm] *n* rydhses *m*
freeze [ˈfriːz] *v* rewi
freezer [ˈfriːzər] *n* rewell *f* +ow
freezing [ˈfriːzɪŋ] *adj* oer
French [ˈfrentʃ] *adj* frynkek; **French language** Frynkek; **French speaker** Frynkeger *m* -oryon
Frenchman [ˈfrentʃmən] *n* Frynk *m* +yon
Frenchwoman [ˈfrentʃwʊmən] *n* Frynkes *f* +ow
frequent [frɪˈkwent] *adj* menowgh: *v* daromres
fresh [ˈfreʃ] *adj* fresk
Friday [ˈfraɪdi] *n* dy' Gwener *m* dydhyow Gwener; **on Friday** dy' Gwener
friend [ˈfrend] *n* kothman *m* +s
frighten [ˈfraɪtn] *v* ownekhe
frog [ˈfrɔg] *n* kwilkyn *m* +yow
from [frɔm] *prep* dhiworth, diworth; **from here** alemma, ahanan
froth [ˈfrɔθ] *n* ewyn *coll* +enn
fruit [ˈfruːt] *n (in general)* froeth *coll* +enn
fuel [ˈfjʊəl] *n* keunys *coll* +enn
full [ˈfʊl] *adj* leun; **Full Moon** loergann *m* +ow; **full**

213

stop hedh *m* +ow
fun [ˈfʌn] *n* ges *m*; **make fun of** gul ges a
funeral [ˈfjuːnərəl] *n* obisow *plur*
funny [ˈfʌni] *adj (amusing)* hwarthus
furious [ˈfjʊərɪəs] *adj* konneryek
furniture [ˈfɜːnɪtʃər] *n* mebel *m*
fury [ˈfjʊəri] *n* konnar *f*
fussy [ˈfʌsi] *adj* fyslek
future [ˈfjuːtʃər] *adj* devedhek: *n* termyn a dheu *m*,
devedhek *m* -ogow

G

gadget [ˈgadʒɪt] *n* darbar *m* +ow
Gaelic [ˈgalɪk] *adj* gwydhelek; **Gaelic language**
Gwydhelek *m*
gain [ˈgeɪn] *n* gwayn *m* +yow: *v* gwaynya
Galicia [gəˈlɪsjə] *place* Galitha
Galician [gəˈlɪsjən] *adj* galithek
gallop [ˈgaləp] *n* peswarlamm *m* +ow: *v* peswarlemmel
game [ˈgeɪm] *n* gwari *m* +ow; *(object of hunt)* gam *m*
garage [ˈgarɪdʒ] *n* karrji *m* +ow
garden [ˈgɑːdn] *n* lowarth *m* +yow
gardener [ˈgɑːdnər] *n* lowarther *m* -oryon
garland [ˈgɑːlənd] *n* garlont *f* +ow
garlic [ˈgɑːlɪk] *n* kennin *coll* +enn
garnish [ˈgɑːnɪʃ] *n* afinans *m* +ow: *v* afina
garret [ˈgaret] *n* talik *m* -igow
gas [ˈgas] *n* gass *m* +ow
gate [ˈgeɪt] *n* yet *f* yetys yetow
gather [ˈgaðər] *v* kuntell

Gaul [ˈgɔːl] *place* Galia

Gaulish [ˈgɔːlɪʃ] *adj* galianek *m*; **Gaulish language** Galianek *m*

gel [ˈdʒel] *n* jell *m* +ow

gene [ˈdʒiːn] *n* genynn *m* +ow

general [ˈdʒenrəl] *n (of army)* pennhembrenkyas *m* pennhembrynkysi: *adj* ollgemmyn

generally [ˈdʒenərəli] *adv* dre vras

generation [ˌdʒenəˈreɪʃən] *n (people in a family)* henedh *m* +ow

generous [ˈdʒenərəs] *adj* hel

genius [ˈdʒiːniəs] *n* awen *f*

gentle [ˈdʒentl] *adj* hwar

genuine [ˈdʒenjuɪn] *adj* gwiryon

geography [dʒɪˈɔgrəfi] *n* doronieth *f*

germ [ˈdʒɜːm] *n (microbe)* korrbryv *m* +es

German [ˈdʒɜːmən] *n (female)* Almannes *f* +ow; *(male)* Almann *m* +ow: *adj* almaynek; **German language** Almaynek *m*

Germany [ˈdʒɜːməni] *place* Almayn

get [ˈget] *v* kavoes, kyrghes; **get married** demmedhi; **get on with someone** omglewes gans nebonan; **get up** sevel

ghost [ˈgəʊst] *n* tarosvann *m* +ow

ghostly [ˈgəʊstli] *adj* tarosvannus

giant [ˈdʒaɪənt] *n* kowr *m* kewri

gift [ˈgɪft] *n* ro *m* rohow

giraffe [dʒɪˈrɑːf] *n* jiraf *m* +es

girl [ˈgɜːl] *n* mowes *f* mowesi

give [ˈgɪv] *v* ri; **give back** daskorr; **give birth** dineythi

glad [ˈglad] *adj* heudh

glass [ˈglɑːs] *n* gweder *m* gwedrow; **drinking glass**

gwedrenn *f* +ow

glasses ['glɑːsɪ] *pl (spectacles)* dewweder *dual*

glisten ['glɪsn] *v* terlentri

glitter ['glɪtər] *v* glyttra

glory ['glɔːrɪ] *n* glori *m*

glove ['glʌv] *n* manek *f* manegow, diwvanek *dual*

glue ['gluː] *n* glus *m* +ow: *v* glusa

gnat ['nat] *n* gwibesenn *f* +ow, gwibes *coll*

gnaw ['nɔː] *v* knias

go ['gəʊ] *v* mos; **go away** mos dhe-ves; **go down**
diyskynna; **go up** yskynna; **go out** mos yn-mes

goal ['gəʊl] *n (sport)* gol *m* +yow

goat ['gəʊt] *n* gaver *f* gever

goblet ['gɔblɪt] *n* hanafik *m* -igow

goblin ['gɔblɪn] *n* kravlost *m* +ow

God ['gɔd] *n* Duw *m*

god ['gɔd] *n* duw *m* +ow

godfather ['gɔdˌfɑːðər] *n* tas-besydh *m* tasow-vesydh

godmother ['gɔdˌmʌðər] *n* mamm-vesydh *f*
mammow-besydh

gold ['gəʊld] *n* owr *m*

golden ['gəʊldn] *adj* owrek

goldsmith ['gəʊldsmɪθ] *n* owrer *m* -oryon

gone ['gɔn] *adj* gyllys

good ['gʊd] *adj* da; *(morally)* mas

goodbye [ˌgʊdˈbaɪ] *int (to one person)* Duw genes;
(to more than one person) Duw genowgh hwi

goodnight! [ˌgʊdˈnaɪt] *int* nos dha!

goods ['gʊdz] *plur* gwara *coll*

goose ['guːs] *n* goedh *f* +ow

gorse ['gɔːs] *n* eythin *coll* +enn

gorsedd ['gɔːseð] *n* gorsedh *f* +ow

gospel ['gɔspəl] *n* aweyl *f* +ys +yow

gourd ['guəd] *n* pompyon *m* +s
government ['gʌvnmənt] *n* governans *m* +ow
gown ['gaʊn] *n* goen *m* +yow
grace ['greɪs] *n* gras *m* grasow
grain ['greɪn] *n (in bulk)* greun *coll* +enn
gram ['gram] *n* gramm *m* +ow
grammar ['gramər] *n* gramer *m* +yow; *(book)*
    yethador *m* +yow
granary ['granəri] *n* greunji *m* +ow
grand ['grand] *adj* brav
grandchild ['gran‚tʃaɪld] *n* flogh-wynn *m* fleghes-
    wynn
granddaughter ['gran‚dɔːtər] *n* myrgh-wynn *f*
    myrghes-gwynn
grandfather ['grand‚fɑːðər] *n* tas-gwynn *m* tasow-
    wynn, hendas *m* +ow
grandmother ['gran‚mʌðər] *n* mamm-wynn *f*
    mammow-gwynn, henvamm *f* +ow
grandson ['gransʌn] *n* mab-wynn *m* mebyon-wynn
granite ['granɪt] *n* growan *m* -enyow
grape ['greɪp] *n* grappa *m* grappys grappow
grass ['grɑːs] *n* gwels *coll* +enn
graze ['greɪz] *v (feed)* peuri
grease ['griːs] *n* blonek *m* -egow
great ['greɪt] *adj* meur; **Great Britain** Breten Veur
Greece ['griːs] *place* Pow Grek
Greek ['griːk] *n (person)* Grek *m* Grekys: *adj* grek;
    Greek language Greka
green ['griːn] *adj* gwyr', gwyrdh; *(of plants)* glas
greet ['griːt] *v* dynnerghi
greetings ['griːtɪŋz] *plur* gorhemmynnadow *m*
grey ['greɪ] *adj* loes
griddle ['grɪdl] *n* men-pobas *m* meyn-pobas

grief ['gri:f] *n* galar *m* +ow

grill ['grɪl] *n* rastell *f* restell: *v* rastella

grip ['grɪp] *n* dalghenn *f* +ow

grocer ['grəʊsər] *n* spiser *m* -oryon +s

groove ['gru:v] *n* ryllik *f* -igow

ground ['graʊnd] *n* dor *m* +yow

group ['gru:p] *n* bagas *m* +ow

grove ['grəʊv] *n* kelli *f* kelliow

grow ['grəʊ] *v* tevi

growl ['graʊl] *v* grommya: *n* grommyans *m* +ow

grumble ['grʌmbəl] *v* krodhvolas: *n* krodhvol *m* +yow

guarantee [garən'ti:] *n* mewgh *m* +yow: *v* mewghya

guard ['gɑːd] *n* gwithyas *m* gwithysi: *v* gwitha

guardian ['gɑːdɪən] *n* gwithyas *m* gwithysi

guess ['ges] *n* dismyk *m* -ygow: *v* dismygi

guest ['gest] *n* gwester *m* -oryon

guide ['gaɪd] *n* kevarwoedher *m* +yon, kowethlyver *m* -lyvrow: *v* kevarwoedha

guilty ['gɪlti] *adj* kablus

guitar [gɪ'tɑːr] *n* gitar *m* -eryow

gulp ['gʌlp] *v* terlenki

gum ['gʌm] *n (in mouth)* kig an dyns

gutter ['gʌtər] *n* londer *m* +yow

gymnasium [dʒɪm'neɪzɪəm] *n* lappva *f* +ow

gymnastics [dʒɪm'nastɪks] *plur* lappieth *f*

H

habit ['habɪt] *n* us *m* +yow

hair ['heər] *n* blew *coll* +enn; *(individual)* blewenn *f* +ow, blew *coll; (head of hair)* gols *m* +yow

218

hairdresser [ˈheəˌdresər] *n* kempennyas gols *m* kempennysi gols, kempennyades gols *f* kempennyadesow gols

half [hɑːf] *n* hanter *m* +yow

half-brother [ˈhɑːfˌbrʌðər] *n* hanter-broder *m* -breder

half-hour [ˌhɑːfˈauər] *n (duration)* hanter-our *m* +yow

half-sister [ˈhɑːfˌsɪstər] *n* hanter-hwoer *f* -hwerydh

hall [hɔːl] *n* hel *f* +yow

hallo! [həˈləu] *int* hou!

ham [ham] *n (meat)* mordhos hogh *f* mordhosow hogh

hammer [ˈhamər] *n* morthol *m* +ow: *v* mortholya

hand [hand] *n (in general)* leuv *f* +yow, diwla, diwleuv *dual*; *(when used as an instrument)* dorn *f* +ow, diwdhorn *dual*

handful [ˈhandfəl] *n* dornas *m* +ow

handicapped [ˈhandɪkapt] *adj* evredhek

handkerchief [ˈhaŋkətʃɪf] *n* lien dorn *m* lienyow dorn

handle [ˈhandl] *n* dornla *m* dornleow

hang [haŋ] *v* kregi

hanging [ˈhaŋɪŋ] *adj* yn krog

happen [ˈhapən] *v* hwarvos

happiness [ˈhapɪnɪs] *n* lowena *f*

happy [ˈhapi] *adj* lowen

harbour [ˈhɑːbər] *n* porth *m* +ow

hard [hɑːd] *adj* kales

hardly [ˈhɑːdli] *adv* skant

hare [ˈheər] *n* skovarnek *m* -ogyon

harm [hɑːm] *n* pystik *m* -igow: *v* pystiga

harp [hɑːp] *n* telynn *f* +ow

harpist [ˈhɑːpɪst] *n* telynnyer *m* -oryon

harsh [hɑːʃ] *adj* asper

harvest [ˈhɑːvɪst] *n* trevas *f* +ow

haste ['heɪst] *n* mall *m*

hat ['hat] *n* hatt *m* +ow +ys

hate ['heɪt] *n* kas *m*: *v* kasa

hateful ['heɪtfəl] *adj* kasadow

hatred ['heɪtrɪd] *n* kas *m*

have ['hav] *v* kavoes; **I have to** res yw dhymm

havoc ['havək] *n* terroes *m* +ow, reudh *m* +ow

hay ['heɪ] *n* goera *m*

hazard ['hazəd] *n* peryll *m* +ow

haze ['heɪz] *n* goniwl *m* +ow

hazel-tree [‚heɪzl'triː] *n* kollwydh *f* +ow, kollwydh *coll* +enn

he [hiː] *pron* ev

head ['hed] *n* penn *m* +ow

headache ['hedeɪk] *n* drog-penn *m* drogow-penn

head-dress ['heddres] *n* pennwisk *m* +ow

health ['helθ] *n* yeghes *m*; **good health!** yeghes da (dhis/dhywgh)!

healthy ['helθi] *adj (person)* yagh

heap ['hiːp] *n* bern *m* +yow, kals *m* +ow; **in a heap** graghellys: *v (put in a heap)* graghella, bernya, krugya

hear ['hɪər] *v* klewes

heart ['hɑːt] *n* kolonn *f* +ow; **by heart** dre gov

hearth ['hɑːθ] *n* oeles *f* +ow

heat ['hiːt] *n* gwres *f*, tes *m*: *v* tesa, toemmhe

heather ['heðər] *n* grug *m* +ow

heating ['hiːtɪŋ] *n* **central heating** toemmheans-kres *m*

heaven ['hevn] *n* nev *m* +ow

heavy ['hevi] *adj* poes

Hebrew ['hiːbruː] *n* Ebrow *m* +yon: *adj* ebrow; *(language)* Ebrowek *m*

hedge ['hedʒ] *n* ke *m* +ow

hedgehog ['hedʒhɔg] *n* sort *m* +es

heel ['hiːl] *n* seudhel *m* +yow, dewseudhel *dual*

heifer ['hefər] *n* denewes *f* +ow

height ['haɪt] *n* ughelder *m* +yow

helicopter ['helɪkɔptər] *n* askell-dro *f* eskelli-tro

hell ['hel] *n* ifarn *m* +ow

helmet ['helmɪt] *n* basnett *m* +ow

help ['help] *n* gweres *m*: *v* gweres *m*: *int* harow!

Helston ['helstən] *place* Hellys

hen ['hen] *n* yar *f* yer

hence ['hens] *adv* alemma

her [hɜːr] *pron (poss.)* hy; **her cat** hy hath; *(obj.)* 's, hi; **we see her** ni a's gwel

herd ['hɜːd] *n* gre *f* +ow

here ['hɪər] *adv* omma; **here is** ottomma; **here are** ottomma

hey ['heɪ] *int* hay

hiccup ['hɪkʌp] *n* hik *m* +ow: *v* hikas

hidden ['hɪdn] *adj* kel, kudh

hide ['haɪd] *v* kudha

high ['haɪ] *adj* ughel; **high ground** ugheldir *m* +yow

hill ['hɪl] *n (eminence)* bre *f* +ow +yer

him [hɪm] *pron* 'n, e', ev

himself [hɪm'self] *n* **by himself** y honan

hinder ['hɪndər] *v* lettya

hippopotamus [hɪpə'pɔtəməs] *n* dowrvargh *m* -vergh

his [hɪz] *pron* y

history ['hɪstəri] *n* istori *m* +ow

hit ['hɪt] *v* gweskel

hoarse ['hɔːs] *adj* kreg

hobby ['hɔbi] *n* hoba *m* +s

221

hold [ˈhəʊld] *v* dalghenna, synsi

hole [ˈhəʊl] *n* toll *m* tell; **bore a hole** telli

holiday [ˈhɒlɪdeɪ] *n* dy'goel *m* +yow

holiday-maker [ˌhɒlɪdeɪˈmeɪkəʳ] *n* havyas *m* -ysi

hollow [ˈhɒləʊ] *n* kow *f* +yow: *adj* kow

holly [ˈhɒli] *n* kelynn *coll* +enn; **holly bush** kelynnenn *f* +ow

holy [ˈhəʊli] *adj* sans

home [ˈhəʊm] *n* tre *f* trevow; **at home** yn tre; **go home** mos tre

homosexual [ˌhɒməʊˈsekʃʊəl] *n* kethreydhek *m* -ogyon: *adj* kethreydhek

honest [ˈɒnɪst] *adj* onest

honesty [ˈɒnɪsti] *n* onester *m*

honey [ˈhʌni] *n* mel *m* +yow

honeycomb [ˌhʌniˈkəʊm] *n* kribenn vel *f* kribennow mel

honour [ˈɒnəʳ] *n* enor *m* +s

hoof [ˈhuːf] *n* karn *m* +ow

hoop [ˈhuːp] *n* kylghynn *m* +ow

hope [ˈhəʊp] *n* govenek *m* -egow: *v* gwaytyas

horizon [həˈraɪzn] *n* gorwel *m* +yow

horn [ˈhɔːn] *n* (*of animal*) korn *m* kern

horrible [ˈhɒrəbl] *adj* euthyk

horse [ˈhɔːse] *n* margh *m* mergh

horseman [ˈhɔːsmən] *n* marghek *m* -ogyon

hospitable [hɒsˈpɪtəbl] *adj* hel

hospital [ˈhɒspɪtl] *n* klavji *m* +ow

host [ˈhəʊst] *n* (*landlord*) ost *m* +ys

hostess [ˈhəʊstɪs] *n* ostes *f* +ow

hostility [hɒsˈtɪlɪti] *n* eskarogeth *f*

hot [ˈhɒt] *adj* **extremely hot** poeth

hotel [həʊˈtel] *n* gwesti *m* +ow

222

hour ['aʊər] *n* eur *f* +yow; *(duration)* our *m* +ys

house ['haʊs] *n* chi *m* +ow

household ['haʊshəʊld] *n* mayni *m* +ow

housekeeping ['haʊski:pɪŋ] *n* gwith chi *m*; *(money)* arghans tiogeth *m*

how ['haʊ] *adv* fatell; **how are you?** fatla genes?; **how far** py par pellder; **how many** pes; **how much** pygemmys

however [haʊ'evər] *adv* byttegyns

howl ['haʊl] *v* oulya

huge ['hju:dʒ] *adj* bras dres eghenn

humanity [hju:'manəti] *n* denses *m*

hump ['hʌmp] *n* both *f* +ow

hundred ['hʌndrəd] *num* kans *m* +ow

Hungarian [hʌŋ'geɪriən] *adj* hungarek; **Hungarian language** Hungarek *m*

Hungary ['hʌŋgəri] *place* Hungari

hunger ['hʌŋgər] *n* nown *m*

hungry ['hʌŋgri] *adj* nownek

hunt ['hʌnt] *n* helgh *m* +ow: *v* helghya

hunter ['hʌntər] *n* helghyer *m* -oryon

hurry ['hʌri] *n* fisten *m*; **I am in a hurry** mall yw genev: *v* fistena

hurt ['hɜːt] *v* shyndya

husband ['hʌzbənd] *n* gour *m* gwer

hush ['hʌʃ] *v* godewel

hut ['hʌt] *n* krow *m* +yow

hymn ['hɪm] *n* hymna *m* hymnys

hypocritical [ˌhɪpəʊ'krɪtɪkl] *adj* fekyl cher

I

I [aɪ] *pron* my

ice ['aɪs] *n* rew *m* +yow; **black ice** rew du: *v* **ice a cake** hwegrewi

ice-cube ['aɪsˌkju:b] *n* kub rew *m* kubow rew

Iceland ['aɪslənd] *place* Rewynys

Icelander ['aɪsləndər] *n* Rewynyser *m* -oryon

Icelandic [aɪs'landɪk] *adj* rewynysek; **Icelandic language** Rewynysek

idea [aɪ'dɪə] *n* tybyans *m* +ow

if [ɪf] *conj* a, mar; **if you please** mar pleg

ignorant ['ɪgnərənt] *adj* diskians

ill ['ɪl] *adj* klav; **be taken ill, fall ill** koedha klav

illness ['ɪlnes] *n* kleves *m* +ow

ill-treat [ɪl'tri:t] *v* tebeldhyghtya

illuminate [ɪ'lu:mɪneɪt] *v (with light)* golowi

illustration [ˌɪlə'streɪʃən] *n* lymnans *m* +ow

image ['ɪmɪdʒ] *n* hevelepter *m* +yow

imagine [ɪ'madʒɪn] *v* tybi

imitate ['ɪmɪteɪt] *v* gul war-lergh

immediately [ɪ'mi:djətli] *adv* a-dhesempis, a-dhistowgh, distowgh

immovable [ɪ'mu:vəbl] *adj (physically)* anwayadow; *(spiritually)* anvovadow

impermeable [ɪm'pɜːmiəbl] *adj* andhewanadow

impervious [ɪm'pɜːviəs] *adj* stanch

importance [ɪm'pɔːtəns] *n* roweth *m*

important [ɪm'pɔːtnt] *adj* poesek

impossible [ɪm'pɒsəbl] *adj* na yll bos, annalladow

improve [ɪm'pru:v] *v* gwellhe

in [ɪn] *prep* yn; **in my** y'm; **in the** y'n; **in thy** y'th

inch ['ɪntʃ] *n* meusva *f* meusvedhi

224

incorrect [ˌɪnkəˈrekt] *adj* ankewar

increase [ɪnˈkriːs] *v* kressya

indeed [ɪnˈdiːd] *adv* dhe wir, devri

independent [ˌɪndɪˈpendənt] *adj* anserghek

index [ˈɪndeks] *n (of a book)* menegva *f* +ow

India [ˈɪndiə] *place* Eynda

Indian [ˈɪndiən] *adj* eyndek

industry [ˈɪndəstri] *n (manufacture)* diwysyans *m* +ow

infant [ˈɪnfənt] *n* fleghik *m* fleghigow

inform [ɪnˈfɔːm] *v* kedhla

information [ˌɪnfəˈmeɪʃən] *n* kedhlow *plur*

informer [ɪnˈfɔːməʳ] *m* kedhlor *m* -oryon

injection [ɪnˈdʒekʃən] *n* skityans *m* +ow

injury [ˈɪndʒəri] *n* pystik *m* pystigow

ink [ˈɪŋk] *n* ynk *m* +ow

insects [ˈɪnsekts] *plur* anpryvyon, hwesker *coll* +enn

inside [ˌɪnˈsaɪd] *n* pervedh *m* +ow: *prep* a-bervedh yn: *adv* a-bervedh, a-ji

insignificant [ˌɪnsɪgˈnɪfɪkənt] *adj* distyr

instead [ɪnˈsted] *prep* yn le: *adv* yn y le

instruction [ɪnˈstrʌkʃən] *n* dyskans *m* +ow

instrument [ˈɪnstrʊmənt] *n (means)* mayn *m* +ys

insult [ˈɪnsʌlt] *n* arvedhenn *f* +ow

insurance [ɪnˈʃʊərəns] *n* surheans *m* +ow

intelligent [ɪnˈtelɪdʒənt] *adj* poellek

intend [ɪnˈtend] *v* mynnes

intention [ɪnˈtenʃən] *n* mynnas *m* +ow

interior [ɪnˈtɪəriəʳ] *n* pervedh *m* +ow: *adj* pervedhel

intermediate [ˌɪntəˈmiːdjət] *adj* kres

international [ˌɪntəˈnaʃənl] *adj* keswlasek

interpreter [ɪnˈtɜːprɪtəʳ] *n* latimer *m* +s

invent [ɪnˈvent] *v* dismygi

invitation [ˌɪnvɪˈteɪʃən] *n* galow *m* +yow

invite [ɪn'vaɪt] *v* gelwel
invoice ['ɪnvɔɪs] *n* reken *m* reknow
involuntary [ɪn'vɔləntəri] *adj* anvodhek
Ireland ['aɪələnd] *n* Iwerdhon *f*
iris ['aɪərɪs] *n (yellow plant)* elestrenn *f* +ow, elester *coll*
Irish ['aɪərɪʃ] *adj* iwerdhonek; **Irish language** Iwerdhonek
Irishman ['aɪərɪʃmən] *n* Goedhel *m* Goedheli
iron ['aɪən] *n (appliance)* hornell *f* +ow; *(metal)* horn *m* hern: *v* hornella
irregular [ɪ'regjʊlər] *adj* anrewlys
island ['aɪlənd] *n* ynys *f* +ow +ys
Israel ['ɪzreɪl] *place* Ysrael
Israeli [ɪz'reɪli] *n* Ysraelyas *m* -ysi
it [ɪt] *pron (m.)* ev; *(f.)* hi; *(m., obj.)* 'n; *(f. obj.)* 's
Italian [ɪ'taljən] *adj* italek; **Italian language** Italek
Italy ['ɪtəli] *place* Itali
itch ['ɪtʃ] *n* debron *m* +ow: *v* debreni
its [ɪts] *pron (m.)* y; *(f.)* hy
ivy ['aɪvi] *n* idhyow *coll* +enn

J

jacket ['dʒakɪt] *n* jerkynn *m* +ow, kryspows *f* +yow
jail ['dʒeɪl] *n* prison *m* +yow
jam ['dʒam] *n* kyfeyth *m* +yow
January ['dʒanʊəri] *n* mis-Genver *m* misyow-G.
Japan [dʒə'pan] *place* Nihon
Japanese [dʒapə'niːz] *adj* nihonek; **Japanese language** Nihonek *m*
jaw ['dʒɔː] *n* awen *f* +ow

jealousy ['dʒeləsi] *n* avi *m* +ow
jersey ['dʒɜːzi] *n* gwlanek *m* gwlanogow
Jew ['dʒuː] *n* Yedhow *m* Yedhewon
jewel ['dʒuːəl] *n* tegenn *f* +ow
Jewish ['dʒuːɪʃ] *adj* yedhowek
jigsaw ['dʒɪgsɔː] *n* **jigsaw puzzle** gwari mildamm *m* gwariow mildamm
job ['dʒɒb] *n* oberenn *f* +ow
John ['dʒɒn] *name* Yowann
join ['dʒɔɪn] *v* junya
joint ['dʒɔɪnt] *n* mell *m* +ow
joke ['dʒəʊk] *n* ges *m* +yow: *v* gesya
journalist ['dʒɜːnəlɪst] *n* jornalyas *m* -ysi
journey ['dʒɜːni] *n* vyaj *m* +yow
joy ['dʒɔɪ] *n* joy *m* joyys, lowena *f*
judge ['dʒʌdʒ] *n* breusydh *m* +yon: *v* breusi
jug ['dʒʌg] *n* podik *m* -igow
juice ['dʒuːs] *n* sugen *m* +yow
July [dʒuːˈlaɪ] *n* mis-Gortheren *m* misyow-G.
jump ['dʒʌmp] *n* lamm *m* +ow: *v* lamma
jumper ['dʒʌmpər] *n (garment)* gwlanek *m* -ogow
June ['dʒuːn] *n* mis-Metheven *m* misyow-M.
Jupiter ['dʒuːpɪtər] *n (planet, god)* Yow *m*
just ['dʒʌst] *adj* ewn; **just now** nammnygen
justice ewnder *m* +yow, gwirvreus *m*

K

kangaroo [kaŋgəˈruː] *n* kangourou *m* +s
keep ['kiːp] *v* gwitha
keeper ['kiːpər] *n* gwithyas *m* gwithysi

kennel ['kenl] *n* kiji *m* +ow

kettle ['ketl] *n* kalter *f* +yow

key ['ki:] *n* alhwedh *m* +ow

keyboard ['ki:bɔːd] *n* bysowek *f* -egi

kidnap ['kɪdnap] *v* denladra

kidney ['kɪdni] *n* loneth *f* -i, diwloneth *dual*

kill ['kɪl] *v* ladha

kind ['kaɪnd] *n* eghenn *f* +ow, sort *m* +ow: *adj* kuv

kindness ['kaɪndnɪs] *n* hwekter *m*, kuvder *m*

king ['kɪŋ] *n* myghtern *m* +edh +yow, ruw *m* +yon

kingdom ['kɪŋdəm] *n* gwlaskor *f* -kordhow

kiss ['kɪs] *n* amm *m* +ow: *v* **kiss someone** amma
    dhe nebonan

kitchen ['kɪtʃɪn] *n* kegin *f* +ow

kiwi ['ki:wi:] *n* **kiwi fruit** froeth kiwi *coll* froethenn
    giwi

knee ['ni:] *n* glin *m* +yow, dewlin *dual*

kneel ['ni:l] *v* (on both knees) mos war benn-dewlin

knell ['nel] *n* **death knell** klogh an marow *m*

knickers ['nɪkəz] *n* islavrek *m* -ogow

knife ['naɪf] *n* kollell *f* kellylli

knit ['nɪt] *v* gwia

knitting ['nɪtɪŋ] *n* gwians *m*

knock ['nɔk] *n* knouk *m* +ys: *v* knoukya

knot ['nɔt] *n* kolm *m* +ow

know ['nəʊ] *v* godhvos; *(persons or places)* aswonn

knowledge ['nɔlɪdʒ] *n* aswonnvos *m*, skians *m* +ow

L

label [ˈleɪbl] *n* libel
laboratory [ləˈbɒrətri] *n* arbrovji
labour [ˈleɪbər] *n* lavur: *v* lavurya
lace [ˈleɪs] *v* lasya
lack [ˈlak] *n* fowt: *v* fyllel a
ladder [ˈladər] *n* skeul *f* +yow
ladle [ˈleɪdl] *n* lo-ledan
lady [ˈleɪdi] *n* arloedhes; **young lady** damsel
ladybird [ˈleɪdibɜːd] *n* bughik-Duw *f* bughesigow-Duw
lake [ˈleɪk] *n (inland)* lynn *f* +yn
lamb [ˈlam] *n* oen *m* eyn
lame [ˈleɪm] *adj* klof
lament [ləˈment] *v* galari: *n* galargan
lamp [ˈlamp] *n* lugarn *m* lugern
land [ˈland] *n* tir *m* +yow; *(country)* gwlas: *v* tira
landlord [ˈlandlɔːd] *n* ost *m* +ys
landscape [ˈlanskeɪp] *n* tirwel *f* +yow
lane [ˈleɪn] *n* bownder *f* +yow
language [ˈlaŋgwɪdʒ] *n* yeth *f* +ow, taves *m* tavosow
lap [ˈlap] *n* barrlenn *f* +ow
large [ˈlɑːdʒ] *adj* bras
last [ˈlɑːst] *adj* an diwettha; **at last** wostiwedh: *v* pesya
late [ˈleɪt] *adj* diwedhes; **later on** a-wosa
Latvia [ˈlatviə] *place* Latvi
laugh [ˈlɑːf] *n* hwarth *m* +ow: *v* hwerthin
laughter [ˈlɑːftər] *n* hwarth *m* +ow
Launceston [ˈlɑːnsn] *place* Lannstevan
law [ˈlɔː] *n* lagha; **law court** breuslys
lawn [ˈlɔːn] *n* glesin *m* +yow

229

lay *v* **lay eggs** dedhwi; **lay the table** restra an voes

lazy ['leɪzi] *adj* diek

lead ['liːd] *v* hembronk, ledya

leader ['liːdər] *n* hembrenkyas *m* -ysi, ledyer *m* ledyoryon

leaf ['liːf] *n (of plant)* delenn *f* delyow, del *coll; (of paper)* lyvenn *f* +ow

league ['liːg] *n (company)* kolmedh *m* +ow; *(3 miles)* lew

lean ['liːn] *v* poesa

leap ['liːp] *n* lamm *m* +ow: *v* lamma

learn ['lɜːn] *v* dyski

lease ['liːs] *n* gobrenans *m* +ow

least ['liːst] *adj* lyha; **at least** dhe'n lyha

leather ['leðər] *n* ledher *m* +ow

leave ['liːv] *n* kummyas *m* +ow: *v* gasa

left ['left] *adj (opposite of right)* kledh; **on the left hand** a-gledh

left-handed [left'handɪd] *adj* kledhek

left-hander [left'handər] *n* kledhek *m* -ogyon

leg ['leg] *n* garr *f* +ow, diwarr *dual*

legend ['ledʒənd] *n* henhwedhel *m* -dhlow

lemon ['lemənz] *n* lymon *m* +yow

lend ['lend] *v* ri kendon; **lend something to someone** ri neppyth yn kendon dhe nebonan

length ['leŋθ] *n* hys, hirder

lengthen ['leŋθən] *v* hirhe

lengthy ['leŋθi] *adj* hir

less ['les] *adj* le

lesson ['lesn] *n* dyskans *m* +ow

let ['let] *v (allow)* gasa

letter ['letər] *n (epistle)* lyther *m* +ow; *(of alphabet)* lytherenn

level ['levl] *n* nivel *m* +yow: *adj* kompes
lexicon ['leksɪkən] *n* gerva *f* +ow
liar ['laɪər] *n* gowek *m* gowogyon
liberate ['lɪbəreɪt] *v* livra
liberty ['lɪbəti] *n* frankedh *m*, rydhses *m*
librarian [laɪ'breərɪən] *n* lyveryas *m* -ysi
library ['laɪbrari] *n* lyverva *f* +ow
licence ['laɪsəns] *n* kummyas *m* +ow
licensee [ˌlaɪsən'siː] *n (of inn)* tavernor *m* +yon
lick ['lɪk] *v* lapya
lid ['lɪd] *n* gorher *m* +yow
lie ['laɪ] *n* gow *m* +yow; **tell a lie** gowleverel
lie ['laɪ] *v* **lie down** gorwedha
lieutenant [lef'tenənt] *n* leftenant *m* +ow
life ['laɪf] *n* bywnans *m* +ow
lift ['lɪft] *n (in car)* gorrans *m* +ow; *(elevator)* jynn-yskynn *m* jynnow-yskynn: *v (lift up)* drehevel
ligament ['lɪgəmənt] *n* giowenn *f* +ow, giow *coll*
light ['laɪt] *n* golow *m* +ys: *adj (not heavy)* skav: *v* **light up** enowi
light-house ['laɪthaʊs] *n* golowji *m* +ow
lightning ['laɪtnɪŋ] *n* lughes *coll* +enn
lily ['lɪli] *n* **lily of the valley** losowenn an hav *f* losow an hav
limb ['lɪm] *n* esel *m* eseli
limit ['lɪmɪt] *n* finweth: *v* finwetha
limpid ['lɪmpɪd] *adj* ylyn
line ['laɪn] *n* linenn *f* +ow
linen ['lɪnɪn] *n* lin *coll* +enn
link ['lɪŋk] *n* kevrenn *f* +ow
lion ['laɪən] *n* lew *m* +yon
lip ['lɪp] *n* gwelv *f* +ow
Liskeard [lɪs'kɑːd] *place* Lyskerrys

list [ˈlɪst] *n* rol *f* +yow

listen [ˈlɪsn] *v* **listen to** goslowes orth

literature [ˈlɪtərətʃəʳ] *n* lyenn *m* +ow

Lithuania [lɪθjuˈeɪnjə] *place* Lithuani

little [ˈlɪtl] *adj* byghan; **little by little** tamm ha tamm

live [ˈlɪv] *v* bywa; *(dwell)* triga

lively [ˈlaɪvli] *adj* bywek

liver [ˈlɪvəʳ] *n* avi *m* +ow

lizard [ˈlɪzəd] *n* pedrevan *f* +es

load [ˈləʊd] *n* begh *m* +yow: *v* beghya

loaf [ˈləʊf] *n* torth *f* +ow

lobster [ˈlɒbstəʳ] *n* legest *m* +i

lock [ˈlɒk] *n (of door)* florenn: *v* alhwedha, prenna

lodge [ˈlɒdʒ] *v* ostya

Loire [ˈlwɑːʳ] *place* Liger

London [ˈlʌndən] *place* Loundres

long [ˈlɒŋ] *adj* hir; **long ago** nans yw pell

longing [ˈlɒŋɪŋ] *n* hireth, hwans *m* +ow

longitude [ˈlɒŋgɪtjuːd] *n (geog.)* dorhys *m* +ow

Looe [ˈluː] *place* Logh

look [ˈlʊk] *n* golok, tremmynn *m* +ow: *v* mires; **look at** mires orth; **look out!** bydh war!

loose [ˈluːs] *adj* lows

lord [ˈlɔːd] *n* arloedh *m* arlydhi

lorry [ˈlɒri] *n* kert *m* +ow +ys

lose [ˈluːz] *v* kelli

loss [ˈlɒs] *n* koll *m* +ow

Lostwithiel [lɒstˈwɪðjel] *place* Lostwydhyel

lot [ˈlɒt] *n (in gambling)* chons *m* +yow; **a lot of houses** meur a jiow, lies chi

louse [ˈlaʊs] *n* lowenn *f* +ow, low *coll*

love [ˈlʌv] *n* kerensa: *v* kara; **be in love with** bos yn kerensa gans

232

lovely ['lʌvli] *adj* hegar
lover ['lʌvəʳ] *n (female)* karores *f* +ow; *(male)* karer *m*
  -oryon
low ['ləʊ] *adj* isel
lower ['ləʊəʳ] *v* iselhe
lowering ['ləʊərɪŋ] *n* iselheans *m*
lozenge ['lɒzɪndʒ] *n* rombenn *f* +ow
luck ['lʌk] *n* chons *m* +yow
luggage ['lʌgɪdʒ] *n* fardellow *plur*
lukewarm [ˌluːk'wɔːm] *adj* godoemm, mygyl
lunch ['lʌntʃ] *n* li: *v* **to have lunch** livya
lungs ['lʌŋz] *n* skevens *plur*
Luxembourg ['lʌksəmbɜːg] *place* Luksemburg
lying ['laɪŋ] *adj* gowek
lyrics ['lɪrɪks] *pl* geryow kan *plur*

M

machine [mə'ʃiːn] *n* jynn *m* +ow +ys
mackerel ['makrəl] *n* brithel *m* brithyli
mad ['mad] *adj* foll, mus
madam ['madəm] *n* madama
madman ['madmən] *n* foll *m* fellyon
magazine [ˌmagə'ziːn] *n (periodical)* lyver-termyn *m*
  lyvrow-termyn
magic ['madʒik] *n* pystri *m*
magician [mə'dʒiʃn] *n* pystrier *m* -oryon
magnifying-glass [ˌmagnɪfaɪŋ'glɑːs] *n* moghweder
  m -wedrow
mainland ['meɪnlənd] *n* tir meur *m*
maintain [meɪn'teɪn] *v* mentena

major ['meɪdʒər] *n (rank)* ughgapten *m* +yon

make ['meɪk] *v* gul

maker ['meɪkər] *n* gwrier *m* -oryon

Malta ['mɔːltə] *place* Malta

Maltese [mɔl'tiːz] *adj* maltek; **Maltese language** Maltek

mammal ['maml] *n* bronnvil *m* +es

man ['man] *n (as opposed to woman)* den *m* tus; gour *m* gwer; *(mankind)* mab-den *m*

Man ['man] *place* **Isle of Man** Manow, Ynys Vanow

manage ['manɪdʒ] *v* dyghtya

management ['manɪdʒmənt] *n* dyghtyans *m* +ow

manager ['manɪdʒər] *n* dyghtyer *m* -yoryon

mankind [man'kaɪnd] *n* mab-den *m*

manner ['manər] *n* gis *m* +yow, maner *f* +ow

mantelpiece ['mantlpiːs] *n* astell an oeles *f* estyll an oeles

manual ['manjuəl] *n* dornlyver *m* -lyvrow: *adj* dornel

manufacture [ˌmanjʊ'faktʃər] *n* gwrians *m* +ow

manure [mə'njuər] *n* teyl *m* +yow

many ['meni] *pron* lies: *adj* lies; **as many** keniver; **many houses** lies chi, meur a jiow

map ['map] *n* mappa *m* mappow

marble ['maːbl] *n (small sphere)* kalesenn *f* +ow

march ['maːtʃ] *n (tune)* ton kerdh

March ['maːtʃ] *n* mis-Meurth *m* misyow-Meurth

mare ['meər] *n* kasek *f* kasegi

mark ['maːk] *n* merk *m* +yow: *v* merkya

market ['maːkɪt] *n* marghas *f* +ow

maroon [mə'ruːn] *adj* gormrudh

married ['marɪd] *adj* demmedhys

marry ['mari] *v* demmedhi

Mars ['maːz] *n (god, planet)* Meurth *m*

marshal ['mɑːʃəl] *n (military)* kaslewydh *m* +yon

martyrdom ['mɑːtədəm] *n* mertherynsi *f*

masculine ['maskjʊlɪn] *adj* gourel; *(grammatical)* gorow

mask ['mɑːsk] *n* visour *m* +s

mason ['meɪsn] *n* ser men *m* seri men

massacre ['masəkər] *n* gorladhva *f* +ow: *v* gorladha

massage *n* ['masɑːʒ] leuvtoesans *m* +ow: *v* [ma'sɑːʒ] leuvtoesa

masseur [ma'sər] *n* leuvtoeser *m* -oryon

mast ['mɑːst] *n* gwern *f* +ow

master ['mɑːstər] *n* mester *m* mestrysi

masterpiece ['mɑːstəpiːs] *n* pennobereth *f* +ow

match ['matʃ] *n (equal)* par *m* +ow; *(game)* fytt *m* +ys +ow; *(lucifer)* tanbrenn *m* -yer

material [mə'tɪərɪəl] *n* devnydh *m* +yow, stoff *m*

mathematics [ˌmaθə'matɪks] *n* awgrym *m*

matter ['matər] *n* mater *m* +yow: *v* **it does not matter** ny vern; **it does not matter to me** ny'm deur

May ['meɪ] *n* mis-Me *m* misyow-Me

maybe ['meɪbi] *adv* martesen

mayor ['meər] *n* mer *m* +yon

me [miː] *pron (obj.)* vy; *(enclitic)* vy; *(emphatic)* -mevy, evy

mead ['miːd] *n (drink)* medh *m* +yow

meadow ['medəʊ] *n* budhynn *m* +ow, pras *m* +ow

meal ['miːl] *n* boes *m* +ow

mean ['miːn] *n (average)* mayn: *adj (stingy)* pith: *v* styrya

meaning ['miːnɪŋ] *n* styr *m* +yow

means ['miːnz] *plur (method)* mayn *m* +ys; *(wealth)* pygans *m*

235

measure ['meʒəʳ] *v* musura

measurement ['meʒəmənt] *n* musurans *m* +ow

meat ['mi:t] *n* kig *m* +yow

mechanic [mɪ'kanɪk] *n* jynnweythor *m* +yon

mediation [mi:di'eɪʃən] *n* maynorieth *f*

mediator [mi:di'eɪtəʳ] *n* medhador *m* +yon

medicine ['medsɪn] *n (as remedy)* medhegneth *f* +ow; *(as science)* medhegieth *f*

medium ['mi:djəm] *adj* kreswedhek

meet *v* dyerbynna, metya

meeting ['mi:tɪŋ] *n* kuntelles *m* +ow

melon ['melən] *n* melon *m* +yow

melt ['melt] *v* teudhi

member ['membəʳ] *n* esel *m* eseli

memory ['meməri] *n* kov *m* +yow

men ['men] *pl (adult males)* gwer *plur*; *(human beings)* pobel *f* poblow

mention ['menʃən] *n* kampoell *m* +ow: *v* kampoella

menu ['menju:] *n* rol-voes *f* rolyow-boes

merchant ['mɜ:tʃənt] *n* marghador *m* +yon, gwikor *m* +yon

Mercury *n (planet)* Mergher *m*

merry ['meri] *adj* heudh, lowenek

messenger ['mesɪndʒəʳ] *n* messejer *m* +s

metal ['metl] *n* alkan *m* alkenyow

metre ['mi:təʳ] *n (unit)* meter *m* metrow

mew ['mju:] *v* miowal

microbe ['maɪkrəʊb] *n* korrbryv *m* +es

microphone ['maɪkrəfəʊn] *n* korrgowsell *f* +ow

midday [ˌmid'deɪ] *n* hanter-dydh *m* +yow

middle ['mɪdl] *n* kres *m*; **in the middle (of)** yn mysk

middleman ['mɪdlmɑ:n] *n* kreswas *m* -wesyon

midnight ['mɪdnaɪt] *n* hanter-nos *f*

mild ['maɪld] *adj* klor
mile ['maɪl] *n* mildir *m* +yow
milk ['mɪlk] *n* leth *m* +ow: *v* godra
mill ['mɪl] *n* melin *f* +yow
million ['mɪljən] *num* milvil *m* +yow
mind ['maɪnd] *n* brys *m* +yow; **state of mind** cher *m*
mine ['maɪn] *n* bal *m* +yow
minister ['mɪnɪstəʳ] *n* menyster *m* -oryon -trys
minority [maɪ'nɒrɪti] *n* minoroleth *f* +ow
mint ['mɪnt] *n (herb)* menta *f*
minute ['mɪnɪt] *n (of time)* mynysenn *f* +ow
miracle ['mɪrəkl] *n* marthus *m* +ow
miraculous [mɪ'rakjʊləs] *adj* barthusek
mirror ['mɪrəʳ] *n* gweder-mires *m* gwedrow-mires
misery ['mɪzəri] *n* anken *m* +ow, poenvos *m* +ow
misfortune [mɪs'fɔːtʃuːn] *n* anfeus *f*
miss ['mɪs] *n (girl)* damsel *f* +s
Miss ['mɪs] *n* Mestresik
mist ['mɪst] *n* niwl *m* +ow
mistake [mɪs'teɪk] *n* kammweyth *m* +ow; **make a mistake** kammwul *v*
mistress ['mɪstrəs] *n* mestres *f* +ow
misty ['mɪsti] *adj* niwlek
mix ['mɪks] *v* kemmyska
mixture ['mɪkstjʊəʳ] *n* kemmysk *m* +ow
moan ['məʊn] *v* oghanas
mobile ['məʊbaɪl] *adj* **mobile telephone** klappkodh *f* +ow
mock ['mɒk] *v* gul ges a, gesya
mockery ['mɒkəri] *n* ges *m* +yow
model ['mɒdl] *n* patron *m* +yow
modern ['mɒdən] *adj* arnowydh
moist ['mɔɪst] *adj* leyth

moisture ['mɔɪstʃəʳ] n gwlygha f

mole ['məʊl] n godh f +ow

moment ['məʊmənt] n pols m +yow, prysweyth m +yow

Monday ['mʌndi] n dy' Lun m dydhyow Lun

money ['mʌni] n arghans m; (cash) mona coll

monk ['mʌŋk] n managh m menegh

monkey ['mʌŋki] n sim m +yon

month ['mʌnθ] n mis m misyow; **period of a month** miskweyth f +ow

monthly ['mʌnθli] adj misyek

monument ['mɔnjʊmənt] n drehevyans kov m +ow kov

moo ['muː] v bedhygla

mood ['muːd] n **in a good mood** pes da; **in a bad mood** drog pes

Moon ['muːn] n Loer f +yow

moonlight ['muːnlaɪt] n loergann m

moor ['mʊəʳ] n hal f halow

Moor ['mʊəʳ] n (person) Sarsyn m +s

moped ['məʊped] n hwil-tan m hwiles-tan

more ['mɔː] adj moy; **more and more** moy ha moy; **more or less** moy po le

moreover [mɔː'rəʊvəʳ] adv kekeffrys

morning ['mɔːnɪŋ] n myttin m +yow; **duration of the morning** myttinweyth f; **good morning!** myttin da!

moss ['mɔs] n kywni coll +enn

most ['məʊst] adj moyha; **for the most part** dre vras

moth ['mɔθ] n goedhan m +es

mother ['mʌðəʳ] n mamm f +ow

mother-in-law ['mʌðərɪnlɔː] n hweger f hwegrow

238

motor ['məʊtər] *n* jynn *m* +ow +ys

motor-bike [ˌməʊtə'baɪk] *n* diwros-tan *m* diwrosow-tan

motorway ['məʊtəweɪ] *n* gorfordh *f* +ow

mould ['məʊld] *n (for casting) n* furvell *f* +ow: *v* furvya

mouldy ['məʊldi] *adj* loes

mount ['maʊnt] *n (horse)* kevyl *m* +es

mountain ['maʊntɪn] *n* menydh *m* +yow

mourning ['mɔːnɪŋ] *n* kynvann *m* +ow

mouse ['maʊs] *n* logosenn *f* +ow, logos *coll*

moustache [mə'stɑːʃ] *n* minvlew *coll* +ynn

mouth ['maʊθ] *n* ganow *m* +ow

move ['muːv] *v* gwaya; *(spiritually)* movya; **move away** ombellhe; **move back** kildenna

movement ['muːvmənt] *n* gwayans *m* +ow

Mr ['mɪstər] *n (abbrev.)* Mr

Mrs ['mɪsɪz] *n (abbrev.)* Mres

much ['mʌtʃ] *adj* meur; **not much** nameur; **as much as** kekemmys; **how much** pygemmys

mud ['mʌd] *n* leys *m* +yow

multicoloured [ˌmʌlti'kʌləd] *adj* liesliw

mum ['mʌm] *n* mammik *f* -igow

murmur ['mɜːmər] *n* hanas *m* +ow: *v* hanasa

muscle ['mʌsl] *n* keher *coll* +enn

museum [mjuː'zɪəm] *n* gwithti *m* +ow

mushroom ['mʌʃrʊm] *n* skavell-groenek *f* skavellow-kroenek

music ['mjuːzɪk] *n* ilow *f*

musician [mjuː'zɪʃən] *n* ilewydh *m* +yon

mussel ['mʌsl] *n* mesklenn *f* +ow, meskel *coll*

must ['mʌst] *v* **I must go** res yw dhymm mos

mutation [mjuː'teɪʃən] *n* treylyans *m* +ow

mute ['mju:t] *adj* avlavar

my [maɪ] *pron* ow

myopic [maɪ'ɒpɪk] *adj* berrwelyek

myrtle-tree [ˌmɜːtəl'triː] *n* myrtwydhenn *f* +ow, myrtwydh *coll*

mystery ['mɪstəri] *n* kevrin *m* +yow

N

nail ['neɪl] *n (metal)* kenter *f* kentrow: *v* kentra

naked ['neɪkɪd] *adj* noeth

name ['neɪm] *n* hanow *m* henwyn; **in the name of** a-barth *prep*; **what's your name?** pyth yw dha hanow?: *v* henwel

named ['neɪmd] *adj* henwys

nanny ['nani] *n* magores *f* +ow

nap ['nap] *n* gogosk *m* +ow

nape ['neɪp] *n* gwarr *f* +ow

napkin ['napkɪn] *n* kwethynn *m* +ow

narrow ['narəʊ] *adj* kul, ynn

nation ['neɪʃn] *n* kenedhel *f* -dhlow, nasyon *m* +s

national ['naʃənəl] *adj* kenedhlek

native ['neɪtɪv] *n* genesik *m* -igyon

natural ['natʃrəl] *adj* naturel

nature ['neɪtʃər] *n* natur *f* +yow

naughty ['nɔːti] *adj* drog

near ['nɪər] *adj* ogas, nes

nearby ['nɪəbaɪ] *adv* yn ogas

nearly ['nɪəli] *adv* nammna, nammnag *(before vowels)*, ogas; **I nearly fell** nammna goedhis

necessary ['nesəsəri] *adj* **if necessary** mars yw res

neck ['nek] *n* konna *m* +ow

need ['niːd] *n* edhomm *m* +ow

needle ['niːdl] *n* naswydh *f* +yow

needlework ['niːdlwɜːk] *n* gweyth naswydh *m*

neighbour ['neɪbər] *n (female)* kentrevoges *f* +ow; *(male)* kentrevek *m* -ogyon

neighbourhood ['neɪbəhud] *n* kentreveth *f* +ow

neither ['naɪðər] *conj* naneyl; **neither ... nor** na ... na

nephew ['nevjuː] *n* noy *m* +ens

Neptune ['neptjuːn] *(planet, god)* Neptun *m*

nerve ['nɜːv] *n* nervenn *f* +ow, nerv *coll*

nervous ['nɜːvəs] *adj* nervus

nest ['nest] *n* neyth *m* +ow

net ['net] *n* roes *f* +ow

Netherlands ['neðələndz] *place* Iseldiryow *plur*

network ['netwɜːk] *n* roesweyth *m* +yow

never ['nevər] *adv (in past)* bythkweth; *(in future)* nevra; **never mind** ny vern

nevermore [ˌnevəˈmɔːr] *adv* nevra namoy

new ['njuː] *adj* nowydh

Newlyn ['njulɪn] *place* Lulynn

Newquay ['njuki] *place* Tewynn Pleustri

news ['njuːz] *n* nowodhow *plur*

newspaper ['njuːsˌpeɪpər] *n* paper-nowodhow *m* paperyow-n.

next ['nekst] *adj* nessa; **next Monday** dy' Lun nessa; **next to** ryb

nibble ['nɪbl] *v* godhynsel

nice ['naɪs] *adj* hweg

night ['naɪt] *n* nos *f* +ow; *(duration)* nosweyth; **last night** nyhewer

nightmare ['naɪtmeər] *n* hunlev *m* +ow

nine ['naɪn] *num* naw

nineteen [ˌnaɪn'tiːn] *num* nownsek

no [nəʊ] *int* na: *adj* **no answer** gorthyp vyth; **no smoking** megi a dhifenner: *adv* **no longer** na fella

noble ['nəʊbl] *adj* nobyl *m* noblys

nobody ['nəʊbədi] *n* denvyth *m*

nod ['nɒd] *v* penn-droppya

noise ['nɔɪz] *n* tros *m* +ow

noisy ['nɔɪzi] *adj* trosek

noon ['nuːn] *n* hanter-dydh *m* +yow

nor [nɔːr] *conj* na, nag *(before vowels)*

north ['nɔːθ] *n* gogledh *m*, kledhbarth *f* +ow, north *m*

north-east [ˌnɔːθ'iːst] *n* north-est *m*

north-west [ˌnɔːθ'west] *n* north-west *m*

Norway ['nɔːweɪ] *place* Norgagh

Norwegian [nɔː'wiːdʒən] *adj* norgaghek; *(language)* Norgaghek *m*

nose ['nəʊz] *n* troen *m* +yow

not [nɒt] *adv* ny, nyns (before vowels in **bos** and **mos**); **do not run** na res; **the one who does not speak** an huni na gows

note ['nəʊt] *n* notenn *f* +ow: *v (take note of)* notya

notebook ['nəʊtbʊk] *n* lyver notennow *m* lyvrow notennow

nothing ['nʌθɪŋ] *n* travyth *f*, mann *m*

notice ['nəʊtɪs] *v* attendya

noun ['naʊn] *n* hanow *m* henwyn

novel ['nɒvəl] *n* romans *m* +ow

novella [nə'velə] *n* drolla *m* drollys

November [nəʊ'vembər] *n* mis-Du *m* misyow-Du

now ['naʊ] *adv* lemmyn; **now and then** war euryow, treweythyow; **till now** bys y'n eur ma

nuance ['njuːɒns] *n* korrstyr *m* +yow

nuisance ['nju:səns] *n* fyslek *m* fyslogyon
number ['nʌmbər] *n* niver *m* +ow, riv *m* +ow; *(of house, telephone)* niverenn *f*
numerous ['nju:mərəs] *adj* niverus, pals
nurse ['nɜ:s] *n (female)* klavjiores *f* +ow; *(male)* klavjior *m* +yon
nursery ['nɜ:səri] *n* **nursery school** skol veythrin
nut-tree [ˌnʌt'tri:] *n* knowwydhenn *f* +ow, knowwydh *coll*

O

oar ['ɔ:ʳ] *n* roev *f* +ow, diwroev *dual*
obey [ə'beɪ] *v* obaya
obscene [əb'si:n] *adj* lyg
obscure [əb'skʊəʳ] *v* tewlhe
obscurity [əb'skjʊərəti] *n* tewlyjyon *m*
obvious ['ɒbvɪəs] *adj* apert
occasion [ə'keɪʒn] *n* gweyth *f* +yow; *(time)* prysweyth *f* +yow
occasionally [ə'keɪʒnəli] *adv* treweythyow
occident ['ɒksɪdənt] *n* howlsedhes *m*
Occitan ['ɒksɪtan] *adj* **Occitan language** Okitanek *m*
Occitania [ˌɒksɪ'teɪnjə] *place* Okitani
occupy ['ɒkju:paɪ] *v* kevannedhi
occur [ə'kɜ:ʳ] *v* hwarvos
ocean ['əʊʃən] *n* keynvor *m* +yow; **Atlantic Ocean** Keynvor Atlantek; **Indian Ocean** Keynvor Eyndek; **Pacific Ocean** Keynvor Hebask
October [ɒk'təʊbəʳ] *n* mis-Hedra *m* misyow-H.

243

odd [ˈɒd] *adj (of numbers)* dibarow; *(strange)* koynt

of [ɒv, əv] *prep* a

offend [əˈfend] *v* divlasa

offer [ˈɒfər] *n* profyans *m* +ow: *v* profya, offra

office [ˈɒfɪs] *n (job)* soedh *f* +ow; *(work-place)* soedhva *f* +ow; **ticket office** tokynva *f* +ow; **tourist office** soedhva dornyaseth *f* soedhvaow tornyaseth

officer [ˈɒfɪsər] *n* soedhek *m* -ogyon; **junior officer** issoedhek *m* -ogyon

official [əˈfɪʃl] *n* soedhek *m* -ogyon: *adj* soedhogel

often [ˈɒfn] *adv* lieskweyth, menowgh

oil [ˈɔɪl] *n* oyl *m* oylys

ogre [ˈəʊgər] *n* kowr *m* kewri

oh! [ˈəʊ] *int* ogh!

old [ˈəʊld] *adj* koth; **old age** kothni *f*; **the old** an re goth

older [ˈəʊldər] *adj* kottha

on [ɒn] *prep* war

once [ˈwʌns] *adv* unnweyth; **at once** desempis, hware

one [ˈwʌn] *num* onan: *pron* **the one** an huni; **the ones** an re; **another one** onan arall

one-eyed [ˌwʌnˈaɪd] *adj* unnlagasek

only [ˈəʊnli] *adv* hepken

open [ˈəʊpən] *adj* igor: *v* igeri

operate [ˈɒpəreɪt] *v* oberi

operation [ˌɒpəˈreɪʃən] *n* oberyans *m* +ow

opinion [əˈpɪnjən] *n* tybyans *m* +ow; **in my opinion** dhe'm brys vy

opponent [əˈpəʊnənt] *n* erbynner *m* -oryon

opportunity [ˌɒpəˈtjuːnəti] *n* chons *m* +yow

oppose [əˈpəʊz] *v* enebi

opposite ['ɔpəzɪt] *n* konter *m* +s: *adj* konter: *prep* a-dal

opposition [ˌɔpə'zɪʃən] *n* enebieth *f*, gorthter *m*

oppress [ə'pres] *v* arwaska

oppression [ə'preʃən] *n* arwask *m* +ow

option ['ɔpʃən] *n* dewis *m* +yow

or [ɔːʳ] *conj* po

orange ['ɔrɪndʒ] *n (fruit)* owraval *m* +ow: *adj (colour)* rudhvelyn

orchard ['ɔːtʃəd] *n (for apples)* avalennek *f* -egi

orchestra ['ɔːkɪstrə] *n* bagas ilewydhyon *m* bagasow i.

order ['ɔːdəʳ] *n (command)* gorhemmynn *m* +ow; **put in order** araya

ordinary ['ɔːdɪnri] *adj* sempel

organ ['ɔːgən] *n (musical)* organ *m* +s

organization [ˌɔːgənaɪ'zeɪʃən] *n (abst.)* restrans *m* +ow

organize ['ɔːgənaɪz] *v* ordena, restra

orient ['ɔːrɪənt] *n* howldrevel *m*, duryen *m*

origin ['ɔrɪdʒɪn] *n* devedhyans *m* +ow

original [ə'rɪdʒnəl] *adj* derowel

orphan ['ɔːfən] *n (female)* omdhivases *f* +ow; *(male)* omdhivas *m* +ow

ostrich ['ɔtɪtʃ] *n* strus *m* +yow

other ['ʌðəʳ] *pron* **the other (f.)** hy ben; **the other (m.)** y gila; **each other** an eyl y gila: *adj* arall, ken; **every other day** pub eyl dydh; **on the other hand** yn fordh arall

otherwise ['ʌðəwaɪz] *conj* poken: *adv* ken

our ['auəʳ] *pron* agan; **and our** ha'gan; **to our** dh'agan

out ['aut] *adv* yn-mes: *adj (of fire)* marow

outcome ['autkʌm] *n* diwedh *m* +ow

outside [ˌaʊtˈsaɪd] *adj* a-ves: *adv* yn-mes

oval [ˈəʊvəl] *n* hirgylgh *m* +yow: *adj* hirgylghyek

oven [ˈʌvən] *n* forn *f* +ow

over [ˈəʊvər] *prep* a-ugh: *adv (ended)* deu, gorfennys

overall [ˈəʊvərɔːl] *adv* dre vras

overalls [ˈəʊvərɔːlz] *plur* gorwisk *m* +ow

overcoat [ˈəʊvəkəʊt] *n* gorhota *m* -hotow

overheat [ˈəʊvəhiːt] *v* gordoemma

overheating [ˌəʊvəˈhiːtɪŋ] *n* gordoemmheans *m*

overthrow [ˌəʊvəˈθrəʊ] *v* domhwel

overturn [ˈəʊvətɜːn] *v* domhwel

owe [ˈəʊ] *v* tyli

owl [ˈaʊl] *n* kowann *f* +ow, oula *m* oulys

owner [ˈəʊnər] *n* perghenn *m* +ow, perghennek *m* -ogyon

ox [ˈɒks] *n* ojyon *m* oghen

P

pace [ˈpeɪs] *n* kamm *m* +ow, pas *m* +ys

pacific [pəˈsɪfɪk] *adj* hebask

packet [ˈpakɪt] *n* fardellik *m* -igow

page [ˈpeɪdʒ] *n (of book)* folenn *f* +ow

pain [ˈpeɪn] *n* payn *m* +ys

paint [ˈpeɪnt] *n* paynt *m* +ow: *v (a surface)* payntya; *(a picture)* lymna

paint-brush [ˈpeɪntˌbrʌʃ] *n* skubyllenn baynt; *(artist's)* pynsel *m* +yow

painter [ˈpeɪntər] *n (artist)* lymner *m* -oryon

painting [ˈpeɪntɪŋ] *n (picture)* lymnans *m* +ow

pair [ˈpeər] *n* kopel *m* koplow

palace [ˈpalɪs] *n* palys *m* palesyow
palate [ˈpalɪt] *n (in mouth)* stevnik *f* -igow
palm [ˈpɑːm] *n (of hand)* palv *f* +ow
pan [ˈpan] *n* padell *f* +ow
panda [ˈpandə] *n* panda *m* +s
pane [ˈpeɪn] *n* **pane of glass** kwarel *m* +s
panel [ˈpanl] *n (of people)* pannell *m* +ow
panther [ˈpanθər] *n* panther *m* +ow
pantry [ˈpantri] *n* talgell *f* +ow
paper [ˈpeɪpər] *n* paper *m* +yow
parachute [ˈparəʃuːt] *n* lammlenn *f* +ow
paradise [ˈparədaɪs] *n* paradhis *f*
paralyse [ˈparəlaɪz] *v* palsya
parasol [ˈparəsɔl] *n* howllenn *f* +ow
parcel [ˈpɑːsl] *n (package)* fardell *m* +ow
parent [ˈpeərənt] *n* kar *m* kerens
Paris [ˈparɪs] *place* Paris
parish [ˈparɪʃ] *n* pluw *f* +ow
park [ˈpɑːk] *n* park *m* +ow: *v* parkya
parliament [ˈpɑːləmənt] *n* senedh *m* +ow
parrot [ˈparət] *n* papynjay *m* +s
parsley [ˈpɑːsli] *n* persil *coll* +enn
part [ˈpɑːt] *n* rann *f* +ow, darn *m* +ow
participant [pɑːˈtɪsɪpənt] *n* kevrenner *m* -oryon
partner [ˈpɑːtnər] *n* kespar *m* +ow
party [ˈpɑːti] *n (feast)* kevywi *m* +ow; *(political)* parti *m* +ow
pass [ˈpɑːs] *n (topographical)* bolgh *m* +ow; *(sport)* pass *m* +ow: *v* tremena
passage [ˈpasɪdʒ] *n (alley)* skochfordh *f* +ow
passenger [ˈpasəndʒər] *n* vyajyer *m* -oryon
passport [ˈpɑːspɔːt] *n* tremengummyas *m* +ow
past [ˈpɑːst] *n* **the past** an termyn eus passys; **in the**

past seulabrys

pasta ['pastə] *n* pasta *m*

paste ['peɪst] *n* past *m* +ow

pasty ['pasti] *n* pasti *m* +ow

path ['pɑːθ] *n* hyns *m* +yow

patience ['peɪʃəns] *n* perthyans *m* +ow

patient ['peɪʃənt] *adj* godhevek

pause ['pɔːz] *v* hedhi, powes: *n* powes *m* +ow

pavement ['peɪvmənt] *n* kons *m* +ow

paw ['pɔː] *n* paw *f* +yow, diwbaw *dual*

pawn ['pɔːn] *n (in chess)* gwerinor *m* +yon

pay ['peɪ] *n (income)* gober *m* gobrow: *v* pe

payment ['peɪmənt] *n* talas *m* +ow

peace ['piːs] *n* kres *m*

peach ['piːtʃ] *n* aval-gwlanek *m* avalow-gwlanek

pearl ['pɜːl] *n* perl *m* +ys

peasant ['peznt] *n* gwerinor *m* +yon

pebble ['pebl] *n* bilienn *f* +ow, bili *coll*

pedal ['pedl] *n* troesell *f* +ow: *v* troesella

peel ['piːl] *n* rusk *f* +enn: *v* diruska

peelings ['piːlɪŋz] *plur* pilyon

peg ['peg] *n* ebil *m* +yer

penalty ['penəlti] *n* spal *m* +yow

pencil ['pensl] *n* pluvenn blomm *f* pluvennow plomm

penetrate ['penɪtreɪt] *v* dewana

penguin *n* penn-gwynn *m* pennow-gwynn

penis ['piːnɪs] *n* kalgh *m* +yow

penny ['peni] *n* diner *m* +ow

penny-piece [ˌpeni'piːs] *n* dinerenn *f* +ow

pension ['penʃən] *n (retirement)* gober omdennans *m* gobrow omdennans

Pentecost ['pentɪkɒst] *n* Penkost *m* +ow

Penzance [pen'zans] *place* Pennsans

people ['piːpl] *n* pobel *f* poblow; **common people**
   gwerin *f*
pepper ['pepər] *n* puber *m* +yow
perceive [pə'siːv] *v* merkya
percentage [pə'sentɪdʒ] *n* kansrann *f* +ow
perch ['pɜːtʃ] *n (for birds)* klus *m* +yow: *v* klusya
perfect ['pɜːfɪkt] *adj* flour, perfydh
perform [pə'fɔːm] *v* gwrythya
perfume ['pɜːfjuːm] *n* melyseth *f* +ow
perhaps [pə'haps] *adv* martesen
period ['pɪərɪəd] *n (of time)* oes *m* +ow; *(menstrual)*
   amseryow *plur*
permission [pə'mɪʃən] *n* kummyas *m* +ow
permit [pə'mɪt] *n* kummyas *m* +ow: *v* gasa
person ['pɜːsn] *n* person *m* +s
personal ['pɜːsnəl] *adj* personel
Peter ['piːtər] *name* Peder
petrol ['petrəl] *n* menoyl *m* +ys
pharmacy ['fɑːməsi] *n (shop)* ferylva *f* +ow
phase ['feɪz] *n (of Moon)* gwedh *f* +ow
photocopy ['fəʊtəʊˌkɒpi] *v* liesskrifa
photograph ['fəʊtəɡrɑːf] *n* skeusenn *f* +ow
physics ['fɪzɪks] *n* fisegieth *f*
piano [pɪ'anəʊ] *n* piano *m* +s
pick ['pɪk] *v (choose)* dewis; *(flowers)* kuntell
picnic ['pɪknɪk] *n* piknik *m* -igow
picture ['pɪktʃər] *n* lymnans *m* +ow
piece ['piːs] *n* tamm *m* temmyn, darn *m* +ow
pierce ['pɪəs] *v* gwana
piercing ['pɪəsɪŋ] *n* gwan *f* +yow: *adj* gwanus
pig ['pɪɡ] *n* hogh *m* -es
pigeon ['pɪdʒɪn] *n* kolomm *f* kelemmi
pill ['pɪl] *n* pellennik *f* -igow; **sleeping pill** pellennik

goska *f* -igow koska

pillow ['pɪləʊ] *n* pluvek *f* pluvogow

pilot ['paɪlət] *n (of aircraft)* lewyer *m* -yoryon

pin ['pɪn] *n* pynn *m* +ow

pinch ['pɪntʃ] *v* pynchya

pineapple ['paɪnapl] *n* pinaval *m* +ow

pink ['pɪŋk] *adj* gwynnrudh

pipe ['paɪp] *n* pibell *f* +ow

pit ['pɪt] *n* pytt *m* +ow

pitiless ['pɪtɪlɪs] *adj* dibita

pity ['pɪti] *n* truedh *m*; *v* kemmeres truedh; **have pity on** kemmeres truedh orth:

place ['pleɪs] *n* le *m* leow, tyller *m* +yow: *v* gorra

plain ['pleɪn] *n* plen *m* +ys: *adj* plen

plane ['pleɪn] *n (aircraft)* jynn-ebron *m* jynnow-ebron

planet ['planɪt] *n* planet *m* +ys +ow

plank ['plaŋk] *n* astell *f* estyll

plant ['plɑːnt] *n* les *m* +yow: *v* plansa

plaster ['plɑːstər] *n* plaster *m* plastrow: *v* plastra

plastic ['plastɪk] *adj* plastek: *n* plastek *m* -ogow

plate ['pleɪt] *n* plat *m* +yow +ys

plateau ['platəʊ] *n* ughelgompesenn *f* +ow

play ['pleɪ] *n* gwari *m* +ow: *v (games)* gwari; *(a wind instrument)* hwytha; *(another instrument)* seni

player ['pleɪər] *n* gwarier *m* -oryon

playtime ['pleɪtaɪm] *n* prys gwari *m* prysyow g.

pleasant ['pleznt] *adj* hweg

please ['pliːz] *v* plesya; *(if you please)* mar pleg

pleasure ['pleʒər] *n* plesour *m* +s

pliers ['plaɪəz] *plur* geveligow

plough ['plaʊ] *n* arader *m* ereder: *v* aras

plug ['plʌg] *n* kanell *m* +ow: *v* ebilya

plum ['plʌm] *n* ploumenn *f* +ow

250

plumber ['plʌmər] *n* plommer *m* -oryon
plural ['pluərəl] *adj* liesplek
plush ['plʌʃ] *n* pali fals *m*
Pluto ['pluːtəʊ] *place* Pluto
Plymouth ['plɪməθ] *place* Aberplymm
pocket ['pɔkɪt] *n* poket *m* +ow
poem ['pəʊɪm] *n* bardhonek *m* -ogow
poet ['pəʊɪt] *n* prydydh *m* +yon
poetry ['pəʊɪtri] *n* bardhonieth *f*
point ['pɔɪnt] *n* bleyn *m* +yow
pointed *adj* minyek
poison ['pɔɪzn] *n* gwenon *m* -enyow: *v* venimya
poisonous ['pɔɪzənəs] *adj* gwenonek
Poland ['pəʊlənd] *place* Poloni
pole ['pəʊl] *n* peul *m* +yow
police [pəˈliːs] *n* kreslu *m* +yow
policeman [pəˈliːsmən] *n* gwithyas-kres *m* gwithysi-gres
policy ['pɔləsi] *n* polisi *m* +s
Polish ['pəʊlɪʃ] *adj* polonek; **Polish language** Polonek *m*
polite [pəˈlaɪt] *adj* kortes
politeness [pəˈlaɪtnɪs] *n* kortesi *m* +s
political [pəˈlɪtɪkl] *adj* politek
politician *n* politeger *m* -oryon
politics ['pɔlətɪks] *pl* politegieth *f*
pollute [pəˈluːt] *v* defola
polluter [pəˈluːtər] *n* defoler *m* -oryon
pollution [pəˈluːʃən] *n* defolans *m* +ow
pond ['pɔnd] *n* poll *m* +ow, lagenn *f* +ow
pony ['pəʊni] *n* hoba *m* +s
pool ['puːl] *n* poll *m* +ow
poor ['pʊər] *adj (lacking money)* boghosek

pope ['pəʊp] *n* pab *m* +ow

popular ['pɒpjʊlər] *adj (of the people)* gwerinek; *(much liked)* meurgerys

population [ˌpɒpjʊ'leɪʃən] *n* poblans *m* +ow

porpoise ['pɔːpəs] *n* morhogh *m* +es

porridge ['pɒrɪdʒ] *n* yos kergh *m*

port ['pɔːt] *n* porth *m* +ow

portable ['pɔːtəbl] *adj* degadow

portion ['pɔːʃən] *n* darnas *m* +ow

portmanteau [pɔːt'mantəʊ] *n* portmantell *m* +ow

Portugal ['pɔːtʃʊgl] *place* Portyngal

Portuguese [pɔːtʃʊ'giːz] *adj* portyngalek; **Portuguese language** Portyngalek *m*

possible ['pɒsəbl] *adj* galladow

post ['pəʊst] *n (pole)* post *m* +ow

postman ['pəʊstmən] *n* lytherwas *m* -wesyon

post-office ['pəʊst,ɒfɪs] *n* lytherva *f* +ow

postwoman ['pəʊswʊmən] *n* lythervaghteth *f* -veghtythyon

pot ['pɒt] *n* pott *m* +ow

potter ['pɒtər] *n* priweythor *m* +yon

pottery ['pɒtəri] *n (craft)* priweyth *m*; *(factory)* priweythva *f* +ow

poultry ['pəʊltri] *n* dovydhyn *plur*

pound ['paʊnd] *n (money or weight)* peuns *m* +ow

pour ['pɔː] *v* diveri

poverty ['pɒvəti] *n* boghosogneth *f*

powder ['paʊdər] *n* polter *m* +yow

power ['paʊər] *n* galloes *m* +ow, nerth *m* +yow

powerful ['paʊəfʊl] *adj* galloesek, nerthek

practise ['praktɪs] *v* praktisya, omassaya

praise ['preɪz] *n* gormola *f* gormoledhow: *v* gormel

pray ['preɪ] *v* pysi

prayer ['preə^r] *n* pysadow *m*

precious ['preʃəs] *adj* drudh

prediction [prɪ'dɪkʃən] *n* dargan *f* +ow

prefer [prɪ'fɜ:^r] *v* **I prefer** gwell yw genev

pregnant ['pregnənt] *adj* beghyek, gans flogh

prepare [prɪ'peə^r] *v* pareusi, darbari

prescription [prɪ'skrɪpʃən] *n* ragsettyans *m* +ow

present ['preznt] *n (gift)* ro *m* rohow: *adj* a-lemmyn

presenter [prɪ'zentə^r] *n* kommendyas *m* -ysi

presently ['prezntli] *adv* y'n eur ma

preserve [prɪ'zɜ:v] *v* gwitha

president ['prezɪdənt] *n* lewydh *m* +yon

press ['pres] *v* gwaska

pressure ['preʃə^r] *n* poes *m* +ow

pressure-cooker ['preʃə͵kʌkə^r] *n* gwaskogforn *f* +ow

pretend [prɪ'tend] *v* omwul

pretext ['pri:tekst] *n* ragskeus *m* +ow

pretty ['prɪti] *adj* teg

prevent [prɪ'vent] *v* lettya, lesta

price ['praɪs] *n* pris *m* +yow

pride ['praɪd] *n* goeth *m*

priest ['pri:st] *n* pronter *m* +yon

primrose ['prɪmrəʊz] *n* briallenn *f* +ow, brialli *coll*

prince ['prɪns] *n* pennsevik *m* -igyon -igyow

princess [prɪn'ses] *n* pennseviges *f* +ow

principal ['prɪnsɪpəl] *adj* penn-

print ['prɪnt] *n* prynt *m* +ow: *v* pryntya

prison ['prɪzn] *n* prison *m* +yow

private ['praɪvɪt] *adj* privedh

privation [praɪ'veɪʃən] *n* esow *m*

prize ['praɪz] *n* piwas *m* +ow

problem ['prɒbləm] *n* kudynn *m* +ow; **no problem** kudynn vyth

253

process ['prəʊses] *n* argerdh *m* +ow: *v (walk)*
  keskerdhes

produce [prə'djuːs] *n* askorr *m*: *v* askorra

product ['prɒdʌkt] *n* askorras *m* +ow

profession [prə'feʃən] *n* galwesigeth *f* +ow

professional [prə'feʃənəl] *n* galwesik *m* -igyon: *adj*
  galwesik

profit ['prɒfɪt] *n* les *m*

programme ['prəʊgram] *n* towlenn *f* +ow

progress ['prəʊgres] *n* avonsyans *m* +ow: *v* avonsya

prohibition [ˌprəʊhɪ'bɪʃən] *n* difenn *m* +ow

project ['prɒdʒekt] *n* ragdres *m* +ow: *v (stick out)*
  balegi

promise ['prɒmɪs] *n* ambos *m* +ow: *v* ambosa

pronunciation [prəˌnʌnsɪ'eɪʃən] *n* gis-leveryans *m*
  gisyow-l.

proof ['pruːf] *n* prov *m* +ow

prophecy ['prɒfɪsi] *n* dargan *f* +ow

proportion [prə'pɔːʃən] *n* kemusur *m* +yow

propose [prə'pəʊz] *v* profya

proposition [ˌprɒpə'zɪʃən] *n* kynnik *m* -igow

proprietor [prə'praɪətəʳ] *n* perghenn *m* +ow

prostitute ['prɒstɪtjuːt] *n* hora *f* horys

protect [prə'tekt] *v* difres; **protect from** gwitha rag

Protestant ['prɒtɪstənt] *n* Protestant *m* -ans: *adj*
  Protestant

proud ['praʊd] *adj* goethus

prove ['pruːv] *v* previ

province ['prɒvɪns] *n* rannvro *f* +yow

prudent ['pruːdənt] *adj* doeth

public ['pʌblɪk] *adj* poblek; **public house** diwotti *m*
  +ow: *n* **the public** an poblek

publish ['pʌblɪʃ] *v* dyllo

254

puddle ['pʌdl] *n* lagenn *f* +ow
puffin ['pʌfɪn] *n* nath *m* +es
pull ['pʊl] *v* tenna
pulverize ['pʌlvəraɪz] *v* mannvrywi
pump ['pʌmp] *n* pompell *f* +ow: *v* pompya
pumpkin ['pʌmpkɪn] *n* pompyon *m* +s
pungent ['pʌndʒənt] *adj* mosek
punish ['pʌnɪʃ] *v* kessydhya
punishment ['pʌnɪʃmənt] *n* kessydhyans *m* +ow
pupil ['pjuːpəl] *n* dyskybel *m* dyskyblon; *(of the eye)*
    byw an lagas
puppet ['pʌpɪt] *n* popett *m* +ow
purchase ['pɜːtʃɪs] *n* prenas *m* +ow: *v* prena
pure ['pjʊər] *adj* pur
purple ['pɜːpl] *adj* glasrudh
purpose ['pɜːpəs] *n* mynnas *m* +ow; **on purpose**
    a-borpos *adv*
purse ['pɜːs] *n* yalgh *f* +ow
pursue [pə'sjuː] *v* pursywya
push ['pʊʃ] *v* herdhya
push-chair *n* kador-herdhya *f* kadoryow-herdhya
put ['pʊt] *v* gorra

Q

quake ['kweɪk] *n* kren *m* +yow: *v* krysya
quality ['kwɒləti] *n* gnas *f* +ow
quarrel ['kwɒrəl] *n* kedrynn *f* +ow: *v* kedrynna
quarry ['kwɒri] *n* *(stone-pit)* mengleudh *m* +yow
quarter ['kwɔːtər] *n* *(space)* kwartron *m* +ys; *(time)*
    kwarter *m* kwartrys; *(of a year)* trymis *m* +yow

quartermaster ['kwɔːtə͵mɑːstər] *n* erberjour *m* +s
quay ['kiː] *n* kay *m* kayow
queen ['kwiːn] *n* myghternes *f* +ow, ruvanes *f* +ow
question ['kwestʃən] *n* govynn *m* +ow: *v* govynn *m* +ow
quick ['kwɪk] *adj (rapid)* uskis, snell
quickly ['kwɪkli] *adv* yn uskis, toeth men
quiet ['kwaɪət] *n* kosoleth *f*: *adj* kosel
quietness ['kwaɪətnɪs] *n* kosoleth *f*
quill ['kwɪl] *n* pluvenn *f* +ow, pluv *coll*
quite ['kwaɪt] *adv* glan, poran; **quite expensive** ker lowr

R

rabbit ['rabɪt] *n* konin *m* +es
rabble ['rabl] *n* rout *m* +ys
rabies ['reɪbiːz] *n* konnar *f*
race ['reɪs] *n* res *m* +ow; *(ethnic)* hil *f* +yow
racist ['reɪsɪst] *n* hilgasydh *m* +yon
rack ['rak] *n* kloes *f* +yow
radio ['reɪdɪəʊ] *n* radyo *m* +yow, diwiver *m* +yow
railing *n* peulge *m* +ow
railway ['reɪlweɪ] *n* hyns-horn *m* hynsyow-horn
rain ['reɪn] *n* glaw *m* +yow; **heavy rain** glaw bras; **light rain** glaw munys: *v* gul glaw; **it is raining** glaw a wra
rainbow ['reɪnbəʊ] *n* kammneves *f* +ow
raincoat ['reɪnkəʊt] *n* mantell-law *f* mantelli-glaw
raise ['reɪz] *v* drehevel
rake ['reɪk] *n* **garden rake** rakan *m* +ow

ram ['ram] *n* hordh *m* +es: *v* herdhya

rank ['raŋk] *n* renk *m* +ow: *v* **rank in order** renka

rape ['reɪp] *v* ravna: *n* ravnans *m* +ow

rare ['reəʳ] *adj* tanow

rasp ['rɑːsp] *n* rathell *f* +ow: *v* ratha

rat ['rat] *n* rath *m* +es

rate ['reɪt] *n* kevradh *m* +ow

rather ['rɑːðəʳ] *adv (sooner)* kyns

raw ['rɔː] *adj (uncooked)* kriv

ray ['reɪ] *n (of light)* dewynn *m* +ow

razor ['reɪzəʳ] *n* altenn *f* +ow

reach ['riːtʃ] *v* drehedhes

read ['riːd] *v* redya; **read aloud** lenna

reader ['riːdəʳ] *n* lenner *m* -oryon

ready ['redi] *adj* parys

real ['rɪəl] *adj* gwir

reap ['riːp] *v* mysi

reason ['riːzn] *n* skila *f* skilys, ken *m* +yow, reson *m* +s; *(intelligence)* poell *m* +ow: *v* resna

rebuild [riː'bɪld] *v* dassevel

recall [rɪ'kɔːl] *v (remember)* perthi kov

receipt [rɪ'siːt] *n* akwityans *m* +ow

receive [rɪ'siːv] *v* degemmeres

recently ['riːsntli] *adv* a-gynsow

reception [rɪ'sepʃən] *n* kemmeryans *m* +ow; **reception room** degemmerva *f* +ow

recipe ['resɪpi] *n* resayt *m* +yow

recipient [rɪ'sɪpɪənt] *n* degemmerer *m* -oryon

recite [rɪ'saɪt] *v* dythya

recognize ['rekəgnaɪz] *v* aswonn

recommend [ˌrekə'mend] *v* kommendya

reconnaissance [rɪ'kɒnɪsəns] *n* aspians *m* +ow

record ['rekɔːd] *n* kovadh *m* +ow; *(sport)* rekord *m*

+ys; *(sound-recording)* plasenn *f* +ow: *v* rekordya, sonskrifa

recover [rɪ'kʌvər] *v (trans.)* daskavoes

rectangle ['rektaŋgl] *n* hirbedrek *m* hirbedrogow

rectify ['rektɪfaɪ] *v* ewnhe

red ['red] *adj* rudh

red-haired [ˌred'heəd] *adj* penn-rudh

Redruth [re'druːθ] *place* Rysrudh

reduce [rɪ'djuːs] *v* byghanhe

reef ['riːf] *n (in sea)* krib *f* +ow

re-enter [riː'entər] *v* dasentra

referee [refə'riː] *n* breusydh *m* +yon

refill [riː'fɪl] *v* daslenwel

refined [rɪ'faɪnd] *adj* fin

reflect [rɪ'flekt] *v* ombrederi; *(of light)* dastewynnya

refrain [rɪ'freɪn] *n* pusorn *m* +ow

refrigerator [rɪ'frɪdʒəreɪtər] *n* yeynell *f* +ow

refuge ['refjuːdʒ] *n* harber *m* +ys

refugee [ˌrefjʊ'dʒiː] *n* fowesik *m* -igyon

refusal [rɪ'fjuːzl] *n* nagh *m* +ow

refuse *v* nagha, skonya

region ['riːdʒən] *n* ranndir *m* +yow

register ['redʒɪstər] *n* kovlyver *m* -lyvrow: *v* kovskrifa

regret [rɪ'gret] *n* edrega *f*: kemmeres edrek *v*

regular ['regjʊlər] *adj* reyth

regulation [ˌregjʊ'leɪʃən] *n* rewl *f* +ys +ow

rehearsal [rɪ'hɜːsl] *n* assay *m* +s

reheat *v* dastoemma

reign ['reɪn] *n* reyn *m* +ys: *v* reynya

related [rɪ'leɪtɪd] *adj* **related by blood** unnwoes

relation [rɪ'leɪʃən] *n (member of family)* kar *m* kerens

relative ['relətɪv] *n* kar *m* kerens

relax [rɪ'laks] *v* diskwitha

release [rɪ'liːs] *v (set free)* livra; *(publish)* dyllo
relieve [rɪ'liːv] *v* difres
religion [rɪ'lɪdʒən] *n* kryjyans *m* +ow
religious [rɪ'lɪdʒəs] *adj* kryjyk
relinquish [rɪ'lɪŋkwɪʃ] *v* hepkorr
remain [rɪ'meɪn] *v* gortos
remake ['riːmeɪk] *v* daswul
remedy ['remədi] *n* kur *m* +yow
remember [rɪ'membər] *v (trans.)* perthi kov a;
  (intrans.) perthi kov
remind [rɪ'maɪnd] *v* kovhe
remote [rɪ'məʊt] *adj* pell; **remote control**
  pellvotonek *f* -egi
remove [rɪ'muːv] *v* dilea
render ['rendər] *v (give)* ri
rent ['rent] *n: v* gobrena
repair [rɪ'peər] *n* ewnheans *m* +ow: *v* ewnhe
repay [riː'peɪ] *v* attyli
repeat [rɪ'piːt] *v* dasleverel
reply [rɪ'plaɪ] *n* gorthyp *m* gorthybow: *v* gorthybi
report [rɪ'pɔːt] *n* derivas *m*: *v* derivas
reporter [rɪ'pɔːtər] *n* derivador *m* +yon
reproach [rɪ'prəʊtʃ] *n* keredh *f* +yow: *v* keredhi
republic [rɪ'pʌblɪk] *n* repoblek *f* -ogow
republican [rɪ'pʌblɪkən] *adj* poblogethek:
  n poblogethek *m* -ogyon
reputation [ˌrepjʊ'teɪʃən] *n* bri *f*
research [rɪ'sɜːtʃ] *n* hwithrans *m* +ow
reservation [ˌrezə'veɪʃən] *n* ragarghas *m* +ow
reserved [rɪ'zɜːvd] *adj (booked)* ragerghys
resew [riː'səʊ] *v* daswrias
residence ['rezɪdəns] *n* treveth *f* +ow
resign [rɪ'zaɪn] *v* omdhisoedha

resignation [ˌrezɪgˈneɪʃən] *n* omdhisoedhans *m* +ow
resist [rɪˈzɪst] *v* sevel orth
resolve [rɪˈzɒlv] *v* ervira
respect [rɪˈspekt] *n* reowta *m*; **with respect to** yn kever
response [rɪˈspɒns] *n* gorthyp *m* gorthybow
responsible [rɪˈspɒnsəbl] *adj* omgemmeryek
restaurant [ˈrestərɒnt] *n* boesti *m* +ow
restore [rɪˈstɔːr] *v* daskorr
result [rɪˈzʌlt] *n* sywyans *m* +ow
retire [rɪˈtaɪər] *v* omdenna
retired [rɪˈtaɪəd] *adj (from work)* omdennys
retirement [rɪˈtaɪəmənt] *n* omdennans *m* +ow
return [rɪˈtɜːn] *n* dehwelyans *m* +ow: *v* dehweles
revise [rɪˈvaɪz] *v* dasweles
revive [rɪˈvaɪv] *v* dasvywa
revolution [revəˈluːʃən] *n (political)* domhwelyans *m* +ow
rewritten [riːˈrɪtən] *adj* dasskrifys
rheumatism [ˈruːmətɪzəm] *n* remm *m*
rhinoceros [raɪˈnɒsərəs] *n* troengornvil *m* +es
rhythm [ˈrɪðəm] *n* resyas *m* +ow
rice [ˈraɪs] *n* ris *coll* +enn
rich [ˈrɪtʃ] *adj* golusek, rych
riches [ˈrɪtʃɪz] *plur* pythow, rychys *m*
ride [ˈraɪd] *v (a horse)* marghogeth
right [ˈraɪt] *n (truth)* gwir *m* +yow; *(law)* reyth *m* +yow: *adj (true)* gwir; *(regular)* reyth; *(opposite to left)* dyghow; **on the right hand** a-dhyghow
rightly [ˈraɪtli] *adv* poran
rigid [ˈrɪdʒɪd] *adj* diwedhyn
ring [ˈrɪŋ] *n (circle)* kylgh *m* +yow; *(for finger)* bysow *m* bysowyer: *v (of a bell)* seni*

rinse ['rɪns] *v* godroghya

ripe ['raɪp] *adj* adhves

ripen ['raɪpən] *v* adhvesi

rise ['raɪz] *v* sevel; *(of tide)* morlenwel

rising ['raɪzɪŋ] *n* sordyans *m* +ow

risk ['rɪsk] *n* argoll *m* +ow: *v* argelli

risky ['rɪski] *adj* argollus

river ['rɪvər] *n* avon *f* +yow

road ['rəʊd] *n* fordh *f* +ow, hyns *m* +yow

roast ['rəʊst] *v* rostya

rob ['rɒb] *v* ladra

robbery ['rɒbəri] *n (in general)* ladrynsi *m*; *(individual crime)* ladrans *m* +ow

robin ['rɒbɪn] *n* rudhek *m* -ogyon

robot ['rəʊbɒt] *n* robot *m* +ow

rock *v* leska

rocket ['rɒkɪt] *n* fusenn *f* +ow

rod ['rɒd] *n* gwelenn *f* gwelynni, gwel *coll*

roedeer ['rəʊdɪər] *n* yorgh *f* yergh

rogue ['rəʊg] *n* sherewa *m* sherewys

roll ['rəʊl] *n (list)* rol *f* +yow: *v* rolya

roller ['rəʊlər] *n (wooden)* rolbrenn *m* +yer; *(stone)* rolven *m* rolveyn

Roman ['rəʊmən] *adj* romanek: *n* Roman *m* +s +yon

Romance [rə'mans] *adj* romanek

Romania [rəʊ'meɪnɪə] *place* Romani

Rome ['rəʊm] *place* Rom

roof ['ruːf] *n* to *m* tohow; *(of mouth)* stevnik *f*

room ['rʊm] *n* stevell *f* +ow

roost ['ruːst] *n* klus *m* +yow: *v* klusya

rope ['rəʊp] *n* lovan *f* lovonow

rot ['rɒt] *n* poder *m*, breynder *m*: *v* pedri, breyna

rotten ['rɒtn] *adj* podrek, breyn

rough ['rʌf] *adj* garow
round ['raʊnd] *adj* kylghyek, rond
roundabout ['raʊndəbaʊt] *n (for traffic)* kylghfordh *f* +ow
row *n (line of objects)* res *f* +yow
rowing-boat ['rəʊɪŋbəʊt] *n* skath-roevya *f* skathow-roevya
rub ['rʌb] *v* rutya
rubbish ['rʌbɪʃ] *n* atal *coll* +enn
rudder ['rʌdər] *n* lew *m* +yow
ruin ['ruːɪn] *n (building)* magor *f* +yow; *(financial)* diswrians *m* +ow: *v* diswul
rule ['ruːl] *n* rewl *f* +ys +ow: *v (trans.)* rewlya
ruler ['ruːlər] *n (head of state)* rewler *m* -oryon; *(tool)* rewlell *f* +ow
rum *n* roemm *m* +ow
ruminate ['ruːmɪneɪt] *v* dasknias
rumour ['ruːmər] *n* kyhwedhel *m* kyhwedhlow
run ['rʌn] *v* poenya; *(of liquids and people)* resek; **run away** diank
runner ['rʌnər] *n* resegydh *m* +yon
rush ['rʌʃ] *n (plant)* broenenn *f* +ow, broenn *coll*
russet ['rʌsɪt] *adj* rudhloes
Russia ['rʌʃə] *place* Russi
Russian ['rʌʃən] *adj* russek; **Russian language** Russek *m*
rust ['rʌst] *n* gossen *f* +yow: *v* gosseni
rye ['raɪ] *n* sugal *coll* +enn

S

sacking ['sakɪŋ] *n (dismissal)* gordhyllans *m* +ow
sacred ['seɪkrɪd] *adj* sans
sad ['sad] *adj* trist
safe ['seɪf] *adj* salow, saw
Sagittarius [sadʒɪ'teərɪəs] *n* An Sether
sail ['seɪl] *n* goel *m* +yow: *v* goelya
sailing-boat ['seɪlɪŋˌbəʊt] *n* skath-woelya *f* skathow-goelya
sailor ['seɪlər] *n (professional)* marner *m* marners marnoryon
saint ['seɪnt] *n (male)* sans *m* syns; *(female)* sanses *f* +ow; **patron saint** tasek *m* tasogyon
salad ['saləd] *n* salad *m* +ys
salary ['saləri] *n* gober *m* gobrow
sale ['seɪl] *n (event)* gwerth *f* +ow
salesman ['seɪlzmən] *n* gwerther *m* -oryon
saliva [sə'laɪvə] *n* trew *m*
salmon ['samən] *n* eghek *m* eghogyon
salt ['sɔːlt] *n* hoelan *coll* +enn; **salt water** hyli *m*
Saltash [sɔlt'aːʃ] *place* Essa
salty ['sɔːlti] *adj* hoelanek
same ['seɪm] *adj* keth; **the same thing** an keth tra
sanction ['saŋkʃən] *n (permission)* kummyas *m*; *(penalty)* kessydhyans *m* +ow: *v* ri kummyas
sand ['sand] *n* tewes *coll* +enn
sandwich ['sanwɪdʒ] *n* baramanynn *m* +ow
Satan ['seɪtən] *name* Satnas
satellite ['satəlaɪt] *n (artificial)* loerell *f* +ow
Saturday ['satədi] *n* dy' Sadorn *m* dydhyow Sadorn
Saturn ['satɜːn] *n (planet, god)* Sadorn *m*
sauce ['sɔːs] *n* sows *m* +ow

saucepan ['sɔ:spən] *n* padell-dhorn *f* padellow-dorn
saucer ['sɔ:sər] *n* padellik *f* -igow
sausage ['sɔsɪdʒ] *n* selsigenn *f* +ow, selsik *coll*
save ['seɪv] *conj* marnas: *v (from danger)* sawya, selwel; *(amass money)* erbysi
savings ['seɪvɪŋz] *plur* erbysyon
saw ['sɔ:] *n (tool)* heskenn *f* +ow: *v* heskenna
say ['seɪ] *v* leverel; **he says/said** yn-medh ev
saying ['seɪɪŋ] *n* henlavar *m* +ow
scab ['skab] *n* krevenn *f* +ow
scaffolding ['skafəldɪŋ] *n* peulweyth *m*
scale ['skeɪl] *n (of map)* skeul *f* +yow: *v* skeulya
scales ['skeɪlz] *n (for weighing)* mantol *f* +yow; *(of fish)* skans *coll* +enn
scarf ['skɑ:f] *n* lien konna *m* lienyow k.
scent ['sent] *n* ethenn *f* +ow
scholar ['skɔlər] *n (female)* skolores *f* +ow; *(male)* skoler *m* -oryon
school ['sku:l] *n* skol *f* +yow; **riding school** skol varghogeth *f* skolyow marghogeth
science ['saɪəns] *n* godhonieth *f* +ow
scientific [ˌsaɪən'tɪfɪk] *adj* godhoniethek
scientist ['saɪəntɪst] *n* godhonydh *m* +yon
scissors ['sɪzəz] *plur* gwelsigow *plur*
scold ['skəʊld] *v* tavosa
Scotland ['skɔtlənd] *place* Alban
Scotsman ['skɔtsmən] *n* Alban *m* +yon
scrape ['skreɪp] *v* kravas, ratha
scratch ['skratʃ] *v* kravas: *n* kravas *m* +ow
scream ['skri:m] *v* skrija: *n* skrij *m* +ow
screw ['skru:] *n* trogenter *f* -gentrow: *v* trogentra
scythe ['saɪð] *n* falgh *f* fylgher: *v* felghya
sea ['si:] *n* mor *m* +yow; **at sea** war vor; **a sea of**

264

people mor a bobel

seagull ['siːgʌl] *n* goelann *f* +es

seal ['siːl] *n (for document)* sel *f* +yow; *(mammal)* reun *m* +yon: *v* selya

search ['sɜːtʃ] *v* **search for** hwilas

season ['siːzn] *n* seson *m* +yow +s

seat ['siːt] *n* esedh *f* +ow; **country seat** plas *m* plasow

seaweed ['siːwiːd] *n* goemmon *coll* +enn

second ['sekənd] *n (of time)* eylenn *f* +ow: *num* nessa, eyl

secret ['siːkrɪt] *n* kevrin *m* +yow: *adj* kevrinek

secretary ['sekrətri] *n (female)* skrifennvades *f* +ow; *(male)* skrifennyas *m* -ysi

section ['sekʃən] *n* tregh *m* +ow

security [sɪ'kjʊərəti] *n* diogeledh *m*

see ['siː] *v* gweles: *int* ott

seed ['siːd] *n (in general)* has *coll* +enn

seek ['siːk] *v* hwilas

seem ['siːm] *v* heveli

seize ['siːz] *v* dalghenna

select [sɪ'lekt] *v* dewis

selection [sɪ'lekʃən] *n* dewis *m* +yow

self ['self] *n* honan *m*

sell ['sel] *v* gwertha

seller ['selər] *n* gwerther *m* -oryon

send ['send] *v* dannvon

sensation [sen'seɪʃən] *n* omglewans *m* +ow

sense ['sens] *n* skians *m* +ow; *(meaning)* styr *m* +yow

sensitive ['sensɪtɪv] *adj* kroghendanow

sentence ['sentəns] *n (grammatical)* lavar *m* +ow

separate *adj* ['sepərət] diblans: *v* ['sepəreɪt] diberth

separation [ˌsepəˈreɪʃən] *n* dibarth *f* +ow

September [sepˈtembər] *n* mis-Gwynngala *m* misyow-Gwynngala

Serb [ˈsɜːb] *n* Serb *m* +yon

Serbia [ˈsɜːbɪə] *place* Serbi

Serbian [ˈsɜːbɪən] *adj* serbek; **Serbian language** Serbek *m*

sergeant [ˈsɑːdʒənt] *n* serjont *m* serjons

serious [ˈsɪərɪəs] *adj* sad, sevur

servant [ˈsɜːvənt] *n* servyas *m* -ysi

serve [ˈsɜːv] *v* servya

service [ˈsɜːvɪs] *n (in general, not in church)* gonis *m* +yow; *(including in church)* servis *m* +yow

serviette [səviˈet] *n* lien diwla *m* lienyow d.

session [ˈseʃən] *n* esedhek *m* +ow

set [ˈset] *v* gorra, settya

settle [ˈsetl] *v (on new land)* trevesiga

settlement [ˈsetlmənt] *n* trevesigeth *f* +ow

seven [ˈsevn] *num* seyth

seventeen [ˌsevnˈtiːn] *num* seytek

seventy [ˈsevntɪ] *num* deg ha tri-ugens

several [ˈsevrəl] *adj* lower

severe [sɪˈvɪər] *adj* sevur

sew [ˈsəʊ] *v* gwrias

sex [ˈseks] *n* reydh *f* +ow

sexual [ˈseksʊəl] *adj* reydhel

shade [ˈʃeɪd] *n* goskotter *m* +yow

shadow [ˈʃadəʊ] *n* skeus *m* +ow

shaft [ˈʃɑːft] *n (rod)* gwelenn *f* gwelynni, gwel *coll*; *(of mine)* shafta *m* +ow

shake [ˈʃeɪk] *v* krena

shallow [ˈʃaləʊ] *adj* bas

shame [ˈʃeɪm] *n* meth *f* +ow, sham *m* +ys: *v* shamya

shameful [ˈʃɪmfʊl] *adj* methus

shampoo [ʃamˈpuː] *n* golslin *m* +yow

shape [ˈʃeɪp] *n* furv *f* +ow, roeth *m* +ow

share [ˈʃeər] *n* kevrenn *f* +ow: *v* kevrenna

shark [ˈʃɑːk] *n* morvleydh *m* +i

sharp [ˈʃɑːp] *adj (not blunt)* lymm

shave [ˈʃeɪv] *v (oneself)* omdhivarva; *(trans.)* divarva

she [ˈʃiː] *pron* hi

shed [ˈʃed] *n* krow *m* +yow: *v* dinewi

sheep [ˈʃiːp] *n* davas *f* deves

sheet [ˈʃiːt] *n (for a bed)* lien gweli *m* lienyow gweli;
   sheet of paper folenn *f* +ow

shelf [ˈʃelf] *n* estyllenn *f* +ow, estyll *coll*

shell [ˈʃel] *n* krogen *f* kregyn; *(explosive)* tanbellenn *f*
   +ow

shelter [ˈʃeltər] *n* goskes *m* goskeusow: *v* goskeusi

shepherd [ˈʃepərd] *n* bugel *m* +edh

shepherdess [ˈʃepədes] *n* bugeles *f* +ow

shine [ˈʃaɪn] *v* splanna

shiny [ˈʃaɪni] *adj* lentrus

ship [ˈʃɪp] *n* gorhel *m* -holyon

shirt [ˈʃɜːt] *n* krys *m* +yow; *(rough)* hevis *m* +yow

shiver [ˈʃɪvər] *v* degrena

shoe [ˈʃuː] *n* eskis *f* +yow; **put shoes on** arghena *v*

shoot [ˈʃuːt] *v* tenna

shop [ˈʃɒp] *n* gwerthji *m* +ow

shopping [ˈʃɒpɪŋ] *n (item bought)* prenas *m* +ow

shore [ˈʃɔːr] *n* morlann *f* +ow

short [ˈʃɔːt] *adj* berr

shorten [ˈʃɔːtn] *v* berrhe

shot [ˈʃɒt] *n* tenn *m* +ow

shoulder [ˈʃəʊldər] *n* skoedh *f* +ow, diwskoedh *dual*

shout [ˈʃaʊt] *n* garm *f* +ow: *v* garma

show [ˈʃəʊ] *n* diskwedhyans *m* +ow: *v* diskwedhes

shower [ˈʃaʊəʳ] *n* kowas *f* kowasow; *(domestic)* kowasell *f* +ow

shred [ˈʃred] *v* frega, skethenna

shrimp [ˈʃrɪmp] *n* bibyn-bubyn *m* bibynes-bubyn

shut [ˈʃʌt] *adj* klos, deges: *v* degea

shuttle [ˈʃʌtl] *n* gwerthys *f* +ow

shy [ˈʃaɪ] *adj* gohelus

sick [ˈsɪk] *adj* klav

sickle [ˈsɪkl] *n* kromman *f* +ow

side [ˈsaɪd] *n* tenewen *m* tenwennow

siege [ˈsiːdʒ] *n* esedhva *f* +ow

sign [ˈsaɪn] *n* arwoedh *f* +yow, sin *m* +ys +yow: *v* sina

signature [ˈsɪgnətʃəʳ] *n* sinans *m* +ow

silence [ˈsaɪləns] *n* taw *m*; *(command)* taw taves!

silent [ˈsaɪlənt] *adj* didros,tawesek; **be silent** tewel

silk [ˈsɪlk] *n* owrlin *m* +yow

silly [ˈsɪli] *adj* gokki

silver [ˈsɪlvəʳ] *n* arghans *m*

similar [ˈsɪmɪləʳ] *adj* haval, hevelep; **similar to** haval dhe

simple [ˈsɪmpl] *adj* sempel

simpleton [ˈsɪmpltən] *n* boba *m* bobys

sin [ˈsɪn] *n* pegh *m* +ow: *v* pegha

since [ˈsɪns] *adv* a-wosa: *prep* a-dhia: *conj* a-ban; **since Christmas** a-dhia Nadelik

sincere [sɪnˈsɪəʳ] *adj* gwiryon

sing [ˈsɪŋ] *v* kana

singer [ˈsɪŋəʳ] *n* kaner *m* -oryon, kanores *f* +ow

singing [ˈsɪŋɪŋ] *n* kenys *m*

single [ˈsɪŋgl] *adj* unnik; *(unmarried)* andhemmedhys

sink [ˈsɪŋk] *n* new *f* +yow

sir [ˈsɜːʳ] *n* syrr *m* +ys

sister ['sɪstə^r] *n* hwoer *f* hwerydh

sister-in-law [ˌsɪstərɪn'lɔː] *n* hwoer dre lagha *f* hwerydh dre lagha

sit ['sɪt] *v* **sit down** esedha; **sitting down** yn y esedh

site ['saɪt] *n* le *m* leow

six ['sɪks] *num* hwegh

sixteen [ˌsɪks'tiːn] *num* hwetek

sixty ['sɪkstɪ] *num* tri-ugens

size ['saɪz] *n* braster *m* +yow, myns *m* +ow

skeleton ['skelətən] *n* korf eskern *m* korfow e.

sketch ['sketʃ] *n* linennans *m* +ow: *v* linenna

ski ['skiː] *v* skia. *n* ski *m* +ow, dewski *dual*

skilful ['skɪlfʊl] *adj* sleygh

skill ['skɪl] *n* sleyghneth *f*

skin ['skɪn] *n* kroghen *f* kreghyn

skirt ['skɜːt] *n* lostenn *f* +ow

skull ['skʌl] *n* klopenn *m* +ow

sky ['skaɪ] *n* ebron *f*

slate ['sleɪt] *n (as a rock)* kyllas *coll* +enn; *(for roofing)* leghenn *f* +ow

slaughter ['slɔːtə^r] *n* ladhva *f* +ow: *v* ladha

Slav ['slɑːv] *n* Slav *m* Slevyon: *adj* slavek

sledge ['sledʒ] *n* draylell *f* +ow

sleep ['sliːp] *n* hun *m* +yow, kosk *m*: *v* koska

sleeping-bag ['sliːpɪŋbag] *n* sagh koska *m* saghow koska

sleeve ['sliːv] *n* breghel *m* bregholow

slice ['slaɪs] *n* lownyans *m* +ow, tregh *m* +ow: *v* lownya

slide ['slaɪd] *n* slynk *m* +ow: *v* slynkya

slim ['slɪm] *adj* moen

slip ['slɪp] *v* slynkya

slipper ['slɪpəʳ] *n* pawgenn *m* +ow

slobber ['slɒbəʳ] *v* glaveri

slope ['sləʊp] *n* leder *f* ledrow

Slovakia [sləʊ'vakɪə] *place* Slovaki

Slovenia [sləʊ'viːnɪə] *place* Sloveni

slow ['sləʊ] *adj* lent

slowly ['sləʊli] *adv* yn lent

slug ['slʌg] *n* melhwenn *f* +ow

sluice ['sluːs] *n* ladres *f* +ow

small ['smɔːl] *adj* byghan; *(of discrete particles)* munys

smell ['smel] *n* blas *m* +ow: *v* blasa

smile ['smaɪl] *n* minhwarth *m* +ow: *v* minhwerthin

smoke ['sməʊk] *n* mog *m*: *v* megi

smooth ['smuːð] *adj* gwastas, leven: *v* levena

smother ['smʌðəʳ] *v* megi

snack ['snak] *n* kroust *m* +yow

snake ['sneɪk] *n* sarf *f* serf

snatch ['snatʃ] *v* kibya

sneeze ['sniːz] *v* striwi: *n* striw *m* +yow

snore ['snɔːʳ] *n* ronk *m* +ow: *v* renki

snow ['snəʊ] *n* ergh *coll* +enn

snuffle ['snʌfl] *v* troenhwytha

so ['səʊ] *adv* mar; *(=so much)* kemmys; **I love you so** kemmys y'th karav; **so old** mar goth: *conj* ytho; **so that** may, mayth; **so that (neg.)** ma na

soak ['səʊk] *v* segi

soap ['səʊp] *n* sebon *m* +ow

social ['səʊʃl] *adj* kowethasel

society [sə'saɪəti] *n* kowethas *m* +ow

sock ['sɒk] *n* lodrik *m* -igow

soft ['sɒft] *adj* medhel, bleudh

software ['sɒftweəʳ] *n* medhelweyth *m*

soil ['sɔɪl] *n* gweres *m* +ow

soldier ['səʊldʒəʳ] *n* souder *m* -oryon

sole ['səʊl] *n (of foot)* godhen *m* godhnow, dewwodhen *dual*

solution [sə'luːʃən] *n (to a problem)* digolm *m*

solve ['sɔlv] *v* digelmi

some ['sʌm] *adj (qualifying a measureable quantity)* nebes *m;* **I would like to drink some milk** my a garsa eva nebes leth; *(qualifying something else)* neb; **let us flee into some hole** yn neb toll fiyn dhe'n fo: *pron (= some people)* re

somebody ['sʌmbədi] *pron* nebonan

someone ['sʌmwʌn] *pron* nebonan

somersault ['sʌməsɔːlt] *n* kryghlamm *m* +ow

something ['sʌmθɪŋ] *n* nep-pyth *m*

sometime ['sʌmtaɪm] *adv* nep-prys

sometimes ['sʌmtaɪmz] *adv* treweythyow

somewhat ['sʌmwɔt] *adv* nebes

somewhere ['sʌmweəʳ] *adv* nep-tu

son ['sʌn] *n* mab *m* mebyon

song ['sɔŋ] *n* kan *f* +ow

son-in-law ['sʌnɪnlɔː] *n* deuv *m* +yon

soon ['suːn] *adv* skon, a verr spys

sooner ['suːnəʳ] *adv* kyns

sore ['sɔːʳ] *n* gwennenn *f* +ow: *adj* brywvannek

sorrow ['sɔrəʊ] *n* keudh *m* +ow

sorry ['sɔri] *adj* keudhesik; **be sorry** kemmeres duwon; **I am sorry** drog yw genev

sort ['sɔːt] *n* par *m* +ow, sort *m* +ow: *v* digemmyska

soul ['səʊl] *n* enev *m* +ow

sound ['saʊnd] *n (noise)* son *m* +yow

soup ['suːp] *n* soubenn *f* +ow

sour ['saʊəʳ] *adj* trenk

source ['sɔːs] *n* pennfenten *f* -tynyow; *(of stream)*

sow ['səʊ] *v* hasa

space ['speɪs] *n (in general)* efander *m*, spas *m* +ow; *(cosmic)* efanvos *m*

spade ['speɪd] *n* pal *f* +yow

Spain ['speɪn] *place* Spayn

Spaniard ['spanjəd] *n* Spayner *m* -oryon

Spanish ['spanɪʃ] *adj* spaynek; **Spanish language** Spaynek *m*

sparrow ['sparəʊ] *n* golvan *m* +es

speak ['spiːk] *v* kewsel; **speak to** kewsel orth

special ['speʃl] *adj* arbennik

specialist ['speʃəlɪst] *n* arbenniger *m* -oryon

species ['spiːʃiːz] *n* eghenn *f* +ow

spectacles ['spektəklz] *plur* dewweder *m* dewwedrow

spectator [spek'teɪtəʳ] *n* mirer *m* -oryon

speech ['spiːtʃ] *n* areth *f* +yow

speed ['spiːd] *n* toeth *m*: *v* toethya

spend ['spend] *v* spena

sphere ['sfɪəʳ] *n* pel *f* +yow

spider-crab ['spaɪdəˌkrab] *n* krygell *f* +ow

spill ['spɪl] *v* skoellya

spirit ['spɪrɪt] *n* spyrys *m* +yon +yow

splash ['splaʃ] *v* lagenna

splendid ['splendɪd] *adj* splann

split ['splɪt] *n* fols *m* +yow: *adj* felsys: *v* folsa

spoke ['spəʊk] *n (of wheel)* asenn *f* +ow

sponge ['spʌndʒ] *n* spong *m* +ow

spoon ['spuːn] *n* lo *f* loyow

sport ['spɔːt] *n* sport *m*; **water sports** sportow dowr

sportsman ['spɔːtsmən] *n (professional)* sportyas *m* -ysi

spot [ˈspɒt] *n (location)* tyller *m* +yow; *(pimple)* kuriek *m* -egi

spouse [ˈspaʊz] *n* pries *m* priosow

spread [ˈspred] *v* lesa; *(intrans.)* omlesa

sprightly [ˈspraɪtli] *adj* bywek

spring [ˈsprɪŋ] *n (season)* gwenton *m* -enyow: *v* lemmel

sprinkle [ˈsprɪŋkəl] *v* dowra

sprout [ˈspraʊt] *n* skyllenn *f* +ow, skyll *coll*

squadron [ˈskwɒdrən] *n* skwadron *m* +ow

square [ˈskweəʳ] *n* pedrek *m* -ogow: *adj* pedrek

squeeze [ˈskwiːz] *v* gwrynna

squint-eyed [skwɪntˈaɪd] *adj* kammlagasek

squirm [ˈskwɜːm] *v* gwynnel

squirrel [ˈskwɪrəl] *n* gwiwer *m* -ow

squirt [ˈskwɜːt] *n* stif *f* +ow: *v* stifa

St Austell [səntˈɒstl] *place* Sen Ostell

St Ives [səntˈaɪvz] *place* Porthia

stable [ˈsteɪbl] *n* marghti *m* +ow

stadium [ˈsteɪdjəm] *n* sportva *f* +ow

stage [ˈsteɪdʒ] *n* gwarila *m* -leow

stain [ˈsteɪn] *n* mostenn *f* +ow: *v* namma

stamp [ˈstamp] *n (postage)* stamp *m* +ys +ow

stand [ˈstand] *n* sav *m* +ow: *v* sevel; **stand against** sevel orth

staple [ˈsteɪpəl] *n* krommgenter *f* -gentrow: *v* krommgentra

stapler [ˈsteɪpləʳ] *n* krommgentrell *f* +ow

star [ˈstɑːʳ] *n* sterenn *f* +ow, ster *coll*

start [ˈstɑːt] *n* dalleth *m* +ow: *v* dalleth

state [ˈsteɪt] *n* studh *m* +yow; *(political)* stat *m* +ow +ys

station [ˈsteɪʃən] *n* gorsav *m* +ow

statue ['statjuː] *n* delow *m* +yow

stature ['statjər] *n* ughelder *m* +yow

stay ['steɪ] *(at a hotel, etc.) n* godrik *m* -igow: *v* godriga

steal ['stiːl] *v* ladra

steam ['stiːm] *n* ethenn *f* +ow

steel ['stiːl] *n* dur *m* +yow

steep ['stiːp] *adj* serth

stem ['stem] *n* garrenn *f* +ow

stench ['stentʃ] *n* fler *m* +yow

step ['step] *n* kamm *m* +ow; *(of stairs)*

stew ['stjuː] *n* bros *m* +ow: *v* stywya

stick ['stɪk] *n* lath *f* +ow

stick ['stɪk] *v* glena; **stick to** glena orth

stiff ['stɪf] *adj* diwedhyn

still ['stɪl] *adj* kosel: *adv* hwath

sting ['stɪŋ] *n* bros *m* +ow: *v* brosa

stir ['stɜːr] *v* kaboli, treylouba

stitch ['stɪtʃ] *v* brosya

stoat ['stəʊt] *n* yewgenn *m* +ow

stocking ['stɔkɪŋ] *n* loder *m* lodrow, dewloder *dual*

stomach ['stʌmək] *n* torr *f* +ow

stone ['stəʊn] *n* men *m* meyn

stool ['stuːl] *n* skavell *f* +ow

stop ['stɔp] *v (intrans.)* hedhi; *(trans.)* stoppya

stopper ['stɔpər] *n* ebil *m* +yer

store ['stɔː] *n* gwithva *f* +ow

stork ['stɔːk] *n* hwibon *m* +es

storm ['stɔːm] *n* tewedh *m* +ow

story ['stɔːri] *n* hwedhel *m* hwedhlow

stove ['stəʊv] *n* forn *f* +ow

straggler ['straglər] *n* treynwas *m* -wesyon

straight ['streɪt] *adj* eun

straighten ['streɪtən] *v* **straighten out** digamma
strange ['streɪndʒ] *adj* koynt, ankoth
stranger ['streɪndʒəʳ] *n* estren *m* +yon
strangle ['straŋgl] *v* taga
straw ['strɔ:] *n (in bulk)* kala' *coll* kalavenn
strawberry ['strɔ:bəri] *n* sevienn *f* +ow, sevi *coll*
streak ['stri:k] *n* ribin *m* +ow
street ['stri:t] *n* stret *m* +ow +ys
strength ['streŋθ] *n* krevder *m* +yow
strengthen ['streŋθən] *v* krevhe
stress ['stres] *n* gwask *f* +ow; *(emphasis)* poeslev *m* +ow
stretch ['stretʃ] *v* ystynn
stretcher ['stretʃəʳ] *n (for carrying)* gravath *f* +ow; **stretcher bearer** deger gravath *m* degoryon g.
strict ['strɪkt] *adj* stroeth
strike ['straɪk] *v (hit)* gweskel
string ['strɪŋ] *n* kordenn *f* kerdyn
strip ['strɪp] *n* skethenn *f* +ow
stroke ['strəʊk] *n* strekys *f* strokosow: *v* palva
stroll ['strəʊl] *n* rosyas *m* +ow: *v* rosya
strong ['strɔŋ] *adj* krev
struggle ['strʌgl] *v* gwynnel
student ['stju:dnt] *n* studhyer *m* studhyoryon
study ['stʌdi] *n (room)* studhva *f* +ow; *(piece of work)* studhyans *m* +ow: *v* studhya
stuff ['stʌf] *n* devnydh *m* +yow, stoff *m* +ys
stuffing ['stʌfɪŋ] *n* stoffyans *m* +ow
stun ['stʌn] *v* basa
stupid ['stju:pɪd] *adj* gokki
stupidity [stju:'pɪdəti] *n* gokkineth *f*
subject [sʌb'dʒɪkt] *n* mater *m* +yow
sub-lieutenant [ˌsʌblef'tenant] *n* isleftenant *m* +ow

submarine [sʌbmə'riːn] *n* lester-sedhi *m* lestri-sedhi
substance ['sʌbstəns] *n* stoff *m* +ys
suburb ['sʌbɜːb] *n* mestrev *f* +ow
succeed [sək'siːd] *v* seweni
success [sək'ses] *n* sewena *f*
such [sʌtʃ] *adj* **such as** kepar ha; **such people** tus a'n par na
suck ['sʌk] *v* sugna
sudden ['sʌdn] *adj* tromm
suddenly ['sʌdnli] *adv* yn tromm
suffer ['sʌfər] *v* godhevel
suffering ['sʌfərɪŋ] *n* godhevyans *m* +ow
sugar ['ʃʊgər] *n* sugra *m*
suicide ['suɪsaɪd] *n* omladhans *m* +ow
suitable ['suːtəbl] *adj* gwiw, delledhek
suitcase ['suːtkeɪs] *n* trog *m* +ow
sulk ['sʌlk] *v* moutya
summer ['sʌmər] *n* hav *m* +ow; **summer visitor** havyas *m* -ysi
summer-time [ˌsʌmər'taɪm] *n* havas *m* +ow
summit ['sʌmɪt] *n* barr *m* +ow
Sun ['sʌn] *n* Howl *m*
Sunday ['sʌndi] *n* dy' Sul *m* dydhyow Sul; **on Sunday** dy' Sul
sunrise ['sʌnraɪz] *n* howldrevel *m* +yow
sunset ['sʌnset] *n* howlsedhes *m* +ow
superior [suː'pɪəriər] *adj (victorious)* trygh
supermarket ['suːpəˌmɑːkɪt] *n* gorvarghas *f* +ow
supper ['sʌpər] *n* koen *f* +yow, soper *m* +yow
supple ['sʌpl] *adj* gwedhyn
support [sə'pɔːt] *n (abst.)* skoedhyans *m* +ow: *v* skoedhya
supporter [sə'pɔːtər] *n* skoedhyer *m* -oryon

sure [ˈʃʊəʳ] *adj* sur, kowgans

surely [ˈʃʊəli] *adv* yn sur

surface [ˈsɜːfɪs] *n* arenep *m* arenebow

surgeon [ˈsɜːdʒən] *n* leuvvedhek *m* -ogyon

surname [ˈsɜːneɪm] *n* hanow teylu *m* henwyn teylu

surprise [səˈpraɪz] *n* sowdhan *m* +ow: *v* sowdhanas

surround [səˈraʊnd] *v* kyrghynna

surroundings [səˈraʊndɪŋz] *pl* kyrghynn *m* +ow

swan [ˈswɒn] *n* alargh *m* elergh

swear [ˈsweəʳ] *v* (*oath*) ti

sweat [ˈswet] *n* hwys *m* +ow: *v* hwysa

Sweden [ˈswiːdn] *place* Sweden

Swedish [ˈswiːdɪʃ] *adj* swedek; **Swedish language** Swedek *m*

sweep [ˈswiːp] *v* skuba

sweet [ˈswiːt] *n* hwegynn *m* +ow: *adj* hweg

sweetheart [ˈswiːthɑːt] *n* keresik *m* -igyon, kuv kolonn *m* kuvyon kolonn

swell [ˈswel] *v* hwythfi

swift [ˈswɪft] *adj* skav

swim [ˈswɪm] *v* neuvya

swing [ˈswɪŋ] *n* lesk *m* +ow: *v* leska

switch [ˈswɪtʃ] *n* (*electric*) skwychell *f* +ow: *v* skwychya; **switch off** skwychya yn farow; **switch on** skwychya yn fyw

sword [ˈsɔːd] *n* kledha *m* kledhedhyow

symbol [ˈsɪmbl] *n* arwoedh *f* +yow

syrup [ˈsɪrəp] *n* sugen *m*

T

table ['teɪbl] *n* moes *f* +ow; *(statistical)* moesenn *f* +ow

table-cloth ['teɪblklɒθ] *n* lien moes *m* lienyow moes

tablet ['tablɪt] *n (stone)* legh *f* +yon; *(pad)* moesik *f* -igow

tail ['teɪl] *n* lost *m* +ow

take ['teɪk] *v* kemmeres; **take a rest** powes *v*

tale ['teɪl] *n* hwedhel *m* hwedhlow

talent ['talənt] *n (natural ability)* roas *m* +ow

talk ['tɔːk] *v* kewsel, kows

tall ['tɔːl] *adj* hir

tame ['teɪm] *adj* dov: *v* dovhe

tan ['tan] *v (sunburn)* howlleski

tap ['tap] *n (for bath)* tapp *m* +ow +ys

tape ['teɪp] *n* snod *m* +ow +ys; **adhesive tape** snod glenus *m*

tar ['tɑː] *n* pyg *m* +ow

target ['tɑːgɪt] *n* kostenn *f* +ow

tart ['tɑːt] *n (food)* tartenn *f* +ow

task ['tɑːsk] *n* oberenn *f* +ow

taste ['teɪst] *n* blas *m* +ow: *v* blasa

tasteless ['teɪstlɪs] *adj* anvlasus

tavern ['tavən] *n* tavern *m* +yow

tax ['taks] *n* toll *f* +ow

taxi ['taksi] *n* taksi *m* +ow

tea ['tiː] *n* te *m* +ow

teach ['tiːtʃ] *v* dyski

teacher ['tiːtʃəʳ] *n (female)* dyskadores *f* +ow; *(male)* dyskador *m* +yon

teaching ['tiːtʃɪŋ] *n* dyskas *m*

team ['tiːm] *n* para *m* parys

278

tease ['ti:z] *v* hyga

teat ['ti:t] *n* teth *f* +i +ow

technical ['teknıkl] *adj* teknogel

technique [tek'ni:k] *n* teknek *m* -ogow

tee-shirt ['ti:ʃɜːt] *n* krys T *m* krysyow T

telephone ['telıfəun] *v* pellgewsel

television ['telı,vıʒn] *n* pellwolok *f* pellwologow

tell ['tel] *v* derivas, leverel; **tell off** keski

temper ['tempər] *v* tempra

temperature ['temprətʃər] *n* tempredh *m* +ow; *(fever)* terthenn *f* +ow

temple ['templ] *n (building)* tempel *m* templow; *(of head)* tal *f* +yow

ten ['ten] *num* deg

tendency ['tendənsi] *n* tuedh *m* +ow

tender ['tendər] *adj* bleudh

tendon ['tendən] *n* giowenn *f* +ow, giow *coll*

tendonitis [,tendən'aıtıs] *n* fagel-giow *f*

tennis ['tenıs] *n* tennis

tent ['tent] *n* tylda *m* tyldow tyldys

tepid ['tepıd] *adj* mygyl

terrace ['terıs] *n* terras *m* +ow

terrible ['terıbl] *adj* euthyk

terribly ['terıbli] *adv* euthyk

terrier ['teriər] *n* dorgi *m* dorgeun

terrify ['terıfaı] *v* euthega

terror ['terər] *n* browagh *m* +ow

terrorism ['terərızm] *n* browaghweyth *m*

terrorist ['terərıst] *n (female)* broweghyades *f* +ow; *(male)* broweghyas *m* -ysi

testicle ['testikəl] *n* kell *f* +ow, diwgell *dual*

testimony ['testıməni] *n* dustuni *m* dustuniow

text ['tekst] *n* tekst *m* +ow

than [ðən] *conj* ages, es

thank ['θaŋk] *v* grassa; **thank you** meur ras

that [ðat] *pron (m.)* henna; *(f.)* honna; **that one** henna *m*, honna *f*: *adj* **that house** an chi na; **that big house** an chi bras na: *conj* y, yth

the ['ði: / ðə] *art* an

theatre [θɪ'etər] *n* gwariva *f* +ow; **open-air theatre** plen an gwari *m* plenys an gwari

theft ['θeft] *n (in general)* ladrynsi *m*; *(individual crime)* ladrans *m* +ow

their [ðeər] *pron* aga

them [ðem] *pron* i; *(infixed)* 's

then ['ðen] *conj* ytho: *adv* ena, y'n eur na

thence ['ðens] *adv* alena

there ['ðeər] *adv (visible)* ena; *(invisible)* eno; *(thither)* di

therefore ['ðeərfɔːr] *conj* rakhenna

thermometer [θɜː'mɔmɪtər] *n* tempredhell *f* +ow

these [ðiːz] *pron* an re ma

they [ðeɪ] *pron* i

thick ['θɪk] *adj* tew

thicken ['θɪkən] *v* tewhe

thief ['θiːf] *n* lader *m* ladron

thigh ['θaɪ] *n* mordhos *f* +ow, diwvordhos *dual*

thin ['θɪn] *adj* moen, tanow

thing ['θɪŋ] *n* tra *f* +ow, pyth *m* +ow, takel *m* taklow

think ['θɪŋk] *v* prederi, tybi

third ['θɜːd] *num* tressa; **the Third World** an Tressa Bys

thirst ['θɜːst] *n* syghes *m*

thirteen [ˌθɜː'tiːn] *num* trydhek

this [ðɪs] *pron (m.)* hemma; *(f.)* homma; **this is** ottomma: *adj* **this house** an chi ma

thorn [ˈθɔːn] *n* dren *m* dreyn

thorough [ˈθʌrə] *adj* kowal

those [ðəʊz] *pron* an re na: *adj* **those houses** an chiow na

though [ðəʊ] *conj* kyn; *(before vowels and h-)* kynth

thought [ˈθɔːt] *n* tybyans *m* +ow

thousand [ˈθaʊznd] *num* mil *m* +yow

thread [ˈθred] *n (in general)* neus *coll* +enn; *(individual)* neusenn *f* +ow, neus *coll*

threat [ˈθret] *n* godros *m* +ow

threaten [ˈθretn] *v* godros, braggya

three [ˈθriː] *num (m.)* tri; *(f.)* teyr

thrice [ˈθraɪs] *adv* teyrgweyth

throat [ˈθrəʊt] *n* bryansenn *f* +ow

through [θruː] *prep* dre; *(before vowel)* der

throw [ˈθrəʊ] *v* tewlel

thrush [ˈθrʌʃ] *n (bird)* molgh *f* +i

thrust [ˈθrʌst] *v* pokya

thumb [ˈθʌm] *n* meus *m* +i

thump [ˈθʌmp] *n* kronk *m* +ys: *v* kronkya

thunder [ˈθʌndər] *n* taran *f*

thunderclap [ˈθʌndəklap] *n* tardh taran *m* tardhow taran

Thursday [ˈθɜːzdi] *n* dy' Yow *m* dydhyow Yow

thus [ˈðʌs] *adv* yndella

ticket [ˈtɪkɪt] *n* tokyn *m* tokynyow toknys

ticket-office [ˈtɪkɪtˌɔfɪs] *n* tokynva *f* +ow

tickle [ˈtɪkl] *v* debreni, kosa

tide [ˈtaɪd] *n* mordid *m* +ys; **high tide** morlanow *m* +yow; **low tide** mordrik *m* -igow, trig *m*; **neap tide** marowvor *m* +yow; **spring tide** reverthi *f* +ow

tidy [ˈtaɪdi] *adj* kempenn; *v* kempenna

tie ['taɪ] *n (clothing)* kolm konna *m* kolmow konna; *(link)* kolm *m* +ow: *v* kelmi

tiger ['taɪgər] *n* tiger *m* tigri

tight ['taɪt] *adj* stroeth, tynn

tighten ['taɪtn] *v* tynnhe

tights ['taɪts] *plur* tynnow

tilde ['tɪld] *n* ughverk tylda *m* ughverkow tylda

tile ['taɪl] *n* prileghenn *f* +ow

timber ['tɪmbər] *n* prenn *m* +yer

time ['taɪm] *n* prys *m* +yow, termyn *m* +yow; *(clock-time)* eur *f* +yow; *(occasion)* gweyth *f* +yow, tro *f* +yow; **in time** a-dermyn; **on time** a-dermyn; **what time is it?** py eur yw?

timid ['tɪmɪd] *adj* ownek

timorous ['tɪmərəs] *adj* ownus

tinner ['tɪnər] *n* stenor *m* +yon

tint ['tɪnt] *n* arliw *m* +ow: *v* arliwya

tip ['tɪp] *n (end)* bleyn *m* +yow; *(money)* grastal *m* +yow

tire ['taɪər] *v* skwitha

tired ['taɪəd] *adj* skwith

tiresome ['taɪəsʊm] *adj* divlas

tiring ['taɪərɪŋ] *adj* skwithus

tissue ['tɪsjuː] *n* gwias *m* +ow

title ['taɪtl] *n (legal)* titel *m* titlow titlys

to [tuː] *prep* dhe; **in order to** rag

toad ['təʊd] *n* lyfans *m* +es

toast ['təʊst] *n (food)* kras *coll* +enn: *v* krasa

toboggan *n* karr-slynk *m* kerri-slynk

today [tə'deɪ] *adv* hedhyw

toe ['təʊ] *n* bys-troes *m* bysies-troes

together [tə'geðər] *adv* war-barth

toil ['tɔɪl] *n* lavur *m* +yow

toilet ['tɔɪlɪt] *n* privedhyow *plur*

tomato [tə'mɑːtəʊ] *n* aval-kerensa *m* avalow-kerensa

tomorrow [tə'mɒrəʊ] *adv* a-vorow; **tomorrow morning** ternos vyttin; **tomorrow evening** a-vorow gorthugher

tongue ['tʌŋ] *n* taves *m* tavosow; **mother tongue** mammyeth *f* +ow

tonight [tə'naɪt] *adv* haneth

too ['tuː] *adv (as well)* keffrys; *(excessively)*; **too big** re vras; **too many people** re a dus; **too much food** re a voes

tool ['tuːl] *n* toul *m* +ys +ow

tooth ['tuːθ] *n* dans *m* dyns

tooth-brush ['tuːθbrʌʃ] *n* skubyllenn-dhyns *f* skubyllennow-dyns

tooth-paste ['tuːθpeɪst] *n* dyenn dyns *m* dyennow-dyns

top ['tɒp] *n (summit)* gwarthav *m* -evyow, barr *m* +ow; **on top** a-wartha *adv*

tor ['tɔːr] *n* torr *f* +ow, karn *m* +ow

torch ['tɔːtʃ] *n* faglenn *f* +ow

Torpoint [tɔː'pɔɪnt] *place* Penntorr

tortoise ['tɔːtəs] *n* melhwyoges *f* +ow

total ['təʊtl] *n* sommenn *f* +ow

totality [təʊ'talɪti] *n* kowalder *m*

totally ['təʊtəli] *adv* kowal

touch ['tʌtʃ] *v* tava

tough ['tʌf] *adj* avleythys

tourism ['tʊərɪzəm] *n* tornyaseth *f*

tourist ['tʊərɪst] *n* tornyas *m* -ysi

tournament ['tɜːnəmənt] *n* tournay *m* +s

towards [tə'wɔːdz] *prep* troha, war-tu ha

towel ['taʊəl] *n* towell *m* +ow

tower ['tauər] *n* tour *m* +yow

town ['taun] *n* tre *f* trevow; **in town** y'n dre

townsman ['taunzmən] *n* burjes *m* burjysi

toy ['tɔɪ] *n* gwariell *f* +ow

track ['trak] *n* lergh *m* +ow

tracksuit ['traksu:t] *n* reswisk *m* +ow

tractor ['traktər] *n* jynn-tenna *m* jynnow-tenna

trade ['treɪd] *n* kenwerth *m* +ow; **trade union** mysterlu *m* +yow: *v* kenwertha

trader ['treɪdər] *n* gwikor *m* +yon

traditional [trə'dɪʃənl] *adj* hengovek

traffic ['trafɪk] *n* daromres *m* +ow; **traffic jam** tag *m* +ow; **traffic lights** golowys *plur*

trail ['treɪl] *n* ol *m* +ow

train *n* railway train tren *m* +ow

training ['treɪnɪŋ] *n* trenyans *m*

trait ['treɪt] *n* gnasenn *f* +ow

traitor ['treɪtər] *n* traytour *m* -s

trampoline ['trampəli:n] *n* lammleur *m* +yow

tramway ['tramweɪ] *n* trammhyns *m* +yow

transfer *n* ['transfər] treusporth *m* +ow: *v* [trans'fɜ:ʳ] treusperthi

translate [trans'leɪt] *v* treylya

translation [trans'leɪʃən] *n* treylyans *m* +ow

transparent [trans'parənt] *adj* treusweladow

transport [tran'spɔ:t] *n* karyans *m*, treusporth *m* +ow

travel ['travl] *v* travalya

traveller ['travlər] *n* tremenyas *m* -ysi

tray ['treɪ] *n* servyour *m* +s

treachery ['tretʃəri] *n* trayson *m*

treasure ['treʒər] *n* tresor *m* +yow +ys

treasurer ['treʒərər] *n* alhwedhor *m* +yon, alhwedhores *f* +ow

284

treat ['tri:t] *v* dyghtya; **treat badly** tebeldhyghtya; **treat kindly** chershya

tree-trunk *n* kyf *m* +yon

tremble ['trembl] *v* krena

trial ['traɪəl] *n (attempt)* assay *m* +ow; *(legal)* trial *m* +s

triangle ['traɪaŋgl] *n* trihorn *m* trihern

tribunal [traɪ'bju:nl] *n* barr *m* +ys

trick ['trɪk] *n* kast *m* +ys, pratt *m* +ys

tricycle ['traɪsɪkl] *n* teyrros *f* +ow

trip ['trɪp] *n* vyaj *m* +yow

triumph ['traɪəmf] *n* trygh *m* +ow

troop ['tru:p] *n* bagas *m* +ow

trouble ['trʌbl] *n* ahwer *m* +yow, trynn *f* +ow

trousers ['traʊzəz] *plur* lavrek *m* lavrogow

trout ['traʊt] *n* truth *m* +ow

true ['tru:] *adj* gwir

trumpet ['trʌmpɪt] *n* hirgorn *m* hirgern

trunk ['trʌŋk] *n (box)* trog *m* +ow

Truro ['truərəʊ] *place* Truru

trust ['trʌst] *n* fydhyans *m*: *v* fydhya

truth ['tru:θ] *n* gwir *m* +yow, gwiryonedh *m*

truthful ['tru:θfəl] *adj* gwiryon

try ['traɪ] *v* assaya, previ: *n* assay *m* +ow

tube ['tju:b] *n* pibenn *f* +ow

Tuesday ['tju:zdɪ] *n* dy' Meurth *m* dydhyow Meurth; **on Tuesday** dy' Meurth

tuft ['tʌft] *n* toes *m* +ow

tune ['tju:n] *n* ton *m* +yow

tunnel ['tʌnl] *n* kowfordh *f* +ow

Turk ['tɜːk] *n* Turk *m* +ys +yon

Turkey ['tɜːki] *place* Turki

Turkish ['tɜːkɪʃ] *adj* turkek; **Turkish language** Turkek *m*

turmoil ['tɜːmɔɪl] *n* tervans *m* +ow

turn ['tɜːn] *n* torn *m* +ow, tro *f* +yow: *v* treylya

turnip ['tɜːnɪp] *n* ervinenn *f* +ow, ervin *coll*

tweezers ['twiːzəz] *plur* gevelik *f* -igow

twelve ['twelv] *num* dewdhek

twenty ['twenti] *num* ugens; **twenty-one** onan warn ugens

twig ['twɪg] *n* barrenn *f* +ow

twilight ['twaɪlaɪt] *n* mo *m* +yow

twin ['twɪn] *n (female)* gevelles *f* +ow; *(male)* gevell *m* +yon; **The Twins (Gemini)** An Evellyon

twist ['twɪst] *v* nedha: *n* nedhans *m* +ow

twisted ['twɪstɪd] *adj* nedhys

two ['tuː] *num (f.)* diw; *(m.)* dew

typewriter ['teɪpreɪtər] *n* jynn-skrifa *m* jynnow-skrifa

U

ugly ['ʌgli] *adj* hager

Ukraine [juːˈkreɪn] *place* Ukrayn

Ukrainian [juːˈkreɪniən] *adj* ukraynek; **Ukrainian language** Ukraynek

umbrella [ʌmˈbrelə] *n* glawlenn *f* +ow

unable [ʌnˈeɪbl] *adj* dialloes

unburden [ˌʌnˈbɜːdn] *v* diveghya

uncertain [ʌnˈsɜːtən] *adj* ansertan

uncle ['ʌŋkl] *n* ewnter *m* ewntres

uncork [ʌnˈkɔːk] *v* digorkynna

uncover [ʌnˈkʌvər] *v* diskudha

under *prep* yn-dann

underground [ˈʌndəˈgraʊnd] *n* **the Underground** an Bib

underline [ˌʌndəˈlaɪn] *v* islinenna

underpants [ˈʌndəpants] *n* islavrek *m* -ogow

understand [ˌʌndəˈstand] *v* konvedhes

understanding [ˌʌndəˈstandɪŋ] *n* konvedhes *m*

undertaking [ˌʌndəˈteɪkɪŋ] *n* omgemmeryans *m* +ow

undo [ʌnˈduː] *v* diswruthyl, diswul

undress [ʌnˈdres] *v* diwiska

uneasy [ʌnˈiːsɪ] *adj* anes

unemployed [ˌʌnɪmˈplɔɪd] *adj* diweyth

unfair [ʌnˈfeəʳ] *adj* anewn

unfold [ʌnˈfəʊld] *v* displegya

unforeseen [ˌʌnfɔːˈsiːn] *adj* anragwelys

unfortunate [ʌnˈfɔːtʃənət] *adj* anfeusik

unfortunately [ʌnˈfɔːtʃənətli] *adv* soweth

unhook [ʌnˈhʊk] *v* dihigenna

uniform [ˈjuːnɪfɔːm] *n* unnwisk *m* +ow

union [ˈjuːnjən] *n* unyans *m* +ow; **the European Union** an Unyans Europek

united [juːˈnaɪtɪd] *adj* unys; **the United States** an Statow Unys; **the United Nations** an Kenedhlow Unys

unity [ˈjuːnɪtɪ] *n* unnses *m*

universe [ˈjuːnɪvɜːs] *adj* ollvys *m* +ow

university [ˌjuːnɪˈvɜːsɪtɪ] *n* pennskol *f* +yow

unknown [ʌnˈnəʊn] *adj* ankoth

unless [ʌnˈles] *conj* marnas, saw

unlike [ʌnˈlaɪk] *adj* dihaval (diworth)

unload [ʌnˈləʊd] *v* diskarga

unmarried [ʌnˈmarɪd] *adj* andhemmedhys

unnecessary [ʌnˈnesəsəri] *adj* diedhomm

unroll [ʌnˈrəʊl] *v* dirolya

unstick [ʌn'stɪk] *v* disklusa
untie [ʌn'taɪ] *v* digelmi
until [ən'tɪl] *prep* bys: *conj* erna; *(before vowels)* ernag; **until tomorrow!** bys a-vorow!
up [ʌp] *prep* yn-bann: *adv* yn-bann
upon [ə'pɒn] *prep* war
upright ['ʌpraɪt] *adj* syth; *(morally)* ewnhynsek
uproar ['ʌprɔːʳ] *n* habadoellya *m*
Uranus ['jʊrənəs] *place* Uranus
urge ['ɜːdʒ] *n* ynni *m* +ow: *v* ynnia
urgency ['ɜːdʒənsi] *n* ynniadow *m*
urgent ['ɜːdʒənt] *adj* ynniadow
urine ['jʊərɪn] *n* pisas *m*
us [ʌs] *pron* 'gan
use *n* ['juːs] us *m* +yow: *v* ['juːz] usya
useful ['juːsfʊl] *adj* dhe les, 'vas
usefulness ['juːsfʊlnɪs] *n* les *m*
usual ['juːʒl] *adj* usadow; **as usual** dell yw usys

V

vacant ['veɪkənt] *adj* gwag
vacuum-cleaner ['vakjʊəm‚kliːnəʳ] *n* skubell-sugna *f* skubellow-sugna
vagina [və'dʒaɪnə] *n* kons *f* +yow
valley ['vali] *n* nans *m* +ow
valuable ['valjʊəbl] *adj* talvosek
value ['valjuː] *n* talvosogeth *f* +ow: *v* talvesa
van ['van] *n* kertik *m* -igow
various ['veərɪəs] *adj* divers, liesek
vase ['vɑːz] *n* lester *m* lestri

veil ['veɪl] *n* kudhlenn *f* +ow

vein ['veɪn] *n (blood)* gwythienn *f* +ow, gwythi *coll*; *(ore)* skorrenn *f* +ow

venom ['venəm] *n* gwenon *m* -enyow

Venus ['viːnəs] *n (planet, goddess)* Gwener *f*

veracious [vəˈreɪʃəs] *adj* gwiryon

very ['veri] *adv* fest, pur

vessel ['vesl] *n (container or ship)* lester *m* lestri

vet ['vet] *n* milvedhek *m* -ogyon

victory ['vɪktəri] *n* trygh *m* +ow

video ['vɪdɪəʊ] *n* gwydhyow *m* +yow

village ['vɪlɪdʒ] *n* gwig *f* +ow

vinegar ['vɪnɪgəʳ] *n* aysel *m* +yow

violence ['vaɪələns] *n* freudh *m* +ow

violent ['vaɪələnt] *adj* freudhek

violet ['vaɪəlɪt] *adj (colour)* glasrudh; *(flower)* mellyonenn *f* +ow, mellyon *coll*

violin [ˌvaɪəˈlɪn] *n* fyll *m* +ow

viper ['vaɪpəʳ] *n* nader *f* nadres

virgin ['vɜːdʒɪn] *n* gwyrghes *f* +ow

virile ['vɪraɪl] *adj* gourel

virtual ['vɜːtjʊəl] *adj* gowir

visit ['vɪzɪt] *n* godrik *m* -igow: *v* godriga

visitor ['vɪzɪtəʳ] *n* godriger *m* -oryon

vocabulary [vəˈkabjʊləri] *n* gerva *f* +ow

voice ['vɔɪs] *n* lev *m* +ow

volcano [vɒlˈkeɪnəʊ] *n* loskvenydh *m* +yow

vomit ['vɒmɪt] *v* hwyja

vote ['vəʊt] *n* raglev *m* +ow: *v* ragleva

vow ['vaʊ] *n* ambos *m* +ow

voyage ['vɔɪɪdʒ] *n* vyaj *m* +yow

vulture ['vʌltʃəʳ] *n* hok karyn *m* hokys karyn

W

waggon ['wagən] *n* kert pedrosek *m* kertow p.

wail ['weɪl] *v* kyni

waist ['weɪst] *n* kres *m* +yow

waistcoat ['weskət] *n* kryspows *f* +yow

wait ['weɪt] *v*; **wait for** gortos

waiter ['weɪtər] *n* servyas *m* -ysi

waitress ['weɪtrəs] *n* servyades *f* +ow

wake ['weɪk] *n (vigil)* goel *m* +yow: *v* **wake up** difuna

Wales ['weɪlz] *place* Kembra

walk ['wɔːk] *v* kerdhes

walker ['wɔːkər] *n* kerdher *m* -oryon

wall ['wɔːl] *n* fos *f* +ow; **party wall** paros *m* +yow

wallet ['wɔlɪt] *n* skryp *m* +ys

walnut ['wɔːlnʌt] *n* knowenn frynk *f* knowennow frynk, know frynk *coll*

wander ['wɔndər] *v* gwandra

want ['wɔnt] *v* mynnes

war ['wɔːr] *n* bresel *f* +yow; **English Civil War** Bresel an Pymp Kenedhel

wardrobe ['wɔːdrəʊb] *n* dillasva *f* +ow

warm ['wɔːm] *adj* toemm: *v* toemma

warmth ['wɔːmθ] *n* toemmder *m*

warn ['wɔːn] *v* gwarnya

warning ['wɔːnɪŋ] *n* gwarnyans *m* +ow

warrior ['wɔrɪər] *n* kasor *m* -oryon

wash ['wɔʃ] *v* golghi; **wash oneself** omwolghi; **wash clothes** kanna; **wash up** golghi an lestri

wash-basin ['wɔʃˌbeɪsn] *n* new *f* +yow

wasp ['wɔsp] *n* goghienn *f* +ow, goghi *coll*

waste ['weɪst] *v* skoellya: *n* skoell *m* +yon

waster ['weɪstər] n skoellyek m -ogyon

watch ['wɒtʃ] n *(timepiece)* euryer f +yow; **keep watch** goelyas v, mires orth v

water ['wɔːtər] n dowr m +ow

watering-can ['wɔːtərɪŋ͵kan] n dowrell f +ow

wave ['weɪv] n tonn f +ow

wax ['waks] n koer *coll* +enn: v koera v

way ['weɪ] n hyns m +yow, fordh f +ow; **in that way** yndellna *adv*; **in this way** yndellma *adv*

we [wiː] *pron* ni

weak ['wiːk] *adj* gwann

weaken ['wiːkən] v gwannhe

wealth ['welθ] n rychys *plur*

weapon ['wepən] n arv f +ow

wear ['weər] v gwiska

weariness ['wɪərɪnɪs] n skwither m

weather ['weðər] n kewer f +yow; **bad weather** hager-awel f

weaver ['wiːvər] n gwiader m -oryon

web-site ['websaɪt] n gwiasva f +ow

wedding ['wedɪŋ] n demmedhyans m +ow

Wednesday ['wenzdi] n dy' Mergher m dydhyow Mergher; **on Wednesday** dy' Mergher m

week ['wiːk] n seythun f +yow

weekend [͵wiːk'end] n pennseythun f +yow

weekly ['wiːkli] *adj* seythunyek

weep ['wiːp] v dagrewi, oela

weigh ['weɪ] v poesa

weight ['weɪt] n poes m +ow

welcome ['welkəm] n dynnargh m +ow; v dynnerghi

well! ['wel] *int* wel!

Welsh ['welʃ] *adj* kembrek; **Welsh language** Kembrek

Welshman ['welʃmən] *n* Kembro *m* +yon

Welshwoman ['welʃwumən] *n* Kembroes *f* +ow

west ['west] *n* west *m*; *(sunset)* howlsedhes *m* +ow

wet ['wet] *adj* glyb: *v* glybya

whale ['weɪl] *n* morvil *m* +es

what [wɒt] *pron* pandra, pyth, py; *(relative pron.)* an pyth: *adj* pana; **what a lie!** pana wow!

wheat ['wiːt] *n* gwaneth *coll* +enn

wheel ['wiːl] *n* ros *f* +ow

wheel-barrow ['wiːl͵barəu] *n* gravath-ros *f* gravathow-ros

wheel-chair [͵wiːl'tʃeəʳ] *n* kador-ros *f* kadoryow-ros

when ['wen] *conj* pan: *adv (interrogative)* p'eur

where [weəʳ] *prep (interrogative)* ple, py le, py tyller; **where is** ple'ma: *conj* le ma(y)

which [wɪtʃ] *pron (interrogative)* py; *(of two)* pyneyl; *(relative pron.)* an pyth, hag

while ['waɪl] *n* pols *m* +ow: *conj* hedre

whinny ['wɪnɪ] *v* kryghias

whip ['wɪp] *n* hwypp *m* +ys: *v* hwyppya

whiskers ['wɪskəz] *plur* minvlew *coll* +enn

whisper ['wɪspəʳ] *n* hwystrenn *f* +ow: *v* hwystra

whistle ['wɪsl] *v (by mouth)* hwibana

white ['waɪt] *adj* gwynn

who [huː] *pron (interrogative)* piw; *(relative pron.)* neb

whoever [huː'evəʳ] *pron* piwpynag, seul

whole ['həʊl] *adj* dien, kowal

whore ['hɔːʳ] *n* hora *f* horys

why [waɪ] *adv* prag

wicked ['wɪkɪd] *adj* drog, tebel

wickedness ['wɪkɪdnɪs] *n* sherewynsi *m*

wide ['waɪd] *adj* ledan

widow ['wɪdəʊ] *n* gwedhwes *f* +ow

292

widower ['wɪdəʊəʳ] *n* gwedhow *m* +yon
width ['wɪdθ] *n* les *m* +yow
wife ['waɪf] *n* gwreg *f* gwragedh
wild ['waɪld] *adj* gwyls
will ['wɪl] *n (volition)* bodh *m*, bolonjedh *m*
willow-plant ['wɪləʊˌplɑːnt] *n* helygenn *f* +ow, helyk *coll*
win ['wɪn] *v* gwaynya
wind ['wɪnd] *n* gwyns *m* +ow
window ['wɪndəʊ] *n* fenester *f* -tri
windy ['wɪndi] *adj* gwynsek
wine ['waɪn] *n* gwin *m* +yow
wing ['wɪŋ] *n* askell *f* eskelli
winger ['wɪŋəʳ] *n* askeller *m* -oryon
wink ['wɪŋk] *n (of eye)* gwynk *m* +ow: *v* gwynkya
winter ['wɪntəʳ] *n* gwav *m* +ow; *(duration)* gwavas *m* +ow
wipe ['waɪp] *v* sygha
wise ['waɪz] *adj* fur; *(knowledgeable)* skiansek
wish ['wɪʃ] *n* hwans *m* +ow: *v* mynnes
witch ['wɪtʃ] *n* gwragh *f* +es
with [wɪð] *prep* gans
wither ['wɪðəʳ] *v* gwedhra
without [wɪ'ðaʊt] *prep* heb, a-der
witness ['wɪtnɪs] *n (person)* dustunier *m* -oryon
wizard ['wɪzəd] *n* pystrier *m* -oryon
wolf ['wʊlf] *n* bleydh *m* +es +i
woman ['wʊmən] *n* benyn *f* +es; **married woman** gwreg *f* gwragedh; **unmarried woman** damsel *f* +s; **young woman** myrgh *f* myrghes
wonder ['wʌndəʳ] *n* aneth *m* +ow, marth *m* +ow
wood ['wʊd] *n (trees)* koes *m* +ow; *(timber)* prenn *m* +yer

woodland ['wʊdlənd] *n* gwydhek *f* -egi
wood-louse ['wʊd‚laʊs] *n* gwragh-oeles *f* gwraghes-o.
wool ['wʊl] *n* gwlan *coll* +enn
word ['wɜːd] *n* ger *m* +yow
work ['wɜːk] *n* ober *m* +ow, gweyth *m* +yow, hwel *m* +yow, lavur *m* +yow; *(opus)* oberenn *f* +ow: *v* oberi
worker ['wɜːkər] *n* gweythor *m* +yon
workman ['wɜːkmən] *n* oberwas *m* -wesyon
works ['wɜːks] *plur* gweythow *plur*
world ['wɜːld] *n* bys *m* +ow; *(Earth)* nor *m*, norvys *m*
worm ['wɜːm] *n* pryv *m* +es
worry ['wʌri] *n* preder *m* +ow: *v* prederi
worse ['wɜːs] *adj* gweth, lakka
worsen ['wɜːsn] *v* gwethhe
worst ['wɜːst] *adj* gwettha
worth ['wɜːθ] *n (value)* talvosogeth *f* +ow; **be worth** talvesa *v*
wound ['wuːnd] *n* goli *m* +ow: *v* golia
wrap ['rap] *v* maylya
wreck ['rek] *n* gwrekk *m* +ys
wrestle ['resl] *v* gwrynya
wrestler ['reslər] *n* gwrynyer *m* -yoryon
wrestling ['reslɪŋ] *n* omdowl *m*
wretched ['retʃɪd] *adj* truan
wrinkle ['rɪŋkl] *n* krygh *m* +yow
wrist ['rɪst] *n* konna-bregh *m* konnaow-bregh
write ['raɪt] *v* skrifa
writer ['raɪtər] *n* skrifer *m* +s -oryon
writing ['raɪtɪŋ] *n* skrif *m* +ow
wrong ['rɔŋ] *n* dregynn *m* +ow: *adj* kamm

Y

yard ['jɑːd] *n (enclosure)* garth *m* +ow; *(3 ft)* lath *f* +ow

yawn ['jɔːn] *v* deleva

year ['jɪər] *n* blydhen *f* blydhynyow; *(year of age)* bloedh *m*; **last year** warlyna; **this year** hevlyna; **next year** nessa blydhen

yell ['jel] *n* us *m* +ow: *v* usa

yellow ['jeləʊ] *adj* melyn

yes ['jes] *int (usually stated by repeating the verb)* ya

yesterday ['jestədeɪ] *adv* de

yet [jet] *adv* hwath

yew ['juː] *n* ywin *coll* +enn

yoghurt ['jɔgət] *n* yogort *m* +ow

you ['juː] *pron (sg. = **thou**)* ty; *(pl.)* hwi

young ['jʌŋ] *adj* yowynk; **the young** an re yowynk

your [jɔːr] *pron (sg. = **thy**)* dha; *(pl.)* agas

yourselves [jɔːˈselvz] *pron* agas honan

youth ['juːθ] *n (abst.)* yowynkneth *f*

Z

zebra ['zebrə] *n* zebra *m* +s

zero ['zɪərəʊ] *n* mann *num*

zigzag ['zɪgzag] *n* kammigell *f* +ow

zone ['zəʊn] *n* parth *f* +ow

zoo ['zuː] *n* milva *f* milvaow

Liligast series (mini dictionaries)
- Alsatian-French
- Breton-Dutch
- Breton-French
- Breton-Italian
- Breton-Portuguese
- Corsican-Italian
- Occitan-French
- Romansh-French
- Romansh-Italian
- Alsatian-German
- Breton-English
- Breton-German
- Breton-Spanish
- Breton-Welsh
- Ladin-German
- Romansh-English
- Romansh-German
- Savoyard-French

Pouloupig series (pocket dictionaries)
- Armenian-French
- Bulgarian-French
- Catalan-French
- Corsican-English
- Corsican-Spanish
- Finnish-French
- Hungarian-French
- Irish-French
- Maltese-French
- Scottish Gaelic/French
- Walloon-French
- Breton-French
- Catalan-Breton
- Cornish-English
- Corsican-French
- Croatian-French
- Galician-French
- Irish-Breton
- Lithuanian-French
- Roumanian-French
- Slovenian-French
- Welsh-French

Website about European nationalities:
http://www.eurominority.eu/

Lakaet er moull e ti CORLET IMPRIMEUR SA
(Condé-sur-Noireau)
—
Disklêriet hervez lezenn
trede trimiziad 2015